# THE EVOLUTION OF THE
# NETHERLANDS INDIES ECONOMY

# THE EVOLUTION OF THE
# NETHERLANDS INDIES ECONOMY

*By*

## J. H. BOEKE

*Professor of Tropical Economics*
*University of Leiden*

I.P.R. INTERNATIONAL RESEARCH SERIES

NETHERLANDS AND NETHERLANDS INDIES COUNCIL
INSTITUTE OF PACIFIC RELATIONS

New York
1946

*Printed in the United States of America*

65

# FOREWORD

This volume embodies the second part of an intensive study of the Netherlands Indies economy by Professor J. H. Boeke, of the University of Leiden, an outstanding authority on that subject. Begun in 1937 at the instigation of the International Research Committee of the Institute of Pacific Relations, this study was seriously interrupted by the war. Nevertheless, the first part of it, entitled *The Structure of Netherlands Indian Economy,* was published by the International Secretariat of the Institute in New York in 1942. Despite his incarceration in a German concentration camp, the author was able to produce a draft of the second part, a preliminary mimeographed edition of which was made available early this year to the author's students at the University of Leiden and to a few scholars and officials. Except for more careful editing and revisions in the first chapter, the present text differs but little from the preliminary draft prepared by Dr. Boeke during his enforced isolation.

Even more than the preceding volume, this work bears closely upon problems with which the whole world is at present concerned—problems which, for example, will occupy the meeting of the International Labor Conference, to be held this autumn. Its subject matter ranges from a historical retrospect upon the forces that have shaped the economic policies of the Netherlands Indies Government to recent changes in the agrarian, trade, and labor policies of both Government and private enterprise. Its special significance lies in the intimate manner in which the author connects basic factors in the support of the colony's economic structure with a vital concern in the ever changing influences that determine the welfare of every section of the population. To those who are in the habit of regarding the statistics of foreign trade, of investment, and of government revenues as sufficient indications of the territory's prosperity or the lack of it, and to those who tend to discuss the burning social and political questions that agitate the Indies as though they were unrelated to questions of world trade, of public finance, or of the social composition of the population—to all such this book may be recommended as holding up the mirror to a reality that is far from simple or easy to appraise.

The author shows that at no time in its modern phase has economic life in the Indies been static; that even the often debated dualism of its economy, with its native and its Western sectors, is not absolute but has more and more come to be modified by the emergence of ever widening and ever more vital common interests and common problems. Since most of this book was written before the end of the war and, as it were, above the battle of contending policies and programs for the reconstruction of the Indies which since has entered a critical stage, it retains the judicious flavor and scholarly tone of the author's previous publications. In its pages, the larger issues are not confused by too much attention to passing conflicts. Instead, the reader's attention is drawn, again and again, to lessons for the future development of the Indies that may be drawn from the colony's experience during the economic depression of the early 'thirties.

With its diagnosis of past misfortunes and of the degree of success that has attended attempted remedial measures, the book has, indeed, a high practical value for the understanding of the task which the Netherlands and Netherlands Indies Governments confront in applying to the economic development of the Indies the great principles of partnership and welfare which, according to their declared purpose, are henceforth to govern the relations of the two countries.

The Netherlands and Netherlands Indies Council of the Institute of Pacific Relations gratefully acknowledges the financial and editorial assistance rendered in the completion of this work by the Institute's International Secretariat. However, neither body shares responsibility for statements of fact or opinion contained in the book. That responsibility rests solely with the author.

FRANS H. VISMAN

*Chairman of the Netherlands and
Netherlands Indies Council,
Institute of Pacific Relations*

New York
August 4, 1946

# CONTENTS

FOREWORD . . . . . . . . . . v
LIST OF TABLES . . . . . . . . . ix
Chapter I—THE EVOLUTION OF THE NETHERLANDS
        INDIES ECONOMICS . . . . . 1
    Western Control and Native Labor . . . . . 3
    Capitalism and Colonialism . . . . . . . 7
    The Period of Consolidation . . . . . . 16
    The Prospect . . . . . . . . . . 19
Chapter II—THE ECONOMIC POSITION OF THE
        NETHERLANDS INDIES BEFORE,
        DURING, AND AFTER THE
        DEPRESSION . . . . . . 22
    Exports and Imports . . . . . . . . 22
    Causes of Intervention . . . . . . . . 28
Chapter III—GOVERNMENT INTERFERENCE WITH
        ECONOMIC LIFE . . . . . 34
Chapter IV—GOVERNMENT INTERVENTION IN
        EXPORTS . . . . . . . 39
    The Promotion of Exports in General . . . . . 39
    Sugar Policy . . . . . . . . . . 40
    Rubber . . . . . . . . . . . 47
    Tea . . . . . . . . . . . . 56
    Cinchona . . . . . . . . . . 65
    Coffee . . . . . . . . . . . 67
    Other Agricultural Products . . . . . . . 71
    Tin . . . . . . . . . . . . 80
    Forestry . . . . . . . . . . . 81
    Advancement of Staple Crop Cultivation . . . . 83
Chapter V—GOVERNMENT INTERVENTION IN
        IMPORTS . . . . . . . 85
    Quota and Licensing Systems in General . . . . 85
    Commodities Subject to Free Quotas . . . . . 93
    Commodities Subject to National Quotas . . . . 94
    Barter Agreements . . . . . . . . . 97
    Commercial Control . . . . . . . . 98
    Shipping and Imports . . . . . . . . 99

Chapter VI—COOPERATION BETWEEN THE NETHER-
LANDS AND THE NETHERLANDS INDIES 101
Chapter VII—GOVERNMENT INTERVENTION IN THE
HOME MARKET . . . . . 109
Food Production . . . . . . . . . 109
Rice Policy . . . . . . . . . . 112
Promotion of Industry . . . . . . . . 116
The Industrial Provisioning of the Netherlands Indies and
the Foreign Share in It . . . . . . . 119
The Textile Industry of the Indies . . . . . 122
Some Other Industries in the Indies . . . . . 125
Regulation of Industry . . . . . . . . 128
Government Intervention in Fisheries and Fish Breeding 131
Chapter VIII—REGULATION OF THE PRICE LEVEL . . 133
Control of Commodity Prices . . . . . . 133
The Control of Wages . . . . . . . . 137
Chapter IX—THE POPULATION PROBLEM . . . 141
Java's Overpopulation . . . . . . . . 141
Native Agricultural Colonization . . . . . . 144
European Agricultural Colonization . . . . . 151
Chapter X—WELFARE AND SOCIAL CARE . . . . 153
The Cooperative Movement . . . . . . . 153
Native Limited-Liability Companies . . . . . 155
Government Intervention in the Provision of Popular Credit 157
The General Popular Credit Bank . . . . . 160
Release from Indebtedness . . . . . . . 161
The Fight Against Usury . . . . . . . 166
Protection of Labor on Western Estates . . . . 168
State Intervention in Unemployment . . . . . 170
Index . . . . . . . . . . . . 173

# LIST OF TABLES

TABLE        I:   Percentage of Netherlands Indian Exports in
                  Total World Exports, 1929, 1933, and 1938        22
TABLE        II:  Value of Netherlands Indian Exports by
                  Branches of Production, 1929, 1933, 1938,
                  and 1940 . . . . . . .                            22
TABLE        III: Percentage of Estate and Native Production
                  in Total Value of Certain Agricultural
                  Exports, 1929, 1933, 1938, and 1940 . .          23
TABLE        IV:  Value of Exported Agricultural Products and
                  Percentage of Each in Their Total Value,
                  1929, 1933, 1938, and 1940 . . .                 24
TABLE        V:   Percentage of Some Important Colonial Prod-
                  ucts Consumed at Home . . . .                    25
TABLE        VI:  Value of Native Agrarian Production, 1939        25
TABLE        VII: Percentage of Certain Netherlands Indian
                  Agricultural Exports in Total Value of
                  World Exports of These Commodities,
                  1929, 1933, 1938, and 1939 . . . .               26
TABLE        VIII: Balance of Trade, 1929, 1933, 1938, and 1940    26
TABLE        IX:  Destination of Netherlands Indian Exports
                  by Value and as Proportion of Total Ex-
                  ports, 1929, 1933, 1938, and 1940 . .            27
TABLE        X:   Origin of Netherlands Indian Imports by
                  Value and as Proportion of Total Imports,
                  1929, 1933, 1938, and 1939 . . .                 28
TABLE        XI:  Quantities of Products Exported, 1928-29,
                  1937-38, and 1940 . . . . .                      39
TABLE        XII: Exported Quantities of Products Subject to
                  Restrictions and Prices Realized, 1929-1940      40
TABLE        XIII: Production and Yield of Sugar Estates Com-
                  pared with Rents, Wages, and Other Pro-
                  duction Costs, 1927-1936 . . . .                 44
TABLE        XIV: Percentage of Total Costs of Sugar Produc-
                  tion Spent on Rent, Wages, and Other
                  Items, 1925 and 1936 . . . .                     45

TABLE        XV:   Quantities and Prices of Estate and Native
                   Rubber Exports, 1929 to 1940  .   .   .        51
TABLE        XVI:  Estimated Productive Capacity for Estate and
                   Native Rubber Plantation and Interna-
                   tional Basic Quota, 1939-1943  .   .   .        54
TABLE        XVII: Coffee Production, Export, and Price, 1929-40   68
TABLE        XVIII: Kapok Exports and Prices, 1934-40  .   .       72
TABLE        XIX:  Estate and Native Share in Exports of Citro-
                   nella Oil, 1931-39  .   .   .   .   .           76
TABLE        XX:   Tin Exports from the Netherlands Indies,
                   1931-40  .   .   .   .   .   .   .              81
TABLE        XXI:  Virgin Forest Area in the Outer Provinces,
                   1938  .   .   .   .   .   .   .   .             82
TABLE        XXII: Monthly Expenditures of Six Types of Fami-
                   lies and Incidence of Import and Excise
                   Duties as Percentages of These Expendi-
                   tures, 1929  .   .   .   .   .   .   .          89
TABLE        XXIII: Effect of Quota and Licensing Regulations
                   on Three Family Budgets, 1935 and 1936         90
TABLE        XXIV: Trade Between the Netherlands and the
                   Netherlands Indies, 1928-1939  .   .   .        105
TABLE        XXV:  Production and Consumption of the Prin-
                   cipal Food Crops in Java per Head of
                   Population, 1929-1940  .   .   .   .            109
TABLE        XXVI: Import and Export Surplus of Rice, 1934-39     112
TABLE        XXVII: Export of 34 Industrial Products Made in
                   Java to the Outer Provinces, 1934-38  .   .     122
TABLE XXVIII:      Number of Improved Looms Distributed to
                   Native Textile Industry by Textile Insti-
                   tute at Bandoeng  .   .   .   .   .            122
TABLE        XXIX: Number of Cooperative Societies, 1930-1938     155
TABLE        XXX:  Price Index of Copra, Rice, and Piece Goods,
                   Manado, North Celebes, 1931-1939  .   .        163
TABLE        XXXI: Age Composition of European Male Popu-
                   lation and of Unemployed Male Europeans
                   in 1934  .   .   .   .   .   .   .             171

# THE EVOLUTION OF THE
# NETHERLANDS INDIES ECONOMY

# CHAPTER I

## THE EVOLUTION OF THE
## NETHERLANDS INDIES ECONOMICS

Three centuries ago, Europeans did not sail to the Indies to collect butterflies. They went to obtain much desired commodities for which that remote region was famous or for the production of which it was reputed to be suitable.

At first the travellers and those who stayed to become the first European colonists in the tropical Far East contented themselves with acquiring in larger quantities those products of which a trickle had reached Western Europe through the ages: pepper, cloves, nutmeg, cinnamon, rice, and others. There seemed to be no limit to the amount of such commodities the land and people were able to supply. One only had to collect, perhaps store for a while until a vessel came into port, then ship away to the homeland; production of the commodities might well be left to the native population. That population could easily be forced to give up part of its produce. The system was simple enough: princes and chiefs were more than willing to obtain for the foreigners in this way a good share of whatever produce they desired. The small farmer considered it perfectly natural that his chief and his prince should take over part of the product of his labor; that right had always been theirs, and what they did with their share was no concern of his—they might sell it locally or they might hand some of it over for a consideration to foreign merchants. Probably the producers were not always aware of what became of this share of their crops.

All went well as long as the trade in these native products was sufficiently lucrative. But the European market was insatiable, and large profits remained unrealized with dearth of supplies. That situation did not last long. Another step was soon taken, and then a third: the small farmers were compelled to plant and raise the desired crops, and experiments were made to find out for what new crops climate, soil, and available skills were suitable. The lands of the tropics, it seemed, had unlimited agricultural possibilities. Any European with enough energy who could gain power over a native chief in the interior now tried to introduce some new crop or to extend in his sphere of influence one that had already proved suitable. On reading the economic records of

1

the Indies in the eighteenth and nineteenth centuries, one is struck with the great variety of crops which at one time or other were hopefully considered or recommended—many of them never to go beyond the experimental stage, to fail forthwith, or soon to be abandoned. Only slowly, from bitter experience, was it learned that the success of a crop depends on a combination of natural factors and painfully exact, often complicated, procedures. Just what that combination was often remained in part obscure; and so repeated experiment in each district was the only way to success.

As a matter of fact, the agricultural pioneers from the West were by no means expert. The indigenous producers themselves were the true entrepreneurs; such leadership as they received from the colonists was founded neither on local experience nor on theoretical knowledge. The indigenous producers could be made to bear the risk of failure; and since little investment of capital was needed, there was every opportunity for light-hearted initiative and for the encouragement of more or less wild experiments. The expansion of a new culture, once it had proved technically possible, presented few difficulties, either. If the natives did not join in the new enterprise of their own accord, seeing no chance of profit in it—and in that respect the farmer in the tropics is no more conservative than his Western colleague, but quite the contrary—then pressure could be applied, again through the intervention of the chiefs. Yet, the development of this policy into a system met with one insuperable obstacle: a culture introduced and maintained under pressure could hardly be intensive. Where the native, the *tani,* enjoyed the growing of a crop, no care or labor was too much for him. But he could find real pleasure only when the product satisfied one of his own needs; and these needs were few, unexacting, and of little variety. As a rule, the *tani* did not, of his own accord, produce for the Western market—or, indeed, for any market; if in an exceptional case he did so it had to be with the slightest possible expenditure of labor and other costs, therefore through some form of quite extensive cultivation. In other words, the exertion was worth his while only if he could gather the harvest without having been obliged to pay much attention to the growing of the crop. Now, as already stated, one could force the *tani* to adopt a more intensive cultivation of the crop; but there is probably no branch of industry in which it is more difficult to intensify production by the application of force. The agricultural producers are spread out over an expanse of fields and gardens where it is difficult to check the thoroughness of their labor, and the diversity of conditions and necessary operations is very great. Intensive guidance which might have produced the desired result is uneconomical in a colonial country like the Indies, because it would have to be Western guidance, imbued with Western energy, therefore either European or at least under close European supervision and consquently paid for in accordance with Western standards. Serious and protracted attempts nevertheless were made to use force in the promotion of native cultivation for export. The policy of the East India Company and later on the "culture system" show this clearly. But these attempts to systematize intensification only served to demonstrate that coercion is not an effective means to procure the growing of crops which demand great care and are technically exacting. Sooner or later, the cultures thus pursued either failed—as, for example, indigo, tea, cotton, tobacco—or they were kept going only with a steadily increasing Western interference in the process of production. This eventually led to private Western organization for production supplanting peasant production under government compulsion —as, for example, in the case of sugar.

Although, therefore, experience has shown that intensive cultivation cannot be secured by means of compulsion, nevertheless, as I shall try to show, the tendency toward intensification persisted and is still to be found in all the Western colonial agricultural enterprises, and not only in these but also in the non-agrarian branches of colonial effort, in industry, mining, and transportation. In short, it is a general characteristic of Western economic development in the Indies.

### WESTERN CONTROL AND NATIVE LABOR

Before proceeding to further explanations of this evolutionary course in its various aspects, let me point out the consequences of this development for the economic position of the indigenous masses. The most important immediate result of the steadily increasing intrusion of Western technique, of Western control and organization, and of Western capital is that native production is more and more pushed into the background and its share in total production is bound to become continually smaller. This result is of the utmost importance because the economic dependence of the Indies on the West grew at a corresponding rate, whether this "West" be regarded as having its seat inside or outside the colony, and whether it be represented by private agencies or by a Western government.

In 1935, an Englishman, Leonard Barnes, made the following statement on the economic development of Africa at a conference of the National Peace Council:

"I can clearly see that this development is consummated by means of a close cooperation between land and labor on the one side, and capital and technique on the other, and that the land and labor will have to be provided by the African population, the capital and the technique by the Europeans. But really, the aim of cooperation must be to give Africa the control over capital and technique, and not to furnish us with the mastery over the labor and the land of the native population."

In this statement a wish is expressed: that Africa in its economic development might secure the control of the production process for its own indigenous population. I am not aware whether Barnes, when he included this point in his economic program, harbored a secret doubt whether this wish might not prove vain. The reader will realize that my view of the economic development of the Indies—at least up to 1930—leads me to the opposite conclusion. And the facts are on my side. Colonial Africa is at the beginning of an evolutionary course along which no colonial territory has advanced as far as have the Indies in the course of three and a half centuries of colonial economic development. I shall now try to describe this development in its nearest phases and for a single branch of industry. Among the consequences on the status of the Indies I shall include the political status. At the end of this chapter, I intend to indicate briefly the direction in which, in my opinion, the economic-political solution of this problem has been sought and must be found.

In a dynamic economic scheme, that is to say, in a scheme which takes as its starting point the desire for a progressive development of the system of production—for our argument the only acceptable point of departure—the function of the entrepreneur must be added to the usual theoretical triad of production factors: nature, labor and capital. This dynamic production factor is most potent when it includes the creative urge, the tenacity, the concentration on the economic result, and the power of organization, all of which characterize the true pioneer—characteristics, incidentally, which the native producer hardly possesses at all unless guided by a modern government.

The Javanese farmer, and no less his counterpart in the Outer Provinces, is attached above all to his individual freedom as a determinant of his economic activity. A single illustration must suffice, one chosen to sketch also the contrasting qualities of the Western entrepreneur and to indicate some of the causes of the intensification of cultures.

When in 1859 George Birnie opened his first tobacco plantation at Djember in the eastern corner of Java, the success of his venture depended entirely on the correct mixture of freedom and coercion in the organization of the indigenous tobacco planters. The two principles had to be so adjusted that the Western manager obtained enough of the product, and this of a satisfactory quality, while the local farmer did not lose interest in his planting of that crop—this last, as has already been pointed out, an essential condition of intensive agriculture. It is understandable that, as more capital was invested in the enterprise, the freedom of the workers engaged in it had to be more and more restricted. When the Birnies had spent some five hundred thousand guilders on irrigation works, the irrigated fields had to be regularly planted with tobacco, and there had to be a larger yield of that crop if the capital invested was to yield a profitable return. For this purpose, five-yearly land-lease and planting contracts were concluded with the tobacco planters who owned the land, and formally signed on stamped papers. After that, the lessors felt themselves bound and no longer masters over their land or over their own labor. In their minds there now was a distinction between two kinds of tobacco. That cultivated under the terms of the lease and planting contracts they called *tembakau segelan*—verbally, "sealed tobacco," so strong was the impression made on them by the formality of the sealed contracts. The tobacco which they continued to grow on their own initiative, on their own account and according to their own lights they now called *tembakau préman*, the tobacco of a freeman. This shows how highly they valued their individual freedom.

Yet, this freedom was inevitably and constantly to decrease. One cause of this I have already mentioned: the large amount of capital invested in the enterprise. Another was the urge of the Western pioneers to expand their enterprise. What has life must grow. The one-man concern soon is brought under a limited-liability company. The European in the tropics knows labor only when it is organized—with himself as leader. But labor so organized is bound labor. Western "leadership" means that there are large numbers of inferiors; otherwise that leadership could not be adequately paid for. In the course of fifty years, the enterprise started by George Birnie grew into a limited-liability company with a staff of sixty Europeans and with 35,000 planters bound by contracts. It became a typical "large concern," with six finishing sheds made of brick, eighty tobacco piling sheds, also of brick, sixty houses for the European staff, a coffee-hulling mill, and 440 drying sheds with a total length of 80,000 feet.

All this capital has to yield a profit. It is thrust like a wedge between the Western "leadership" and the simple natives' executive labor. That labor, indeed, must be made so productive that it pays not only its own costs and those of the management but also the interest on the capital.

Hence a sterner commitment, further intensification and also further departure from the freedom of a worker who previously was responsible only to himself and kept control over the whole process of production from start to finish. Now that process is split up into all sort of separate categories of work, both in the cultivation of the product and in its preparation for the market. Division of labor is more widely applied in the enterprise, and the share of the individual farmer in the final product is less than it used to be. Five hundred native supervisors, *mandurs,* are needed to instruct the 35,000 planters; and the drying, piling, and packing sheds have, in part, their own specialized staffs.

The native farmer is also pushed out of the market. No longer is there a final local price for a significant portion of the *tembakau segelan;* the leaf tobacco is sold in Rotterdam. So the distance between the free native tobacco planter and the tobacco grower who works under contract becomes ever greater. The latter is hardly more than a wheel in a machine that is becoming more and more intricate. He remains an individual in his attitude toward his work, but he faces an organization that constantly expands in breadth and in depth. He no longer even plays his part in a separate agricultural enterprise, though this was large enough: there is a cartel now that can dictate working principles and conditions, wages, the terms of leases, and the intermediate prices to be paid. In short, the worker faces a monopoly.

Considering the mentality of the Javanese farmer, alluded to above, one might expect that this shrinkage of the share he takes in the production as a whole, this lessened attractiveness of tied tobacco-growing, would result in an extension of "free" native cultivation. But this has not been the case. The free cultivator is no longer able to compete and, moreover, has had to put up with all kinds of limitations placed on his freedom to dispose of his product by a government bound to protect the more weighty interests of the Western enterprises. These limitations—all perfectly justifiable when considered one by one—impeded the rise and extension of a free native tobacco-growing industry. In so far as he finds no opportunity to bring to the market a distinct product of his own, one satisfactory to his own class and therefore meeting a local demand, whether for cut tobacco or for *krosok,* the native "freeman" tobacco grower gets the worst of it.

This course of affairs is typical of economic development in the Indies. The European takes the initiative, experiments, introduces new crops or varieties, takes risks—and then starts organizing. The native free farmer, who is not swept into the whirlpool of Western enterprise, copies but suits his practice to his own ideas, remains alone without capital or technical help, and then finds himself hindered in reaping the results of his labor and in developing his paltry little business by the competition of the much more powerful and efficient Western enterprise and perhaps even by the measures which the authorities take to advance its interests. So it was in the tobacco, sugar, coffee, rubber and cocoa industries. But in the years before the second world war there came a change, as will presently be explained.

CAPITALISM AND COLONIALISM

Daniel H. Buchanan, a writer on British Indian economics, in prosaic contrast to the idealist Leonard Barnes, comes to the conclusion that British India has not become more and more capitalistic but is only exploited more and more in a capitalistic way. The distinction is fundamental and applies in even greater measure to the Netherlands Indies because here capital is almost entirely foreign. Here, therefore, Western enterprise is almost without exception European enterprise; and this, by reason of its predominatingly agrarian character, has penetrated even more deeply into the life of the indigenous society than it has in India. Yet, in both Indias Western enterprises remain enclaves in native society, and the boundaries of these enclaves constantly become more clearly defined. On the one side, Western enterprises are extended, grow more complicated in techniques, organization, finance, and sales procedures, while the share in them of native production factors becomes more and more modest. On the other side, the native crofter industries shrink and decline. A striking example of this in the Netherlands Indies is the development of the sugar industry. In other branches of production the enclave character of European enterprise was there from the beginning: e.g. in mining, for example, and in the cultivation of oil palms, fibers, and cinchona.

It may be objected that there has also been an extension of various native agricultural industries and small manufactures. Is not the share of native production for the export market, and of native cultivation of commercial crops, on the increase—both absolutely and relatively? Is not a tendency opposite to that described above illustrated by the "tropical growth" of native rubber cultivation in the Indies, by the wide distribution of native coconut cultivation, by the ability of native lemongrass cultivation to compete with Western plantation production? Do we not have native tea and native coffee, and have not both for some time managed to hold their own? And what about pepper, kapok, and diverse tree fruits—have they not been left almost entirely to the native growers?

All this is true enough. But here, too, the contrast with the Western concerns is too great to present a picture of some sort of balance. The difference is not only one of degree of development but fundamental; and what is even more to the point, it seems as if the contrast steadily increases. The native cultivations, one is inclined to suppose, lack all too much the solid economic foundation that would enable them to withstand a changing tide; they call up only too vividly the picture of the old-time sailing ship which, even today, sailing before the wind, is an impressive sight but which, in truth, can be kept afloat only with aid from all sides. Is it still possible to equip it with a modern engine?

To begin with there is the question of size of operations. The Western concerns are, without exaggeration and strictly speaking, some two or more thousand times as extensive as are the corresponding native concerns—and this not only in the thinly peopled Outer Provinces but also in densely populated Java, not only in the perennial cultures of rubber, coffee and tea but also in such annual cultures as sugar and tobacco. Moreover, the Western concerns rest on a firm capital foundation, thus are capable of sustaining heavy losses and of enlarging at will, when the need arises, the range within which production costs can be cut down. The small native industries, on the other hand, are almost entirely without capital investment—at most take into account their own unremunerative labor that has been used to clear the land and to exploit it—and can bring down their production costs only by economizing on this labor. Besides, the Western concerns are in direct touch with the world market; the small native concerns on the contrary, when left to themselves, remain at a great distance from it and must depend on a chain of middlemen, finishers, and dealers to connect them with it. That chain, long or short, stretches between the two poles, the primitive one-man concern and the world market. When prices fall, each link in it needs for its support a larger part of the proceeds. Finally, Western enterprises reap the rich—often fabulously rich—fruits of modern science and technique, while the small native industries are for the most part wholly deprived of their benefits, unless government comes to their aid.

*Contrasts between Western and Native Methods of Operation.* With all this, it is difficult to realize the enormous contrast between the Western concerns and the small native enterprises—a contrast which, as has already been mentioned, is steadily increasing. It was sharpened by the world economic depression of the 'thirties. The unprecedented drop in prices and the crushing overproduction had opposite effects on the two poles of economic enterprise in the Indies. The Western concerns were obliged to give up their independence and to adopt far-reaching measures of organization. Many of them were merged with larger concerns, had to buy their survival by sacrificing their independence. But of all of them it may be said that the restriction of their planted areas, or the restriction of their export quotas, has been a sharp spur to further intensification of their operations. No longer expansion but lowering the cost of production now was the parole. This meant not only a drastic reduction of wages but also continued technical improvement, rationalization, more efficient organization, above all a strictly scientific economic policy. In this way the capitalistic character of these concerns was further emphasized. Western enterprise in the Indies is a proud and splendid structure; its mighty pillars rest in the confederations of owners, in national and international regulations, in banks and estate companies, in syndicates and unions, in holding companies and managing agencies, in experiment stations and laboratories.

Compare with all this the structure of native industry. How differently must one focus one's eyes to be able to distinguish the individual units! There is practically no organization here. The few modest cooperative societies are like coral reefs in the ocean. Each small unit struggles on, relying only on its own resources. State intervention, however incisive, seldom comes in direct touch with the individual producers, is obliged to deal with the collecting groups, the wholesalers, the manufacturers of native raw materials, and the exporters. All the small producer experiences is the drop in prices—unless, perchance, he finds himself altogether unable to sell his product. What can he do about it, without capital, ignorant of market conditions, and thrown on his own resources? With the basis of his business in his own labor, with his technical helplessness, and with his lack of capital, it is natural that he looks for a solution of his problem in extensification of his operations; he will economize on the labor spent, will try to save on the little he is obliged to pay out. His fields or gardens will become still poorer, less cared for. His means to employ helpers will be even smaller than before, and the owner may not be able now to give as much of his own time as formerly to his plantation. In this way the contrast of his holding with the Western estate will become more pronounced than ever; with the economies forced on him by circumstances, the small man comes to a bad end. The fierce tropical nature, subjected, bound and harnessed on the Western estate, reclaims its own on the native plantation, once more becomes almighty, wild, irresistible—unless a resourceful government finds a way to help the native producers.

*The Dependence of Native Enterprise.* There is still another important reason for emphasizing the Indies' growing dependence on Western capital: the dependence also of the native agricultural industries on that capital. It is customary to contrast the agricultural industries under native and under foreign management; and I have tried to make it clear that there is every reason for doing so. But this contrast leaves out of account one important category of Western enterprise—concerns that buy up native raw materials which processing or manufacture in the Indies can render suitable for the Western market, that merely assemble such products in sufficient quantity and in the desired form for export when the individual indigenous producer can offer them for sale only in small quantities. For, as soon as a native product can be used to fill a demand more remote than that expressed in the nearby village bazaar, the producers no longer can market it themselves in suitable forms or are willing to learn how to do so. The farther the market is from the place of cultivation, the more completely the trading is centralized in Western hands.

This further centralization usually is associated with a more thorough industrial processing or fabrication of the native material, and this entirely in Western hands. The term "Western" here takes on a broader meaning. It denotes that the manufacture of the agrarian product and the trade in it take place without participation of the native producer of the raw material. The two operations belong to the Western side of the economy, even when carried on by Asiatics. This phenomenon may be observed in connection with almost all the agricultural crops of the indigenous farmers—not only those produced entirely for the market but also those partly produced for home use. For example, when rice, pre-eminently a native crop, was to be distributed from Java over the whole archipelago, as has been the Government's aim since 1933, rice hulling mills and Chinese rice dealers seemed to be springing out of the ground. The same thing occurred with the second chief food crop, cassava. Not only did small and large cassava factories spring up as non-native enterprises, as soon as fabricated cassava appeared on the world market, but even large concerns made it an estate crop and placed on the market tapioca products of a superior quality at a correspondingly high price quite out of the native producer's reach.

Naturally, this is even more the case with crops raised to be marketed: tobacco, kapok, tea, essential oils, coffee, coconut, fruits, vegetables, and so forth. Here it is easy to see how Western commercial interests have tried to penetrate more deeply into native production. The process begins with money advances through which the trader tries to assure delivery and to influence the price. Soon he intervenes in the production itself, and this especially at a time of economic depression. We should not forget that when the balance between supply and demand is disturbed with the approach and the growing materialization of overproduction, the demand for quality becomes stronger than that for quantity. This is true of the supply of raw materials as well as of manufactures. But the native farmer often cannot or will not satisfy this new demand unless he is forced to do so. What happens then is, first, that the finishing process is entirely taken out of the native producer's hands; soon he is provided with seed and seed plants; the purchaser insists on controlling the cultivation, may supply artificial manure, and, after a time, to protect his increased capital interest in the native enterprise, acquire a right to the land so as to bind the farmer still more firmly. By such steps, the Western entre- preneur finally may assume all the risk of production; the native planter then becomes a wage-earner in all but name; and a native type of agri- culture changes into a Western kind of enterprise. This last phase, however, is far from general.

To illustrate this course of events one might point to the development of both sugar and tobacco cultivation. These industries also happen to demonstrate that the steps mentioned in the preceding paragraph can also be taken in a more roundabout way. Thus, instead of granting credit and securing a right to the land himself, the interested trader may leave these actions to a separate agency. An example of this is the cultivation of Virginian tobacco in Bodjonegoro (Rembang) through the cooperation of a few large cigarette factories and the General Popular Credit Bank. But once these preliminary phases have been passed, it is a question whether the Western concern will decide to continue some such division of functions or to take the whole business into its own hands from start to finish. The outcome of this calculation will depend on the degree of appreciation shown on the market for quality (a ques- tion of market development, as I have pointed out), on the degree to which the native producer is able to meet the new and stricter demands on the efficiency of his production, and eventually on the resistance or compliance of the Government which can influence the decision through its power to confer long leases and area licenses, power also to set condi- tions for the drawing up or registration of ground-lease contracts. Besides, it is possible—as will be shown below in Chapter IV, p. 71 ff.—for the Government to take the native producers' interest into its own hands and thereby to alter the line of development here described.

As a result, the dependence of the native producer on the wholesaler can be very great. Their actual relationship is influenced also by the nature of the product and by other factors: the durability of the raw material, its potential uses in the producer's own household or its saleability in the local market, his need of credit, the monopolistic position of the buyer. In any case, a considerable part of the export price for the processed product does not reach the original producer. Sometimes, as in the case of tea, his share is fifty per cent—and this only thanks to government intervention; sometimes it is much less, as in the case of kapok, or considerably more, as in that of rubber. But in all these industries examples can be found of the development of entire large-scale Western enterprises, either through the absorption of native independent cultivation or carried on by the same concerns that buy its product; that is, sometimes the small cultivator is helped to string along, sometimes he is crowded out. Even such typical native crops as rice and cassava are no absolute exception; there are a few Western rice and cassava estates. And, as is well known, the Western cane-sugar industry has well-nigh taken the place of the long-standing arrangement under which the mills bought up the cane planted by native farmers, so that the combination of Western industry and native agriculture in this important branch has now practically ceased to exist. Such native sugar growing as has developed since this absorption has remained a humble plant; indeed, it can maintain itself only by the grace of the sugar factories and thanks to the active interest of the Government—advantages which it enjoys only, however, as long as it confines itself to an inferior product.

This is common knowledge in the Indies. Less well known is the fact that the Deli tobacco culture, now often proclaimed as the pride of Western technical agricultural achievement in the tropics, also began as a business of buying from Asiatic farmers, though this phase did not last long. Originally, Chinese planters were allowed to choose a piece of ground on which to grow tobacco, from an area allotted for that purpose by the Sultan of Deli. These Chinese planters usually worked in groups, *kongsis,* and sold the leaves to the Western concession holders.

*The Capitalists' Reluctance.* It should not be imagined that the change to complete estate cultivation of commercial crops took place by voluntary agreement. The Western entrepreneurs at first preferred to leave the risk of planting to the native farmers, as they dreaded to have to put so much capital into an uncertain business. In 1864, Jacob Nienhuys, the pioneer of the Deli tobacco industry, declared to his financial backers that he expected to receive permission to buy up the tobacco; if this were not forthcoming he would liquidate the Deli expedition and return to Loemadjang, East Java. In 1866 he urged abandonment of the system of estate tobacco growing in favor of the system of contracting with Chinese growers. He wrote to his principals: "As soon as I see that this does not work, it will be best to put an end to it." Again a month later he gave them a choice between tobacco production by contract with culti-vators or his own release from the project, a release granted him on January 20, 1867.

Capital was little prepared at that pioneer stage to follow the business firms in their transition from purchase of raw materials to their direct production, a transition which involved a change from trade credit to industrial credit, from short-term to long-term advances. An example may serve as illustration. The Amsterdam Trading Society (H.V.A.) stipulated at the time of its foundation that it would not purchase, or take part in purchasing or otherwise acquiring, any rural enterprise; it wished to remain purely a trading company and to advance short-term loans only. As a rule, there are reverses: bankruptcies of concerns that are indebted for important sums; the financing company is forced to enter into the debtor's business territory, which it does reluctantly. Once arrived at that point, it cannot draw back but is obliged to go further and further. The H.V.A. offers a striking example of this course. In 1890, eleven years after its foundation, difficulties in the settlement of a sugar consignment contract led to an agreement under which the society took over seven-eighths of the property of a concern called Giran. Three years later, two other sugar factories which had received mortgage credit changed hands, "as a result of an execution which had to be decided upon when the Chinese owners could not meet the demand to repay the loan." So it went on. But more and more it was a new spirit of enterprise which seized capital and loosened the purse strings that hastened the process. Not only are rural concerns, already organized as Western large-scale businesses, swallowed up, but the former trading companies set up enter-prises of their own—in some instances even for the purpose of raising with Western techniques and on large estates traditionally native crops.

*The Slow Growth of Capitalist Expansion.* With this change of economic policy a new era of development may be said to have started, that of capitalist expansion. This went so far that in 1910 the Amsterdam "Trading" Society, the H.V.A., decided to liquidate its original business of import and export, although the annual turnover in merchandise still amounted to more than twelve million guilders. In 1929, fifty years after its foundation, the H.V.A. had no capital in rural enterprises except those in its own exclusive possession. They included in Java fifteen sugar plantations, four tapioca plantations, three of which also produced fiber, two rubber plantations, one of which also produced coffee; in Sumatra, five tea plantations, four fiber plantations, four rubber plantations and two palm-oil plantations—altogether thirty-six plantations. At that time it had a European staff of 1,050 and a working personnel of 150,000 non-Europeans.

The point of the story is that the transition to complete estate or plantation cultivation of the desired products under direct Western management during the colonial pioneer period and the pushing back of the native share in agricultural production for the world market did not take place deliberately and on purpose. Capital accepted this form of investment only after much hesitation and resistance. What induced both entrepreneur and capitalist to take the business entirely into their own hands was the inadequacy of the buying-up system. Its shortcomings came more clearly to light as the processing of the raw materials grown became technically more complicated and the working capacity of the plants increased, also as the market made higher demands on the quality of the final product. Moreover, in order to meet transportation difficulties and to keep down costs, it became necessary to limit the area to be planted as much as possible—which could only be done by intensification. One had to be sure of large enough stretches of serried plantation, so that the technical processes might be effectively applied and the necessary direction and supervision be given without waste of time. A raw material of uniform and high quality is needed to make manufacture profitable. Large quantities of this material must regularly be available to insure continuity of the mechanical process. It must be possible to improve the crop systematically and efficiently to make it immune to the ever-threatening diseases and pests and so to keep the risks within compass. And one must be able to estimate with certainty what quantities of the product can be counted upon to satisfy the foreign demand. Experience had shown that these requirements could not be met by the buying-in system. Moreover, with the growth of the Western share in production, the difference in power between the Western entrepreneur and the small native producer of raw material became so large, and consequently the association of the two parties in the system dominated by the buyers and manufacturers of such dubious equity, that the Government no longer could acquiesce in it and had to take measures either to seal the transition to complete Westernization—large-scale production under direct management—where this was technically, socially, and legally possible, or to make the relation of native production to world markets a matter of government concern.

*From Planter Initiative to Planned Capital Enterprise.* In the first decades of the era which opened the Indies up for private Western exploitation, roughly the beginning of the twentieth century, or the period preceding the first world war, it was the Western planter who took the initiative. He carried the investor along with him; it was not a case of capital looking for investment possibilities in the tropics or perhaps even, as has been the case at other times, sending its own representatives to discover such opportunities. Because of this, there is continual lack of capital: the entrepreneur again and again has to beg, threaten, protest, to get the necessary working capital together. One of the causes of this relation was that people in Europe, the potential investors, at first knew so little about the kinds of crops for which the soils and climates of different parts of the archipelago might be considered especially suitable. We have become so used to regarding the agricultural products of the Indies as typically of the country's, as belonging there, that we lose sight of the fact that practically all of the crops have originated elsewhere, and that their introduction in the Indies has resulted from much investigation and experiment—sometimes long and costly experiment. Even the choice of territory and the planning of a plantation project often was a jump in the dark. To a certain extent that still is true today; and it would be possible to draw up, in contrast with the series of successful crops and of flourishing enterprises, a much longer list of failures: of agricultural industries imported and later abandoned, of methods adopted and later given up. Formerly, all such experiments were conducted exclusively by the planter himself who thankfully accepted every tip, from whatever source it came, and allowed luck a large place in his schemes. An example or two will illustrate this. Mention has been made of Jacob Nienhuys, the pioneer Western tobacco planter of Deli. When in 1861 he was sent out with a credit of at most sixty thousand guilders to start a tobacco-growing project, it was to "somewhere in Java" and not to Sumatra. He did not succeed there; but he happened to meet at Surabaya an Arab who introduced himself as a prince from the East Coast of Sumatra and who spoke of the excellent tobacco grown in Deli. It was on the strength of this bit of information that Nienhuys made a journey there; and it was there that he established himself when he found the tobacco grown in Deli that he could get hold of to be much to the taste of his creditors. But while he was in Deli, Nienhuys also tried a number of other things, the growing of black pepper, nutmeg, rice, opium, coffee, and cocoa. Furthermore he entered into contracts for the supply of salt and shirtings. It was years before the knowledge ripened that Deli lent itself particularly well to the cultivation of tobacco, and knowledge of the methods of success in that line of enterprise was achieved.

Another example. In 1935, the estate company Bandoeroto issued a history of its activities on the occasion of its fiftieth anniversary. The record begins with the growing of Java coffee in 1885. This crop was gradually replaced by Liberia coffee and cocoa, which were followed by the planting of *robusta* and *quillou* coffee, and by experiments with pepper and cubeb. In the course of years, cocoa appears and disappears several times, and experiments are recorded with nutmeg, kapok, cotton, agave, and coca. Then, in 1900, *ficus elastica* and other latex-producing trees, such as *castelloa, ceara* and *hevea,* appear on the scene. Finally *hevea* wins; but in 1932 the *hevea* gardens once more give way to coffee plantations—a change which in the meantime probably has again been undone. And this certainly is not an extreme example.

It will be seen that with such a kaleidoscopic policy it is impossible to draw a clear line of demarcation between capitalist and planter. In this wild, hazardous beginning of Western enterprise in the Indies, the entrepreneur in the person of the hardy planter stood at the forefront as pioneer and leader. The self-opinionated planter of this period is the entrepreneur à la Schumpeter: the man who creates new combinations, the captain of industry who takes risks and turns to the best advantage the little capital he has been able to get hold of.

But as the calmer period of expansion follows the hectic days of pioneering, this personal element of the planter in the evolution of Western enterprise falls into the background. The limited-liability company appears; capital flows in a turgid but wide stream into the Indies and carries everything with it. The isolated enterprise is caught up in a larger relation, becomes part of an estate company, a colonial bank, a combine, or whatever the larger entity may be called. The planter becomes manager, administrator, a kind of head-employee, who has to accept his instructions from a board of directors and, in the last instance, from the owners of the capital, abroad. He no longer walks with a sun helmet on his head and a planter's stick in his hand, if necessary barefoot, through the gardens and fields—through *his* gardens and fields—but is enthroned behind a desk in a large office building in Batavia, Surabaya, or Medan. Yes, in many cases the real entrepreneur, the man who takes the initiative, who has the reins in his hands, has climbed still a step higher and now resides in Amsterdam, Rotterdam, London, or New York.

### THE PERIOD OF CONSOLIDATION

This introduces a new phase in the colonial economic evolution. Its opening is connected with the consolidation and restriction of the main agricultural industries of the tropics, which at the end of the 'twenties of this century replaced the period of expansion.

In the industrial plan of the new entrepreneur, the separate estates are mere pawns to be moved about at will in a larger game. He may put an end to their production, parcel them out, take over, bring in, abandon, combine or split them, or steer them in a new direction. He conveys the capital to any place where he sees a chance of profit, organizes it in complicated structures. Where the planter thought of his estate as a concrete business with a special product, the new entrepreneur thinks in abstract terms of his assets. In the Indies this stage has brought us the more comprehensive capital constructions: the mother and daughter companies, the syndicates, the managing agencies, the holding companies, the investment trusts, and yet other kinds of financing concerns.

Such has been the evolution of the agricultural export industry of the Indies. But the factors which determined it are not especially derived from agriculture, and a similar course of developments may be expected in other branches of Indian industry. Indeed, to some extent that is already the case. Although in the Indies industry in the limited sense of the term and especially industrial production for the world market does not exist as a force, and although as yet there has been little Westernization of industry or concentration in large business units, we find that here, too, the crowding-out process goes on and cannot be stopped, since it is dominated by coercive economic forces—in the spinning and weaving of textiles, in the metal industry, in the processing of foods, in the manufacture of leather goods, in the cigarette factories, and many more.[1] Here no less than in commercial agriculture, it costs the Government a never slackening and constantly increasing effort of intervention to slow up and ease the process of change at least to some degree.

As for trade, shipping and land transportation, the general course of development is similar. We shall not here pursue this theme any further. It would be a rather cheerless study, with such sub-titles perhaps as "From trading *prahu* to loading *prahu*," "From tilt-cart and pack-horse to rail and car," "From cottage industry to factory and import trade." The case of mining, however, is quite different. This industry is of Western origin and scarcely ever has assumed any importance in native hands. Only, it is worth noting that the process of concentration operates here too, in the same degree as in the branches of industry already mentioned.

---

[1] Although before the war the industrial firms of the Indies produced almost exclusively for the home market, it must be expected that the elimination of Japan from world markets will fundamentally alter this situation.

Taking the general development as a whole—all too briefly sketched and analyzed in these pages—one may say that the distance which separates the Western entrepreneur from the individual native producer increases immeasurably, that Western capital and Western capitalism determine the economic structure of Indian society and give it an appearance of prosperity and wealth. The small native business is dependent on this Western economic framework, can maintain itself only with its assistance even when it is capable of self-development within its limits. Yet, the relation of that business to the world economic situation as it is now advancing toward an even closer unity urgently requires that self-reliance and flexibility which have so largely been lacking. With the overproduction and the resulting low prices, which will return when world peace has been restored and when the excessive war production, with the accompanying urgent need for raw materials, will have disappeared, the final word will come from the technical and organizational perfection of the process of production.

*Is Native Enterprise Doomed?* How well is native business equipped to answer this call? Will not the small native producers under the stress of this increased competition lag more and more behind? Will they at last give up the unequal struggle and return to the raising of crops for their own provision? Government, at least, refuses to share this expectation: it has challenged private Western business in its relations to native primary production; it has resumed the control of native agrarian affairs; has instituted a new kind of "culture system" without indentured labor or restraint and in a new spirit—this time no longer only in its own behalf but in the interest of hundreds of thousands of small, free producers. It has tried to imbue them with the Western urge of enterprise and faculty of organization. It has made it worth the cultivators' while to improve the quality of their products and to make use of some of the devices that have given Western business its start.

Government has undertaken all this under abnormal conditions and is still uncertain whether the native producers will persevere in answering the "call of the West" when the relation between supply and demand changes and prices again fall to a lower level. But in any case, these native agriculturists are being harnessed to withstand a future slump. At the same time, the Government is gathering valuable experience.

I return now to my quotation from Buchanan (p. 7), to the effect that India has not become more capitalistic but is only more and more exploited in a capitalistic way. Applied to the Netherlands Indies, this statement had to be interpreted as meaning that the mass of the popula-

NETHERLANDS INDIES ECONOMICS

tion takes an ever more modest and slighter share in the economic development of the country. It appears now that this view can be accepted only with an important reservation—although possibly it may become true in the long run. The strength of the capitalistic system should not be underestimated; but no more should we fail to give full weight to the new spirit that has been fostered among the native producers by the Government. The most likely solution of the basic problem is a division of labor between Western estates and native planters along a line dividing the more exacting from the less exacting crops.

This conclusion holds true for those branches of commercial agriculture with regard to which we already have examined the statement; but it applies just as much to industrial production which I have practically passed by in silence. One likes to speak of the industrialization of the Indies and to enumerate proudly the various industries that have been started. I do not wish to belittle the importance of this development which still has magnificent prospects. But, however impressive the long list of new factories and new branches of industry, it should be remembered that Indonesia today is further removed from self-sufficiency than it was a century ago; and that the industry of the nation, its self-provisioning with manufactured products, has for the most part been ruined in the course of modern development. Here, too, the economic development of the country has increased its dependence—the dependence, that is, of the native population, of those born and bred in the country, of the workers with little or no capital.

### THE PROSPECT

This conclusion, in point of fact, also contains the answer to the thesis advanced by Leonard Barnes (see above, p. 3) : the Indies can only in part satisfy his demand that the native population should possess the control over capital and technique. Here, as he observed in Africa, the actual development leads in the opposite direction: the Indies is becoming more dependent on capital which, wherever it comes from, still never is native Indonesian capital.

Fortunately, this pessimistic conclusion does not necessarily mark the final phase of the evolutionary process. The economic policy of the Indies has taken a new direction since the depression of the 'thirties, and in many ways has accomplished what it set out to do. In the most recent phase of economic development, that of consolidation and restriction, there has been a turning point, soon after the crisis of 1931, when the center of gravity of Western industrial life came to be partially transferred again to the Indies—this time, however, to the Netherlands Indian Government offices in close cooperation with the Colonial Department in the Netherlands. In the writer's opinion, it is symptomatic that the purely private organization of the United Java Sugar Producers, commonly known as VISP, which dates from before 1918 and had its seat in the Netherlands, was in 1932 replaced by the NIVAS, the Netherlands Indian Association for the Sale of Sugar, established by ordinance, seated in the Indies, and working under Government patronage—a symptom that a turning point was reached about that time in the development which may come to be seen as having been of first importance for the future of the Indies' economy.

This does not mean that other tendencies have been altogether arrested. Economic life continues to grow in a capitalistic direction; the share taken by the native population, by the mass of the people, in the provisioning of the home and the supply of the foreign markets generally is still lessening in volume and relative importance. Of that I am sure. On the one hand, capital has come to the conclusion that it cannot do without the help of the Government in its further organization; it has called upon the Government to intervene on an ever larger scale in the industrial life of the Indies. But on the other hand, faced with this new task, the Government has not shown itself a willing instrument of capitalistic interests but has acted as the protector and promoter of what it regards as Netherlands Indian interests—as the interest of each part concerned in the country's industrial life, in its production in the widest sense. This is the new economic policy of the authorities, a policy extended in a few years on all sides with enormous speed, a regulative policy in really grand style. It is my conviction that this new economic policy does not ring out the capitalistic development of the Indies; rather, it consolidates it and at the same time bends it in a direction in which it may be expected to benefit the whole society of the Indies.

In this sense, then, the statement of Leonard Barnes, quoted as a point of departure for this brief general survey of the economic development of the Netherlands Indies, would be acceptable, though in a somewhat modified form and sense. It does not appear to be possible to give a more important place to either native mass labor or native land uses in the process of colonial production. Capital, science, and technique, in the hands of the Western entrepreneur, have not abandoned their control over that process. But these factors will have to permit an increasing influence of the Government over their sphere of activity, an influence which will result in making that domination increasingly more beneficial to the Netherlands Indian community. And they will have to take into account an expanding native competition, led and inspired by the authorities.

It would not, of course, be realistic to suppose that industrial life will henceforth steer by the compass of the common good; that the industrial leaders will come to regard their business as a kind of social task—as theoretically national socialism does, making this the starting point for its system. The Romans already were aware of this: *vulpes pilos mutat non mores*: the fox may change his hair but not his tricks. Certainly, private industry assumes new airs of authority by conferring with the Government, by making joint decisions and by helping to regulate. It learns how to find its way among the government offices and gradually comes to feel at home there. On the other hand, the Government gives it to understand, by setting up a new department, that it will engage in "economic affairs," and shows itself able to move with gusto and authority in industrial life—in the Western as well as the Eastern sector. In this way both parties grow nearer together. But underneath this mutual approach the fundamental difference in attitude between them remains as strong as ever. Industrial enterprise, still driven forward by self-interest and the desire of gain, could not exist without these aims; and the Government is obliged, more strongly than ever, to remain true to its principles of unselfish and exclusive devotion to the common good. But this does not alter the fact that a form of cooperation has been created which will determine the economic future of the Netherlands Indies.

# CHAPTER II

# THE ECONOMIC POSITION OF THE NETHERLANDS INDIES BEFORE, DURING, AND AFTER THE DEPRESSION

## EXPORTS AND IMPORTS

The international economic position of the Netherlands Indies can best be expressed by a few statistical tables. Four years have been chosen to display the salient features: 1929, the year before the crisis, 1933, the year in the middle of the depression, 1938, the year of recovery and 1940, the last year of peace. Comparison of statistical data for these years brings to light important trends and may also serve to explain the economic policy which arose from the crisis.

The importance of the Netherlands Indies as a producer country appears from its share in the value of the total export of the world:

TABLE I: PERCENTAGE OF NETHERLANDS INDIAN EXPORTS IN TOTAL WORLD EXPORTS, 1929, 1933, AND 1938

| | |
|---|---|
| 1929 | 1.7 |
| 1933 | 1.61 |
| 1938 | 1.69 |

This proportional value of the Netherlands Indian exports was spread over different branches of production in rapidly changing proportions:

TABLE II: VALUE OF NETHERLANDS INDIAN EXPORTS BY BRANCHES OF PRODUCTION, 1929, 1933, 1938, AND 1940

*In million guilders*

| | 1929 | | 1933 | | 1938 | | 1940 | |
|---|---|---|---|---|---|---|---|---|
| Type of Export | Value | Per cent | Value | Per cent | Value | Per cent | Value | Per cent |
| Estate agricultural products | 688 | 47.7 | 181 | 38.7 | 257 | 39.0 | 368 | 42.1 |
| Native agricultural products | 395 | 27.4 | 125 | 26.7 | 169 | 25.7 | 225 | 25.8 |
| Total agricultural products | 1,083 | 75.1 | 306 | 65.4 | 426 | 64.7 | 593 | 67.9 |
| Mining products | 264 | 18.3 | 130 | 27.8 | 203 | 30.9 | 252 | 28.9 |
| Forest and other products | 96 | 6.6 | 32 | 6.8 | 29 | 4.4 | 28 | 3.2 |
| Total | 1,443 | 100.0 | 468 | 100.0 | 658 | 100.0 | 874 | 100.0 |

It will be remarked that in this table manufacturing industry has not been considered worthy of special mention. It is true, nearly all agricultural and mining products have undergone a more or less radical transformation before they are exported; but independent branches of manufacture, producing for the world market with domestic or imported raw materials, scarcely exist in the Netherlands Indies.

The previous chapter will have shown that the distinction between estate and native products is one of major importance. The estates are without exception large-scale Western businesses built up with imported capital, under Western direction and organized on capitalistic lines. The native products, on the other hand, are only partly brought forth by anything that could be called "business." Where this is the case, the units of business are without exception small and work with a minimum of capital or no capital at all. They are mostly family businesses, and the measure of their remunerativeness is the degree to which they make profitable use of the family's labor services. The exported mining products derive entirely from Western enterprise, while the forest products are without exception collected by natives.

As the following table shows, the division is less clear in the allocation of agricultural products. But in reality native products in this branch, too, differ greatly from estate products—either in nature and quality, as with sugar and tobacco, or in that the native products must undergo a more or less important industrial process before they are ready for export, as with tea, essential oils, kapok, and coffee. The table does not include products which entirely derive from estates, such as cinchona, palm-oil products and agave, or those cultivated exclusively by natives, such as rice, maize, groundnuts, and soybeans. Where there is most competition between estate and native production, as in the case of cocoa, nutmeg and coconut, the table indicates some shift—but not all in the same direction. It happens more frequently that the product of the estates ousts the native crop than the reverse. For the rest, this movement is kept in check and sometimes altered by the policy of restrictions.

TABLE III: PERCENTAGE OF ESTATE AND NATIVE PRODUCTION IN TOTAL VALUE OF CERTAIN AGRICULTURAL EXPORTS, 1929, 1933, 1938, AND 1940

| Product | 1929 | | 1933 | | 1938 | | 1940 | |
|---|---|---|---|---|---|---|---|---|
| | Estate | Native | Estate | Native | Estate | Native | Estate | Native |
| Sugar | 99 | 1 | 99 | 1 | 99 | 1 | 99 | 1 |
| Cocoa | 87 | 13 | 98 | 2 | 98 | 2 | 94 | 6 |
| Tea | 78 | 22 | 84 | 16 | 82 | 18 | 82 | 18 |
| Gambier | 62 | 38 | 61 | 39 | 64 | 36 | 67 | 33 |
| Rubber | 59 | 41 | 60 | 40 | 52 | 48 | 50 | 50 |
| Tobacco | 55 | 45 | 54 | 46 | 70 | 30 | 95 | 5 |
| Essential oils | 38 | 62 | 38 | 62 | 43 | 57 | 43 | 57 |
| Nutmeg | 35 | 65 | 33 | 67 | 20 | 80 | 28 | 72 |
| Coffee | 27 | 73 | 31 | 69 | 42 | 58 | 70 | 30 |
| Coconut products | 10 | 90 | 5 | 95 | 5 | 95 | 9 | 91 |
| Kapok products | 4 | 96 | 9 | 91 | 17 | 83 | 25 | 75 |
| Pepper | 1 | 99 | 1 | 99 | 1 | 99 | 1 | 99 |

Table III does not show the general importance of the various agricultural products in the export trade of the Indies. This is indicated by Table IV, below, which shows both the value of exported agricultural products and the percentage of these products in their total value.

TABLE IV:    VALUE OF EXPORTED AGRICULTURAL PRODUCTS AND PERCENTAGE OF EACH IN THEIR TOTAL VALUE, 1929, 1933, 1938, AND 1940

*In million guilders*

| | 1929 | | 1933 | | 1938 | | 1940 | |
|---|---|---|---|---|---|---|---|---|
| Product | Value | Per cent | Value | Per cent | Value | Per cent | Value | Per cent |
| Sugar | 312 | 28.5 | 62 | 20 | 45 | 11 | 53 | 9 |
| Rubber | 235 | 21.5 | 37 | 12 | 134 | 31 | 328 | 55.5 |
| Coconut products (copra) | 116 | 11 | 42 | 14 | 44 | 10 | 14 | 2.5 |
| Tea | 86 | 8 | 26 | 9 | 56 | 13 | 49 | 8.5 |
| Tobacco | 86 | 8 | 32 | 10 | 39 | 9 | 38 | 6.5 |
| Coffee | 68 | 6 | 26 | 9 | 13 | 3 | 8 | 1.5 |
| Pepper | 49 | 4.5 | 13 | 4 | 9 | 2 | 3 | 0.5 |
| Fiber products | 21 | 2 | 9 | 3 | 9 | 2 | 11 | 2 |
| Cassava products | 21 | 2 | 9 | 3 | 9 | 2 | 12 | 2 |
| Kapok products | 16 | 1.5 | 9 | 3 | 7 | 2 | 5 | 1 |
| Palm oil products | 13 | 1.2 | 12 | 4 | 19 | 4 | 10 | 2 |
| Maize | 12 | 1.2 | 3 | 1 | 3 | 1 | 3 | 0.5 |
| Cinchona products | 10 | 1 | 6 | 2 | 12 | 3 | 27 | 4.5 |
| Essential oil products | 3 | 0.3 | 3 | 1 | 3 | 1 | 3 | 0.5 |
| Rice products | 3 | 0.3 | 1 | — | 2 | 1 | 6 | 1 |
| Remaining products | 32 | 3 | 16 | 5 | 22 | 5 | 20 | 2.5 |
| Total | 1,083 | 100 | 306 | 100 | 426 | 100 | 590 | 100 |

Here, too, diverse movements may be perceived. There is no stability at all, and the danger of dependence on the world market, and thereby on the commercial policy of foreign countries, is disclosed.[1] This danger is all the more serious because in most of the agricultural industries the portion of the product destined for export is very large. The circumstance that all the capital for the estates comes from abroad—which makes export essential—together with slight buying power of the home market, leads to a choice of crops and products that is entirely dominated by consideration of the foreign market.

Only the autarchic policy of most of the countries, which took shape in the 'twenties and early 'thirties, attracted the attention of Netherlands-Indian entrepreneurs to the importance of their home market; but the consuming power of that market has remained small, as will appear from Table V.

---

[1] This table should be compared with Table XI in Chapter IV, which gives the exported quantities. The fluctuations of the prices are much greater because they reflect the influence of the deflation policy, which lasted until September 1936, and of the world depression, also of the preparation for and waging of the world war, which in 1940 justified a distinction between "strong" and "weak" products.

TABLE V:  PERCENTAGE OF SOME IMPORTANT COLONIAL PRODUCTS
CONSUMED AT HOME*

| | | | |
|---|---|---|---|
| Rubber | 1 | Sugar | 20 |
| Leaf tobacco | 4 | Paraffin | 20–40 |
| Petrol | 6–10 | Copra | 30 |
| Tea | 10 | Coffee | 34 |
| Cinchona | 4.5 | | |

* Annual average. An annual percentage would be of no use because laying in and disposing of stocks may increase or decrease the divergence between production and export.

The case is very different with the native products. In so far as they are staple food crops, they are mainly intended for home use. Still, a part of these products, too, must find its way to the foreign market. The native people no longer can manage without money. They all have taxes to pay in money and need to import certain products. In Java this money income can be obtained, although to a rapidly lessening degree, from wages earned on the Western plantations, in the towns, and in government employment. But elsewhere produce must be brought to the market for that purpose; and as far as the home demand is insufficient, these products must find their way to a foreign market. This, too, may be illustrated by a few figures.

TABLE VI: VALUE OF NATIVE AGRARIAN PRODUCTION, 1939*

*In guilders*

| | Total (million) | | Per head of agrarian** population | | Per family** (4.5 persons) | |
|---|---|---|---|---|---|---|
| | Java and Madura | Outer Provinces | Java and Madura | Outer Provinces | Java and Madura | Outer Provinces |
| Market crops | 57 | 232 | 1.90 | 14.40 | 8.55 | 64.80 |
| Food crops (incl. compound crops) | 550 | 280 | 17.40 | 17.50 | 78.30 | 78.75 |
| Total | 607 | 512 | 19.30 | 31.90 | 86.85 | 143.55 |

* This table no doubt is instructive and of interest; but were it not that the Netherlands-Indian Government has published it, we should not have dared to reproduce it. Its positiveness is somewhat arbitrary. Indeed, how can one determine the exchange value of products which are only in small part brought to the market, and then often under the force of necessity? And how can one accurately determine the value of the exported native products when these, as is sometimes the case, are mixed with the estate products? It is only with difficulty that the Javanese farmer's family is able to add a few guilders to its income by wage labor and handicraft.
** For the purpose of this calculation it is roughly assumed that the agricultural population of Java and Madura contains 70 per cent, and that of the Outer Provinces 80 per cent, of the respective total population.

Clearly, export is of vital importance to the Indies. "Export or die" would be a device which the Netherlands Indies, more perhaps than any other country in the world, might make her own. This accounts for the large place taken up by the agricultural produce of this country in total world exports, as shown by Table VII:

TABLE VII: PERCENTAGE OF CERTAIN NETHERLANDS INDIAN AGRICULTURAL EXPORTS IN TOTAL VALUE OF WORLD EXPORTS OF THESE COMMODITIES, 1929, 1933, 1938, AND 1939

| Product | 1929 | 1933 | 1938 | 1939 |
|---|---|---|---|---|
| Cinchona bark | 94 | 89 | 90 | 91 |
| Kapok | 73 | 81 | 64 | 72 |
| Pepper | 69 | 80 | 85 | 86 |
| Rubber | 30 | 33 | 33 | 37 |
| Copra | 29 | 29 | 29 | 27 |
| Agave | 22 | 30 | 25 | 38 |
| Tea | 17 | 19 | 17 | 19 |
| Sugar | 11 | 6 | 5 | 6 |
| Coffee | 6 | 5 | 4 | 4 |
| Palm oil | 5 | 15 | 24 | 24 |
| Cocoa | 0.2 | 0.3 | 0.2 | 0.2 |

Here, too, there is movement: a fluctuation in the percentage figures for most of the products named. It results from world competition, from international restriction, in some instances, from national restriction, but also from a dogged persistence.

There is another set of figures which shows the great importance of export for the Netherlands Indies, the balance of trade. For a territory that serves as a field of investment for foreign capital, such as the Indies, export is a first necessity. Speaking broadly from a capitalistic point of view, export provides the gross profit of that capital, while import on the contrary represents a cost of capital investment and production; the export surplus therefore indicates the net return. The amount of capital invested in the Netherlands Indies can hardly be determined. Every estimate that has been made is too arbitrary in character. But the export surplus gives a rough idea of the volume of invested capital which must find its reward in that surplus.

TABLE VIII: BALANCE OF TRADE, 1929, 1933, 1938, AND 1940

In million guilders

| | 1929 | 1933 | 1938 | 1940 |
|---|---|---|---|---|
| Export | 1,443 | 468 | 658 | 882 |
| Import | 1,052 | 318 | 478 | 432 |
| Export surplus | 391 | 150 | 180 | 450 |

The preceding tables are intended to give a general impression of the value and composition of Netherlands Indies exports. To recognize the country's position in world trade, yet other types of information are needed. We must know, for example, to what countries the Indies' exports go and the changes produced by the economic crisis of the 'thirties in the destination of these exports.

All export is the result of specific business relations; but every business relation has two sides, and with the vigorous growth of the nationalist principle in commercial policy this twosidedness determines the balance of imports and exports between each country in active trade relations with another. This is the reason why a replacement of export from the Netherlands Indies will, sooner or later, cause a shift of import—or the reverse; and when something goes wrong with this reciprocity, a strong tendency arises for its recovery. In this adjustment, the colonial structure of the Netherlands Indies forms a complicating factor. For, as has been stated, export is of primary importance for the foreign capital invested in the Indies, while import figures mainly as part of the production cost. Now, capital can be indifferent to the origin of the imports as long as they are cheap; export naturally seeks the most profitable markets. But in the Indies these rational principles of commercial policy are crossed by two less rational principles, and these in recent years have greatly increased in power: the principle of national twosidedness—the bilateral commercial policy already mentioned, and the principle of the unity of the empire, that is, the principle that the colony and the motherland, historically joined together as they are, should stretch out their hands to each other in economic as well as in political matters. From these crossings of principles all kinds of compromises arise which will have our attention later: the quota system and the licensing policy and such as are connected with them. But first of all let us look at the export figures, grouped according to countries of destination:

TABLE IX: DESTINATION OF NETHERLANDS INDIAN EXPORTS BY VALUE AND AS
PROPORTION OF TOTAL EXPORTS, 1929, 1933, 1938, AND 1940

*In million guilders*

| Destination | 1929 Value | 1929 Per cent | 1933 Value | 1933 Per cent | 1938 Value | 1938 Per cent | 1940 Value | 1940 Per cent |
|---|---|---|---|---|---|---|---|---|
| The Netherlands | 231 | 16 | 86.7 | 18.5 | 134.1 | 20.4 | 49.1 | 5.5 |
| The rest of Europe | 330 | 23.1 | 96.2 | 20.6 | 111.5 | 16.9 | 80.3 | 9.1 |
| U.S.A. | 165 | 11.4 | 54.5 | 11.7 | 89.3 | 13.6 | 293.6 | 33.4 |
| The rest of America | 1 | 0.1 | 1.3 | 0.3 | 9.9 | 1.5 | 8.7 | 1.0 |
| Japan | 48 | 3.3 | 21.6 | 4.6 | 20.6 | 3.1 | 50.4 | 5.7 |
| The rest of Asia | 587 | 40.5 | 155.9 | 33.3 | 171.4 | 26.1 | 282.6 | 32.0 |
| Australia | 37 | 2.6 | 18.0 | 3.8 | 36.3 | 5.5 | 37.8 | 4.3 |
| Africa | 3 | 0.2 | 11 | 2.4 | 37.3 | 5.7 | 19.6 | 2.2 |
| Unknown | 41 | 2.8 | 22.7 | 4.8 | 47.3 | 7.2 | 59.7 | 6.8 |
| Total | 1,443 | 100.0 | 467.9 | 100.0 | 657.7 | 100.0 | 881.8 | 100.0 |

The strengthening of the tie with the motherland, before it was broken by the war, is clearly shown in these percentages. So also are the turning away of the exporters from Europe and Asia, the slight importance of Japan, and the increasing significance of America, Australia and Africa as recipients of Netherlands Indian exports. The figures for 1940 show the consequences of the state of war.

The import figures, grouped in the same way, give still stronger outlines to this changing picture. Here, too, one notes the turning away from Asia, which contributed more than one-half of the imports in 1933 but less than a third in 1938, the large increase for the Netherlands, and America's coming to the fore.

TABLE X:   ORIGIN OF NETHERLANDS INDIAN IMPORTS BY VALUE AND AS
PROPORTION OF TOTAL IMPORTS, 1929, 1933, 1938, AND 1939*

In million guilders

| | 1929 | | 1933 | | 1938 | | 1939 | |
|---|---|---|---|---|---|---|---|---|
| Region of Origin | Value | Per cent | Value | Per cent | Value | Per cent | Value | Per cent |
| The Netherlands ...... | 187 | 17.7 | 39.4 | 12.4 | 106.2 | 22.2 | 99.3 | 21.1 |
| The rest of Europe ..... | 297 | 28.2 | 73.3 | 23.0 | 133.6 | 27.9 | 118 | 25.0 |
| U.S.A. ........ | 130 | 12.3 | 15.6 | 4.9 | 60.2 | 12.6 | 63.7 | 13.5 |
| The rest of America ... | — | — | 1.7 | 0.5 | 4.2 | 0.9 | 4 | 0.8 |
| Japan ........ | 115 | 10.9 | 97.1 | 30.6 | 71.8 | 15.0 | 85 | 18.0 |
| The rest of Asia | 273 | 26.0 | 77.9 | 24.5 | 82.5 | 17.2 | 79 | 16.7 |
| Australia ..... | 26 | 2.5 | 10.2 | 3.2 | 13.3 | 2.8 | 15.4 | 3.2 |
| Africa ...... | — | — | 2.2 | 0.7 | 4.4 | 0.9 | 6.5 | 1.4 |
| Unknown .... | 24 | 2.4 | 0.2 | 0.2 | 2.2 | 0.5 | 1.5 | 0.3 |
| Total ....... | 1,052 | 100.0 | 317.6 | 100.0 | 478.4 | 100.0 | 472.4 | 100.0 |

*1939 was chosen instead of 1940 because in the latter year important government imports were not inserted in the statistical returns.

CAUSES OF INTERVENTION

*Overproduction.* The production of all goods supplied by the Indies to the world market increased enormously after the first world war. This was partly because of an increase of productivity but to a still larger degree because of extension of the cultivated area, hence expansion. In this respect, the Indies followed a line of conduct pursued by the whole world, but the colony was in a far less favorable position than most countries, one might even say, in an exceptionally unfavorable one, to do so because, for the sale of this increased output, the Indies were for the most part dependent on foreign markets and were, therefore, especially liable to suffer from measures of national protection. Thus, the most important foodstuff export, sugar, was very hard hit, even before

1930, by the complete or partial closing of its most important markets. There was no question of the Indies being able to force any of the doors closed to her. In many cases, the imperial policy of foreign customers did not even permit the free play of such power of competition as the colony possessed, and nothing could be done about it except to cut down the supply, to lessen production.

*Commercial Organization.* In a country like the Netherlands Indies, where foreign trade plays so important a role that relations must be maintained with all sorts of foreign markets, a country moreover consisting of a group of islands remote from all these markets, trade which serves import and export will naturally be concentrated in large-scale business houses. On the other hand, export goods, in so far as they are of native origin, are, as it were, produced bit by bit and offered for sale from many remote places in the interior; while import goods, in so far as they are intended for the native population, must be dispersed in diminutive quantities over an enormously extended area. All this is possible only with the help of an extensive carrying trade with many branches, and with the help of many buyers of native products and of many salesmen. This intermediate trade in the Netherlands Indies is almost entirely the domain of the Chinese. It includes lines of business in which credit is raised to alarming heights; and through long years of experience it has been weighted by debt to the utmost of its capacity. The depression and the deflation policy of the 'thirties appreciably increased the difficulties that beset this commercial organization. Especially imports suffered heavily; not only the constantly decreasing retail prices of imported goods but also the quickly depreciating buying power of the native consumers made almost superhuman the task of keeping the import trade going and up to the mark. Under these circumstances, the cheap Japanese goods were a real blessing for the Indian importers, and Japan's share in the total imports went up by leaps and bounds. The share of 10 per cent which the Empire had gained in the first world war and had maintained through the 'twenties rose to about 16 per cent in 1931, almost 21 per cent in 1932, 31 per cent in 1934, and over 32 per cent—almost one-third of total imports—in 1934. But the ambitions of Japanese commerce went beyond this expanded outlet for Japanese manufactures. In the long chain that linked the Japanese producer with the Netherlands Indian consumer, every link had to be forged by the Japanese: passing over the existing commercial apparatus, Japanese organization had to penetrate to the interior of the archipelago. It is easy to understand that such aspirations could not be respected. Not only political reasons forbade this, but the disturbance of the efficient import mechanism that had been built up with heavy financial sacrifices could not possibly be regarded as in the lasting interest of the consumer, and the danger that an import monopoly of foreign nationality might be operated to the disadvantage of the consumer could not lightly be dismissed. Moreover, this intermediate trade as a rule combined the sale of imported goods with the buying up of native produce; therefore, the native producers, too, were in imminent danger of being hit by the disturbance of the import trade apparatus.

Here, then, government interference was urgent, but here, too, that intervention was bound to be in the nature of a compromise. In a country where imports form the capital and furnish the production costs of exports, where everything must be staked on keeping cheap the population's standard of living, in such a country the wish to do without cheap Japanese goods could hardly be entertained. The Asiatic price level of articles for mass consumption offered at least some relief in the straitened circumstances; and only the desire to support the existing commercial apparatus could make acceptable even the partial relinquishment of the obvious advantages of cheapened imports. But that this concern over the commercial apparatus must lead to some moderation of Japan's share in imports was self-evident. This, indeed, was the immediate consequence of a new policy which reduced Japanese imports to only one-fourth (25.3 per cent) of total imports in 1937. A further sharp drop to 15 per cent in 1938 had other causes, chiefly in connection with the Sino-Japanese war and Japanese war policy.

*Movement of Prices and Wages.* The deflation policy, put into practice in both the Netherlands and the Netherlands Indies, kept up the gold price and, combined with the depression and the shrinkage of free markets, kept down export prices. The entrepreneurs, seeking to lower their production costs, found the least resistance in the wages of their laborers, which were considerably decreased. At the same time, the prices of native products—both those destined for export and those intended for the home market—could hardly be raised at all if indeed these products were not altogether unsaleable. Living became very cheap for the mass of the population; but the native farmer had great difficulty, sometimes found it impossible, to acquire the money he needed to meet his debts and to buy things he needed. Especially in Java, where money traffic had permeated more deeply into the economic life of the people, the drop in prices and wages caused serious social dislocations; and the Government could not leave matters as they were. Here intervention was necessary on several grounds: deliverance from debt, price fixing, protection of wages, and these measures could not wait.

*The Population Problem.* The problem of overpopulation may be regarded as the reverse of the problem of unemployment, to be discussed below. While the latter relates to the individuals who live in the Western sphere of the colonial economy, or strive to enter it, the population problem concerns the native masses living in the Eastern sphere. Both problems are localized in Java, the main island of the archipelago.

The population problem may also be seen as a problem arising from the business cycle and as a structural problem. When during the depression more than a hundred thousand laborers from the estates in the Outer Provinces were sent back to Java, and when, again in Java, native laborers from the towns, from the sugar estates (now shrunk to one-fifth of their original size) and from the various upland plantations returned to their villages without means of subsistence—returned, that is to say, to the very parts of the country which by reason of their dense population had supplied the labor armies of Western enterprise—many feared that the interior of Java would not be able to accommodate this influx and that serious disturbances would result. This apprehension, however, turned out to be unfounded; at least this depression problem solved itself. The community spirit in the *desas* (villages) still proved so strong, the absorbing power of the population still so elastic, that all these numbers could once more find their place in village life. They shared their new poverty with those whose lives also were poor; the lack of markets for native foodstuffs at least made it possible for the producers and all their dependents to eat. In some localities, however, which had to rely on imported foodstuffs and therefore on a money income, the people had a very bad time.

So much for the effect of the business cycle on the lives of the people. The structural population problem is quite another matter. For many years, a chorus of voices had made itself heard, warning that Java was getting overcrowded. The census of 1930 revealed a surprisingly rapid increase of the population. Every year the native population had grown by 500,000 to 600,000. But a survey of unused arable land had shown that, with such an addition to the number of farmers all the land available for clearance and new cultivation would be exhausted in a few years. The question is whether this structural problem, too, was influenced by the economic crisis, and whether, more urgently than ever before, it now demanded a short-term solution. The answer must be in the affirmative.

What is the actual situation? The Western enterprises in the archipelago have passed their period of expansion. Even the maintenance of the limits they have reached is no longer possible for most of them; they are obliged to curtail their area. The growing native population, therefore, cannot find a living on the estates or even expect to be as well paid when employed for wages as they were before the crisis. But this implies that one of the main channels supplying a money income for the native household is slowly becoming choked up, and just at a time when all of the Western administrative organization must more than ever rely on the money contributions of the native population.

Is it possible, it may be asked, for the Javanese farmer to acquire this essential income in his own agricultural business? The density of the population forms an insurmountable barrier to that possibility. Through lack of cultivable land, native agriculture already is developed to an intensity far beyond the optimum: there is no more place for those money crops that require a more extensive cultivation. This circumstance greatly limits the choice of crops. But where and how may other sources of money income be found? Is the advancement of native manufacturing industry one? It is, but only as long as those industries require no capital and as long as markets with sufficient purchasing power, lacking in Java, can be found elsewhere; and, another primary condition, provided that export is in some way helped by such a movement, for the problem is how to increase the total of native earnings, and ultimately this is possible only by an increase of sales abroad.

Here, then, is the structural population problem. It is essentially part of the problem of developing a money economy for the mass of Java's population. It is only one side of that problem, but it is the side which also brings it into direct contact with the economic depression, the side moreover to which too little attention has been paid, and finally the side where solution of the problem as a whole probably will meet its greatest difficulty.

*Unemployment.* With the shrinkage of production, retrenchment, as we have seen, became an imperative need for the authorities as well as for industry. It could not be brought about without making victims. On all sides people were dismissed. Netherlands Indian society suddenly confronted a problem which it had been spared up to that time: the problem of widespread unemployment. "Unemployment" is a Western concept; it assumes a social division of labor, paid labor as an exclusive means of existence, and entire dependence of the worker on this labor. The victims, therefore, were principally those who, of whatever nationality or occupation, were working as regular wage-earners in Western business. That the unemployment problem became especially acute among the European personnel has a colonial explanation. For the European the colony is a place to work, not a place to live in; if he cannot find work he becomes an outlawed exile; for there is no social refuge to which he can have recourse, able and ready to shelter him. Even for the Eurasian, who remains in the Indies all his life, the social environment at such a time proves insecure and of little help; all too soon he is forced to fall back on native society and becomes a "kampong-European," a resident in a native quarter.

The unemployment here described is often called conjunctural. In addition, the Indies has to fight against a more permanent form of unemployment, the structural unemployment which, likewise, has its own colonial imprint. A rapidly growing class of natives with a Western education underbids the European applicant for certain types of employment and pushes him out of the more modest professions; a native middle class begins to form, encouraged by the authorities, with its nucleus in the civil service—at the expense of the Eurasian group. The supply of graduates with a Western education proved much greater in the prewar decade than the shrunken Western labor market could digest. The solution of this problem is more difficult than that of the overproduction of goods in that it is hardly possible to apply a policy of restriction; to limit the opportunities for education and thereby to lessen the supply of educated labor would not be in the public interest.

CHAPTER III

GOVERNMENT INTERFERENCE WITH ECONOMIC LIFE

In 1937, at a conference of agricultural, industrial, and trade advisers in Batavia, the director of the Department of Economic Affairs of the Netherlands Indies made the following declaration about government interference with the economic life.

"We all, I believe, are beginning to realize how greatly we have in our younger years underestimated the world's capacity to undergo far-reaching changes, how wrong we have been in regarding our society as static, as fundamentally not very susceptible to radical change.

"It is true, more than a few of us have had social ideals whose realization would have effected more or less violent earthquakes in our society. For others these same ideals foreshadowed alarming pictures of future social degeneration. Still, if we are quite honest most of us admit that in our hearts we did not expect to live long enough to see the fulfillment of these ideals—or these nightmares. But behold, the world today offers a sample card, as it were, a specimen collection of utopias and of millennia of the most diverse designs. Every economic reformer of the last three centuries should be able to find his ideals realized somewhere in this present world, with the exception perhaps of Adam Smith, the founder of the liberal school.

"Throughout the world, and not only in the authoritarian states but certainly in the democratic states, people look at the government with different eyes than some years ago. Its authority is greater, its task is different: more comprehensive, more idealistic, and at the same time more realistic. This is strikingly the case in the field of economics. Under the force of circumstances, the spirit everywhere has changed especially in this respect. In the Netherlands Indies, too, people have been willing to give the Government an authority not dreamed of in former times—to give it power, sometimes readily with an open hand, sometimes reluctantly and under protest. In my opinion, the Netherlands Indian Government has never misused or exploited this authority; generally speaking, I believe, it has acted with self-control and objectivity. I am of the opinion also that in the years to come—under changed, more favorable conditions for lasting prosperity and for free international trade—this Government should have ample authority in the economic field. But I am no less convinced that, while retaining this competency, it will have to aim at limitation of its activities; those of the present are, in the long run, both too drastic and too extensive for our Indian society. As this society again acquires more resistance, and as the threats from outside diminish, we should systematically strive to put out of action the *de facto* use of some of the powers conferred upon the Government by recent statutes. The tensions of and within the government apparatus have become too great, in my opinion, for permanent use; these tensions today exist in many new domains where they cannot be maintained over a long period. The attraction of doing something new, of the call to action and the opportunity for showing results, attraction too of the chance to provide leadership and to support helpful movements, cannot in the long run be kept alive in scores of domains and for a relatively small group of live and versatile persons. There is the danger that the proper care for a number of important projects will drop to a mediocre level of devotion and skill, that the great evils of routine performance, formalism, red tape and ossification will appear. Further, it is undeniable that intensive government intervention, even under the best of circumstances, leads to a certain rigidity in the relations between the authorities and the people, to a certain lowering of energy, love of ease, too easy acquiescence, and a weakening of the personal power of perception and initiative among members of the community. There arises a tendency for the ambitious and industrious to see the most important tasks in government offices and not on the ships, in the commercial houses and on the estates."

The speaker cited was at the time head of the Department of Economic Affairs of the Netherlands Indian Government whose economic policy is the subject of the present chapter. His verdict is symptomatic for the responsible leader in the application of a new, more or less revolutionary, authoritative policy. Such an officer gladly convinces himself that only special circumstances necessitate a drastic government intervention, and that this is exceptional and temporary. All measures taken are marked as "crisis" measures and, at least at first, are designed to be of the shortest possible duration. Those who believe this behave as though the traditional liberal principles of government had retained unweakened their lasting validity. Even in 1937, the Governor General declared emphatically that the Indian Government, on principle, was remaining true "to the free play of spontaneous forces." But was this more than a phrase or, if you will, a handshake of farewell? Or were the authorities— and the quoted effusions of the director of the Department of Economic Affairs point in that direction—thinking with anxiety of the proverb, "In for a penny, in for a pound"? Was their real hope a return to the freedom to choose the best economic policy? But has such freedom to initiate policies really ever existed in any country, anywhere? In the previous chapter some problems have been reviewed which compelled government intervention in the Indies. It could not stay behind as the whole world went by without suffering ill consequences. Indeed, private interests impelled government intervention and emphatically insisted on it. This happened in regard to some private agricultural experiment stations and with the regulation of such products as sugar, rubber, cement, tea, cinchona, and others. Similarly, commerce, shipping, and various industrial concerns at first urged the Government to act. If it had readily followed all the wishes and demands of private interests, government interference would have been far greater than it actually was or is.

Be that as it may, people have come to the conclusion that government, whether as a matter of free choice or by force of circumstance, is able to regulate the economic life, to direct prices, to canalize the disposal of products, and to shift the population. In the Indies, where society is in some ways simpler and easier to control than elsewhere, where regulative measures as a rule can be confined to a limited number of large enterprises already in touch one with another, where the position of the central government forty years ago was purely autocratic and still is paramount, where economic problems need not be complicated by insolvable problems of higher politics, where everyone wishes to live in peace and friendship with the whole world—in the Indies the success of such government intervention can be more complete than almost anywhere else.

Therefore, unless compelled to follow in the tracks of all the countries with which the country entertains trade relations, the Netherlands Indian Government cannot be expected to go back on its policy and to give back their former freedom to private, individual profit hunters. What has once been regulated remains regulated. The Government itself apparently desires to clear away all illusions on that score. In a budget memorandum addressed to the Volksraad it declares:

> "The Government does not shape its policy toward the restoration of an uncontrolled industry or that of free trade. As it has explained many times, it must take into account that within a measurable space of time there will be no possibility for an entirely free industry, either in the interests of the community or in those of industry itself. Trade obstructions, however, are in themselves undesirable, in small as well as large business. They should not be confused with limitations of freedom in the interest of the community or in the interest of all who work together against undesirable influences from without."

Still more circumstantially, the Director of Economic Affairs, previously mentioned, stressed the same note in the speech quoted. Having previously declared that under normal circumstances one should strive systematically to put out of action some of the new provisions enacted for government intervention, he too appeared unwilling to give up the new system and to return to the old, if one may judge from the political confession with which he wound up that speech:

> "Do I wish, then, gradually to go back to the former situation—
> to a passive government, to the principle of non-intervention in
> the play of economic forces, to the unimpaired rule of the law of
> free competition?
> "No, decidedly not. I can see clearly a many-sided and extensive
> task for the Government in the Netherlands Indies. As I judge the
> situation, it will be obliged to continue, and even to intensify, the
> coordinating function which it has assumed during the period of
> depression. It will have to continue to bring and keep together
> groups of the community which in the general interest should work
> together, and if necessary to link such groups to one of its own
> organizations. It cannot tolerate that opposing groups should
> weaken our international economic position or harm the interests
> of other groups in this country through either controversy or too
> intensive a collaboration. It will still have to control the activities
> of certain interest groups, even *bona fide* activities, if they are in
> a position to cause serious damage to the concerns of the community, at home or abroad. It will have to continue to help the
> economically weaker groups become stronger; and to this end it
> will occasionally have to hold in check the activities of other groups
> if the general public interest demands it, even though these activities may be valuable in themselves. It will have to take care that
> economic interests do not under all circumstances and as a matter
> of course take precedence over social interests. . . ."

One gets the impression that not very much of the Government's present interference with the economic life of the Netherlands Indies is left out in what the speaker has in mind for the future. On the contrary, as a system it is to be supplemented: as he sees it, the Government will have to concern itself not only with the execution of plans derived from private initiative, it will have to take the lead as representative of the common weal.

An example will show this change in position and help to explain it. In 1933, people still were of the opinion that intervention of the authorities in industrial life was justified only when a majority of the private interests concerned were in favor of it and had agreed upon it beforehand. The task of the Government then was confined to carrying out the known wishes of industry, though this at times involved compulsion of unwilling outsiders to follow the demands of the majority, in so far as these were in the general interest. In such an atmosphere originated the tea restriction scheme. This is the reason why the international negotiations were not conducted by government representatives but by private persons, and why the agreement when reached was signed by representatives of the planters' organizations. Still, government agencies were needed to promulgate the regulations. A first step toward a change in these relations was the reorganization of 1935, by which governmental representatives were included as observers in the International Tea Committee, so that the governments at least were kept directly informed of the international planters' organization's proposed policies and no longer needed to hang on its apron strings in the hope of catching this or that bit of information. This step, however, was not enough: the governments wished to determine the restriction policy independently and in consultation with each other. Therefore, a second reorganization soon followed: the private delegates on the International Tea Committee made room for government delegates. It is to be expected that a final step will follow in due time: that the renewal of the international agreement will no longer be signed by the planters but by the governments concerned.

This illustration will help to confirm the point made in the introductory chapter, that the Netherlands Indian Government's interference with industry is not to be considered as an incidental, voluntary, and temporary policy, but has to be understood as a fundamental, necessary and lasting fulfillment of its task. The following chapters will indicate the directions in which the new government activities are moving. Here, however, a few words must be devoted to the executive organs through which this new government policy finds expression. Because of the speed with which the new direction was followed, and because of the temporary character which it was intended to attach to the new economic policy, which by preference still was called the "crisis policy," the organs for its execution were left constitutionally unarranged. All conceivable kinds of committees were conjured up. In 1937, the Economic Affairs Department counted about forty of them.

# Chapter IV

# GOVERNMENT INTERVENTION IN EXPORTS

## THE PROMOTION OF EXPORTS IN GENERAL

As has been pointed out before, export is a matter of life and death for the Netherlands Indies; and this is true not only with regard to estate products but also for native products. It is, therefore, understandable that, in spite of the inauspicious times and the difficulties caused by the restrictive trade policies adopted abroad, the Government, with these interests in mind, tried to find methods to stimulate export, to complement and reinforce what was already being done in this matter by private initiative. These methods have been of the most divergent kinds:

1. Advancement of sale and consumption through trade agreements, appointment of trade observers, export boards for various native products, propaganda for tea and coffee, exhibitions, and annual fairs;
2. Attempts to raise prices through international and autonomous restriction and export regulations;
3. Improvement of the products through agricultural and industrial advice, agricultural experiment stations, and research;
4. Increase of the variety of exportable products, through investigation of new industrial crops and promotion of the export of new products.

The results of these activities may broadly be gauged from Table XI, below, but cannot clearly be shown because restriction measures, adopted to meet overproduction, curtailed the quantities of some of the products exported, so as to improve prices.

TABLE XI: QUANTITIES OF PRODUCTS EXPORTED, 1928-29, 1937-38 AND 1940
*In million kilograms*

| Products | Average 1928-29 | Average 1937-38 | Percentage Decrease (—) Increase (+) | Average 1940 |
|---|---|---|---|---|
| Sugar | 3,025 | 1,100 | — 63 | 938 |
| Tobacco | 74 | 50 | — 32 | 29 |
| Tapioca products | 393 | 357 | — 9 | 241 |
| Tea | 81 | 69 | — 15 | 82 |
| Coffee | 101 | 85 | — 16 | 41 |
| Rubber and getah | 307 | 407 | + 32 | 596 |
| Vegetable oils and fats | 591 | 889 | + 50 | 537 |
| Drugs and spices | 95 | 124 | + 30 | 106 |
| Fibres | 77 | 113 | + 47 | 116 |
| Not specified vegetable products | 964 | 966 | + 0 | 857 |
| Earth oil | 4,039 | 6,362 | + 57 | 7,139 |
| Other minerals | 109 | 452 | +315 | 551 |

That the restrictions answered their purpose is shown in Table XII, below, in which the changes in the exported quantities of certain commodities over a ten-year period are set side by side with the changes in prices. Italicized figures show years restrictions were imposed.

TABLE XII: EXPORTED QUANTITIES OF PRODUCTS SUBJECT TO RESTRICTIONS AND PRICES REALIZED, 1929-1940

| Year | Sugar Million Kg. | Million Guilders | Plantation Rubber Million Kg. | Million Guilders | Native Rubber Million Kg. | Million Guilders |
|---|---|---|---|---|---|---|
| 1929 | 2,403 | 312 | 154 | 151 | 109 | 84 |
| 1930 | 2,222 | 244 | 156 | 128 | 90 | 43 |
| 1931 | 1,553 | 125 | 173 | 65 | 89 | 16 |
| 1932 | 1,502 | 97 | 153 | 28 | 62 | 5 |
| 1933 | 1,152 | 62 | 171 | 26 | 116 | 11 |
| 1934 | 1,089 | 45 | *200* | *58* | *186* | *62* |
| 1935 | 1,029 | 35 | 142 | 40 | 145 | 40 |
| 1936 | 869 | 34 | 163 | 68 | 151 | 68 |
| 1937 | *1,129* | *50* | 230 | 152 | 209 | 145 |
| 1938 | 1,071 | 45 | 156 | 74 | 147 | 59 |
| 1939 | 1,606 | 78 | 170 | 102 | 186 | 93 |
| 1940 | 938 | 53 | 276 | 173 | 269 | 155 |

| Year | Tea Million Kg. | Million Guilders | Cinchona Million Kg. | Million Guilders | Tin and Tin-ore Million Kg. | Million Guilders | Native Tea Million Guilders |
|---|---|---|---|---|---|---|---|
| 1929 | 73 | 86 | 10.3 | 10 | 42 | 79 | — |
| 1930 | 72 | 70 | 11.1 | 12 | 43 | 58 | — |
| 1931 | 79 | 70 | 6.1 | 7 | 34 | 37 | 3 |
| 1932 | 79 | 32 | 6.9 | 8 | 19 | 18 | *1.4* |
| 1933 | 71 | 26 | 6.5 | 6 | 17 | 22 | *3.4* |
| 1934 | 64 | 45 | *6.5* | *6* | 23 | *33* | 3.4 |
| 1935 | 66 | 37 | 6.6 | 8 | 28 | 36 | 2.7 |
| 1936 | 70 | 43 | 9.2 | 11 | 39 | 46 | 3.3 |
| 1937 | 67 | 49 | 6.5 | 10 | 51 | 84 | 4.8 |
| 1938 | 72 | 56 | 7.2 | 12 | 27 | 33 | 4.4 |
| 1939 | 84 | 57 | 6.9 | 11 | 39 | 59 | 4.5 |
| 1940 | 82 | 49 | 8.6 | 27 | 53 | 72 | 3.7 |

### SUGAR POLICY

Although Java is one of the lowest-cost producers of sugar, the fact that it depends on foreign markets for the sale of four-fifths of its production has had the result that this industry, though under normal conditions able to withstand powerful competition, has found the greatest difficulty in disposing of its output. The free sugar market has become continually smaller, as one country after another—the United States, Great Britain, British India, Japan—closed their frontiers or made competition impossible through measures of imperial preference. Since 1918, a voluntary and incomplete union of sugar producers in Java had tried to protect itself as best it could against the disintegration of the market by centralizing the sale in one agency. Moreover, in 1931 the producers' organizations of several important sugar-exporting countries concluded the so-called Chadbourne Agreement whereby exports were as far as possible adapted to the absorbing capacity of the remaining free markets. However, Java was not nearly able to dispose of its quota, and so its sugar stocks accumulated until in 1932 they reached the formidable height of two and a half million tons, almost the entire harvest of a year without restrictions.

Looming above the market, these supplies forced down prices. No one knew how to get out of this vexing situation, and a unanimous decision as to the policy to be followed seemed unattainable. The sale cartel threatened to fall through. In this crisis, with the day drawing near on which the sales organization was to end, the Government was appealed to. It set up a central sales commission to whose directions all the sugar estates had to submit and on which the Government acted in an advisory capacity with the right of veto. The main task of the commission, the N.I.V.A.S., was to clear up the enormous sugar stock at the highest possible prices that could be realized. Production, to be sure, was not legally placed under restraint, but in practice it was limited by the sales regulations of the central commission. The agencies set up, or "Nivas," actually succeeded in liquidating the surplus stock, although this was at the cost of a radical shrinkage of production during four years (a shrinkage that brought production down to less than one-fifth of what it had been) ; at the cost also of an enormous loss of income to the native population (a reduction of income from 138 million guilders to a little over 10 million guilders a year) ; and at the cost of severe capital losses to the sugar companies (the value of shares dropped by nearly 86 per cent below the level in 1928).

Even so, the provisions of the legal regulation in 1934 were clearly not radical enough to assure healthy conditions. The so-called free market for sugar could be estimated at only two and a half or three million tons per year in 1935; and on this market Java, Cuba, Peru, San Domingo, Czechoslovakia, Poland, Hungary, and other countries competed with a collective offer of 3.2 million tons. Moreover, among them were competitors who had a protected and extremely remunerative home market for a large part of their output and could therefore offer their surplus product on the free market at a loss.

In all this, Java was very much at a disadvantage. On the other hand, Java's natural market, Southeast Asia, had practically unlimited possibilities in that sugar here was more or less of a luxury, which made the demand very sensitive to price fluctuation, and the denseness of the population in some parts of this region could turn even a slight increase of average consumption into an important addition to sales.

Java could not alienate such a market by an inconstant price policy or risk losing it to rivals by holding out for too large a gain. The circumstances here demanded a carefully controlled production and a controlled market satisfied with moderate prices—a market, that is, which would not unnecessarily stimulate production and competition.

This could not be achieved without state intervention. Nor could the domestic struggles between the producers, which inevitably resulted in the victimization of both owners and native land lessors and workers, be averted without the authority of government. A "controlled" production, however, with the shrunken free market, meant a restricted production; and this could best be brought about by eliminating a number of enterprises altogether from the production process. This elimination had to take place as smoothly, as quickly, and as fairly as possible. The total production had to be determined annually. And that was no easy matter. For, because of the duration of the production process, the annual production of sugar cane had to be determined about two and a half years in advance; and once the figure had been set it could not be altered. Further, during the period of transition there had to be an opportunity for the re-arrangement of the production machinery. Not all of this could be managed without government regulation and direction. Moreover, it was essential to place a ban on the importation of sugar: as long as it was necessary to export this commodity at unremunerative prices, there was always the threat that from one or other of the markets it might be re-imported and so make it impossible to maintain a reasonable price on the home market.

Re-arrangement of the machinery of production involved a number of touchy questions. How could part of that machinery be put out of action? The exceptionally good and exceptionally poor units of production were only few in number; the great majority of sugar estates seemed to show only small differences between each other. To the concerns having more than one plant it was possible to leave, as a matter of internal adjustment, the task of putting one plant out of action. But what to do about isolated factories? Then, the interests of particular districts had to be considered, too. For example, in some of them it might be of crucial importance to have at least one sugar estate remain in operation as a source of money income which the growers could not afford to lose. In short, the problem could not be treated as though its solution involved simply a demolition of every production center which could be spared without too much damage; there was also the constructive task of building up a strong, firm, and well-connected whole. Rivalry had to make room for general cooperation.

While in the period 1933-1935 state intervention served only to supplement the work of the parties concerned and was based on the idea that the difficulties were of a temporary nature and that the Government would soon be able to withdraw, now the Government realized that it must act in the permanent interest of the Indies' national economy as a whole. A process of natural selection, resulting from a struggle between the various estate owners, would not only weaken these owners but also bring with it an intense search for further means of lowering costs and thus—perhaps even in the first place—bring heavier pressure to bear on land rents, wages, and buying prices. And not only the regulation of production needed the firm hand of government; the sales, too, needed the support which only their control by a monopoly could insure. Only by that means could the crowding out of Javanese exports from foreign markets be systematically counteracted and improvements of position, as soon as gained, be quickly and effectively consolidated. To counter any attempts at self-sufficiency which must be assumed to be a constant tendency of the sugar consuming countries, the price policy had to be moderate and cautious; and that was possible only with a firm and unanimous organization of sales. Finally, the sugar problem could be solved permanently only through international agreement; and for successful participation in international regulation a firm national organization was an inescapable prerequisite.

For all these reasons, the Netherlands Indian Government held its ground against the sugar factories; and so, after prolonged investigations and consultations, a new regulation came to light in January 1936. As a result of it, all production was placed under restraint, and the production apparatus was gradually adjusted to the new proportions of the trade. On this basis, the harvestable crops of 1937 and 1938 were brought back to the 1.4 million ton level—rather less than one-half of the potential production.

The losses suffered by the estate owners in the years in which sales were difficult amounted to about 150 to 200 million guilders. This means that in an important part of the industry the prices realized did not compensate for the expenses incurred, including wages and rents. A comparison of the course of payments that directly benefited the population in the depression years with the output of the plantations and the value of the harvests will be instructive. It reveals that, as a result of the production system under the estates' responsibility, the lowering of this category of costs followed only with a considerable time lag the decrease of prices and yield. If it has been truly observed that a strong boom reacts comparatively slowly and—if it lasts only a short time—incompletely on rents and wages, this is equally true of the reaction of a sharp fall of prices, a lag obviously of advantage to the lessors and wage-earners. Table XIII clearly shows this lag:

TABLE XIII: PRODUCTION AND YIELD OF SUGAR ESTATES COMPARED WITH RENTS, WAGES, AND OTHER PRODUCTION COSTS, 1927-1936

*In thousand tons\* and million guilders\*\**

| Harvest Year | Production * | Value ** ‡ | Rents ** | Payments to Javanese Wages† ** | Compensation ** | Total ** | Per cent of Yield |
|---|---|---|---|---|---|---|---|
| 1927-28 | 2,990 | 400 | 22.9 | 111.3 | — | 134.2 | 34 |
| 1928-29 | 2,935 | 350 | 23.9 | 105.7 | — | 129.6 | 37 |
| 1929-30 | 2,971 | 213 | 25.0 | 100.9 | — | 125.9 | 59 |
| 1930-31 | 2,839 | 178 | 25.9 | 86.2 | 0.1 | 112.2 | 63 |
| 1931-32 | 2,611 | 128 | 21.7 | 53.8 | 0.8 | 76.3 | 60 |
| 1932-33 | 1,401 | 64 | 11.9 | 22.2 | 2.7 | 36.8 | 57 |
| 1933-34 | 644 | 23.5 | 6.5 | 9.9 | 2.6 | 19.0 | 81 |
| 1934-35 | 513 | 19.5 | 3.5 | 6.0 | 2.5 | 12.0 | 61 |
| 1935-36 | 565 | 25 | 3 | 6.2 | 1.0 | 10.2 | 41 |
| 1936-37§ | 1,400 | 60 | 6 | 15.4 | — | 21.4 | 36 |

† Wages and other labor payments.

‡ On account of the slow sales of sugar, the price given is the middle price of the following harvest period, so as to make it comparable with the production costs. For example, the Fl. 400.00 entered for 1927-28 actually is the middle price made in the harvest year 1928-29.

§ Figures for the harvest year 1936-37 are rough estimates.

The circumstance that in Java sugar production does not take place through contracts of sugar centrals with native cane growers, it will be seen, has slowed up and mitigated the effect of the depression on the native population, as the decline in rents and wages lagged behind that of prices realized. If the system that obtains in Cuba had existed in the Indies, the full weight of decreased prices would immediately have fallen on the cane planters; and this indeed did take place in the case of other products that were bought by the European enterprises and not produced under their own auspices. This difference certainly should be taken into account in judging the Javanese system of sugar cane production. And this is not the only danger. The system of sugar manufacture from cane bought from the farmers involves the disadvantages that it requires a larger land area for planting (and irrigated land for food crops is exceedingly scarce in Java), and that the factories would be far less certain of being regularly supplied with the right amount of standard-quality raw material.

The following table shows that even with the production system which actually obtains in Java a large part of the cost represents payments to the native population. The table gives comparative figures for a boom year, 1925, and a depression year, 1936.

TABLE XIV: PERCENTAGE OF TOTAL COSTS OF SUGAR PRODUCTION SPENT ON RENT, WAGES, AND OTHER ITEMS, 1925 AND 1936

|                                                              | 1925 | 1936 |
|--------------------------------------------------------------|------|------|
| Rents                                                        | 7    | 10   |
| Wages to native population                                   | 30   | 27   |
| Salaries, pensions, bonus, European and higher native staff  | 14   | 11   |
| Upkeep, repairs, renewal of machines and buildings           | 14   | 5    |
| Manure, bags and auxiliary materials for manufacture         | 13   | 19   |
| Transport to harbor                                          | 7    | 8    |

It appears that, in spite of boom or depression, the share of the native population remains about the same. Another recent calculation, drawn from about thirty industrial accounts, shows that, out of a cost price (not including depreciation) of about 3.75 guilders per quintal, about 3 guilders (80 per cent) stay in the country and about 1.50 guilders (40 per cent) benefit directly the inhabitants of the sugar districts.

At the same time, it should be realized that it may be of the utmost importance to develop the native economy by giving it a more prominent place in the production process; and that therefore one should be pre- pared, even at the cost of maximum efficiency, to return—partly at least and under certain conditions—to the buying-up system.

To return to the sugar regulation of 1936, what exactly were its pro- visions?. Each year the maximum production was to be determined by the Government and assigned in production quotas to the units of the industry, the quotas being in proportion to the former production capa- city of each unit. These production quotas were made transferable for a period of four years, so as to give the industry an opportunity to re-organize itself as economically as possible. The expectation originally was that in 1940 the industry would have stabilized its basis of produc- tion, and that this basis would be suitable to consolidate in legal form. This expectation was not, however, realized. Notwithstanding the London Sugar Convention of 1937, the market for Java sugar re- mained uncertain, influenced as it was by political developments abroad, the output of sugar cane in British India, the war in China, and other events. For example, as a result of the sales campaign, fully 244 thousand tons of sugar could be shipped to British India in 1938-39, as compared with only 32 thousand tons in the previous year. Another source of uncertainty was the fact that the London convention was to come to an end in 1942; and no one knew what effects the changed world position at that time might have on sales.

Because of these uncertainties, the Javanese sugar industry thought it advisable to keep a reserve by not letting the active units work at full capacity and by having ready an additional number of idle units. And it was still considered necessary to leave production quotas transferable—

but in such a way that the units closed for the time being would not be definitely shut off from possible future participation.

Although the Netherlands Indian Government had already in February 1935 fixed the maximum productive capacity at 17.5 million quintals, only about 50 of the 178 factories, with a normal total capacity of 29.5 million quintals of sugar, were to be regarded as definitely closed. This means that, besides the 84 factories which had part in the harvest of 1939, 44 factories still were kept ready, entirely or in part, to begin producing again if necessary and desirable. Moreover, the 84 factories mentioned produced to 96 per cent of their normal capacity; 22 isolated factories out of these 84 produced only to 75 per cent. One cannot therefore say that the situation has already been reached where the amount of Java sugar which the Indies can sell is entirely and exclusively manufactured by the economically best situated factories, working at full capacity.

In conclusion, one may state that the organization of sugar production in Java has settled down, although still keeping its essential elasticity. The producers will certainly retain the principle of the "single seller," of a monopolistic sales organization. Seen from a statistical point of view, one may consider about two-thirds of the manufacturers, counted according to their interests in the production, as supporters of the continuation of this system. Counted as companies, the supporters are far more numerous, however, because the smaller companies profit most by the monopolized selling organization. The chief considerations in favor of the continuation of the "single seller" are the necessity (a) of a common, purposeful sales policy for retaining and strengthening foreign sales, (b) of preventing destructive competition on the home market, which still takes 20 per cent of the production, and (c) of establishing guarantees against a wrong application of stocks arising from eventual miscalculation in the estimation of the year's production.

Finally, a few words more about the international sugar export regulation, the previously mentioned London Sugar Convention of May 1937. This convention, too, is an example of how governments, in fixing an international economic policy, take over the task of private initiative. The London Convention, the result of informal deliberation between the English and the Netherlands Governments, can be regarded as successor to the private so-called Chadbourne Agreement, which succumbed as the result of its imperfections. Twenty-one countries took part in the conference. An International Sugar Board, set up by the authority of the convention, and composed of government representatives, has the right to fix the annual export quota. The Netherlands and the Netherlands Indies are regarded as one in this convention, but practically speaking only Java comes into consideration for sugar export.

Professor J. Van Gelderen, who (as Netherlands representative) signed the sugar convention, declares in his book, *The Recent Development of Economic Foreign Policy in the Netherlands East Indies* (London and New York, 1939), about the sugar regulations (p. 62): "The recent history of the Java sugar industry . . . is a good example of a system of national planning . . . containing elements which can hardly be neglected in the further development of international economic policy."

RUBBER

The first restriction on rubber production introduced in the Netherlands Indies was a result of the international agreement of May 7, 1934, between the Netherlands Indies, Great Britain and Siam, to restrict exports for about four and a half years. As described in the preamble, the purpose of this agreement was to regulate production and export, so that world stocks might fall to normal levels, supply would systematically be adjusted to demand, and a reasonable price could be maintained, sufficient to remunerate producers with efficient working procedures. The means utilized to put rubber cultivation on a sound basis were limitation of stocks, prohibition of new planting, and international organization for scientific research, for the consideration of new applications, and for promotion to stimulate demand. The execution of this international program was put in the hands of an International Rubber Regulation Committee, composed of government delegates.

The first phase of the rubber restriction agreement's operation was marked by various difficulties. At the start, speculation drove up prices on the rubber market and so stimulated production, that the restriction measures lost part of their effect. About the middle of 1935 there began to be an improvement in this respect. Under the influence of the gradual reduction of the export quotas and the increase in consumption, world stocks decreased by degrees. After that, however, a disturbance of the balance was threatened from the side of the world demand. The strained political situation led to the accumulation of rubber reserves in several countries, the export quotas had to be raised again, and the available world supplies decreased to the low level of 396 thousand tons at the end of May 1936. The International Rubber Regulation Committee after that did not succeed in preventing price fluctuations. The fact that the export percentage has to be fixed some time before it comes into force, and that the production apparatus can adapt itself only very slowly, makes impossible a prompt response of restrictive action to changes in demand. Moreover, the rubber trade continued to show a strong tendency toward speculation.

In spite of all this, the international working of the restriction scheme may be considered satisfactory. To finance investigations and the promotion of increased rubber consumption, most of the countries concerned with the restriction have since 1936 raised a levy on exporters, now uniformly fixed at one cent per 100 pounds. The administration of the fund collected in the Netherlands Indies is entrusted to the "Crisis Rubber Centrale," the financial center of rubber research work. The executive work is done in the Netherlands by the Rubber Institute and in the Indies by the research section of the rubber experimental station in West Java. Originally, the national regulation of the restriction plan made a distinction between three groups of producers. The first group consisted of all the Western rubber estates in Java and the Outer Provinces, the second of native rubber areas in Java, and the third of native rubber plantations in the Outer Provinces. It was thought at the time that each of these groups required a somewhat different system of restrictive regulation.

Under the system that rules restriction for the first group, a standard production is annually fixed for each estate, to serve as a basis for sharing out the total volume of production for which licenses are available each year. Each estate receives a production license in proportion to its standard quota and must, when exporting, procure an export certificate. The licenses are transferable with permission of the director of the Department of Economic Affairs.

The situation of the second group was rather different. Whereas in the Outer Provinces native rubber had since 1925 been subject to a separate export tariff and the total extent of native rubber production was therefore fairly accurately known, in Java the Government, having no such customs statistics to fall back upon, was entirely in the dark as to what part of the total rubber exports came from native gardens. However, because of the concentration of the plantations in Western Java a rough survey and registration was possible, and the approximate productive capacity could be estimated. In the second half of 1936, these native plantations in Java were re-registered, and it was shown that they contained 7,956,332 trees distributed over a total planted area of 15,049 hectares. The valuation of these plantations was based on the results of a large number of test tappings which, meanwhile, had taken place in the native rubber areas of the Outer Provinces. In this way the productive capacity of this group was determined with some degree of accuracy. A harvesting license was issued monthly to the native producers of rubber in Java, and these could be changed for export certificates. Both harvesting licenses and export certificates are transferable on a limited scale.

The system used for the third group was quite different. Here the principle of a special export tariff was adopted as an emergency measure in 1934; by raising the tariff it was possible to lower the price level of native rubber, so that production in native areas would not exceed the proportionate volume of exports permitted by the restriction regulations. The Government expected that the amount of rubber supplied by the native growers would be directly proportional to the price of rubber. This proved to be an error, since it left out of account the fact that the native producer often depends for his living on the sale of rubber. Such a man will intensify the tap and increase the supply every time the price he receives per unit of rubber goes down. The supply by these producers, therefore, was *inversely* proportional to the price of rubber minus export duties.

The Government was not blind to the faults and the unfairness of this threefold system of regulation which necessity had forced upon it. From the first, it provided that the yield of the special export tariff should, as far as possible, benefit the rubber-growing districts. At the same time, it declared that it would leave no stone unturned to discover a better system. This was all the more necessary when it appeared that, after all, the Government could not control production with the help of the export tariff. In spite of a gradual increase of the special export tariff rate from 5 cents per half kilogram to 14.5 cents (end of 1935), the quota was repeatedly exceeded.

At the end of 1934, the excess amounted to 8.5 thousand tons, a little more than 10 per cent of the quota of native rubber allotted to the group. Considering the difficulties experienced at the start of the restriction when the special tariff had to be put into force, this deviation from the intended effect cannot be regarded as very serious. Less favorable was the fact that the year 1934 closed with a stock of 17,000 tons of native rubber in the hands of the recognized exporters.

During the following year this became much worse. Although the export tariff was screwed up higher and higher, the excess amounted to 29,000 tons at the end of May 1935, 34,000 tons at the end of September, and 44,000 tons at the end of November. It was then decided to buy up estate licenses and to take native harvest licenses off the market to the amount of twenty thousand tons, payment to be made from the returns of the special export tariff. In this way the export of an equal quantity of native rubber could be covered. The Government succeeded in buying up 19,667 tons of estate rubber licenses and in taking 330 tons of native licenses off the market at a cost of about 5,625,000 guilders. At the same time it conducted international discussions to obtain an increase of the Netherlands Indies' basic quota as a means of meeting the great difficulty it had encountered with the restriction of native rubber production. This step, too, was successful: for the years 1936 to 1938, the basic quota was increased successively by 57, 53, and 55 thousand long tons, and the international committee acquiesced in the excess of the Netherlands Indies' quota which still existed at the end of 1935.

In September 1936, depreciation of the guilder made necessary a further increase of the special export tariff; the rate rose as high as 29.5 cents per half kilogram. In the meantime a beginning had been made with preparations for an individual licensing system for the third as well as for the second group of producers. Because of the tree count made in North Sumatra, which has previously been mentioned, that area was already available in 1935 for a possible introduction of individual restriction. Toward the end of that year, a general registration and classification of native rubber holdings was started at full speed in accordance with a scheme devised by the central government, to cover all districts. This survey included the property of about 750,000 owners with a total of about 582 million rubber trees. The productivity of these plantations was ascertained by means of test tappings. Thus, on January 1, 1937, individual restriction could be introduced in all the important rubber areas.

The new system of native-rubber restriction in the Outer Provinces has so far worked well. The owners of the groves obtain the necessary licenses, called "harvest licenses" or "rubber coupons." These are distributed every quarter in connection with the three-monthly determination of the total restriction quota set by the International Rubber Regulation Committee. The rubber coupons are very popular in the interior; in fact, they have become a valued object of commerce and are generally used as a means of paying accounts. The money value of the coupons has practically taken the place of the former special export tariff as an index of the fluctuations of rubber quotations on the world market. For example, in mid-January 1937, the price obtained in Palembang for such coupons was 50 cents per kilogram. Taking also into consideration the rise in the price of copra and other native products, it was possible to compute that the receipts of the population in the Outer Provinces had increased by about 12 million guilders per month. As a result, banks and commercial firms opened or re-opened offices in the rubber districts, and the Java Bank brought large quantities of bank-notes and currency into circulation. Moreover, a substantially increased movement of manufactured goods of better quality, including smokers' requisites, packed provisions, preserves, milk products, bicycles, and automobiles, took place from Java to the rubber districts. And in the same year, 1937, prices of batik work increased by 30 per cent.

The rubber coupons finally reach the hands of the exporters who now can buy up rubber supplies not previously covered with export certificates and export these supplies on the strength of the coupons. There is, therefore, a separate market for rubber that is and is not covered by coupons in each of the different rubber areas. The price paid for the "uncovered" rubber gives the measure of the extent of the production. The separate trade in coupons and in uncovered rubber has a very speculative character which is quite to the taste of Orientals. (See *The Structure of Netherlands Indian Economy*, New York 1942, chapter X.)

So much for the restriction system as it applies to different groups of rubber producers. Something more should be said about the financial results of restriction measures. Since the basic quota allotted to the Netherlands Indies under the international scheme during the first restriction period was considerably higher than the volume of rubber exports had been in the preceding years, the restriction did not lead to a decrease of exports, but by effecting an improvement in prices it furnished the Netherlands Indies with an important increase of income and helped in no small degree to strengthen the country's balance of payments and financial position.

TABLE XV: QUANTITIES AND PRICES OF ESTATE AND NATIVE RUBBER EXPORTS, 1929 TO 1940*

In thousands of tons and cents per half kilogram of standard sheets in Batavia

| Year | Estate Rubber | Native Rubber | Total | Price |
|---|---|---|---|---|
| 1929 | 154.4 | 108.6 | 263.0 | 54 |
| 1930 | 155.5 | 90.5 | 246.0 | 30½ |
| 1931 | 172.6 | 88.7 | 261.3 | 15 |
| 1932 | 153.3 | 62.4 | 215.7 | 8½ |
| 1933 | 171.2 | 115.6 | 286.8 | 11 |
| 1934 | 199.6 | 185.9 | 385.5 | 20 |
| 1935 | 142.5 | 144.9 | 287.4 | 18½ |
| 1936 | 163.2 | 151.4 | 314.6 | 27 |
| 1937 | 230.0 | 208.6 | 438.6 | 37 |
| 1938 | 160.0 | 146.6 | 306.6 | 27 |
| 1939 | 189.6 | 186.2 | 375.8 | 31½ |
| 1940 | 262.0 | 266.0 | 528.0 | 32 |

* One should not try to calculate the income of the native rubber planters for any one year by multiplying the quantity of native rubber exported with the standard price, since these growers receive only a fraction of the price realized in Batavia.

In the first three years of restriction, 1934 to 1937, the direct and favorable effect which it might have had on the native welfare was impeded by the levy of the special export tariff. In these few years, that special tax yielded no less than 85.2 million guilders. Part of this amount served to pay for the cost of the individual registration and licensing system; the greater part, however, benefited the rubber districts since it was spent on relief and to carry on social work and economic improvement generally. In 1937 it was decided to set apart from the general budget a sum of about fifteen million guilders, drawn from the returns of the special export duty on native rubber, and deposit it in a "rubber fund." Specific allocations from that fund have kept pace with the progress in the planning of relief measures which investigation revealed as necessary. Such measures included road and irrigation works, a study of the "yellow disease" of pepper, the construction of military hospital barracks in Bandjermasin and Palembang, a polyclinic in Djambi, a campaign to combat framboesia and other native diseases in the Dayak regions, grants in aid of individual native states to make up budget deficits, agricultural and industrial research, soil investigations, and other projects. A central advisory board and regional committees were set up to guide the expenditure of the fund. By far the largest part of the income from the export duty was used, however, on projects, such as those named, that had been pursued before the fund came into being.

As has already been pointed out, the introduction of individual restriction came at about the same time as higher prices; both together brought large sums to the rubber districts. The value of native-grown rubber exports in 1937 could be estimated at 145 million guilders; and although 1938 brought a reaction, both in quantity and prices, the export value of that year still reached about 76 million guilders. The effects of this increased income were noticeable in the rubber districts. Clothes and food improved both in quality and quantity, road transportation increased considerably, a reduced stock of cattle was replenished, there was much activity in the construction and furnishing of houses, new articles of daily use were procured, debts were paid off, festivities became more splendid. More care was spent on the rubber gardens themselves. Many thousands of rolling presses were imported to improve the quality of the product; large areas of reserve rubber gardens were opened up; areas under operation were better kept; better tapping tools were purchased; more owners built smoking houses. The proportion of wet rubber in the total exported, which was about 40 per cent at the beginning of the restriction, was reduced to a very small figure, so that returns from remilling now remain for the most part in the country. The improvement of the general welfare begun in these ways has had a stimulating influence throughout the districts affected and beyond them. Thus, the increased export of piece goods from Java to the Outer Provinces roused the sarong weaving and batik industries to new life. The larger demand for tap knives, iron bedsteads, furniture, and other articles brought great activity in the small metal goods- and furniture-making shops. A cattle-producing district such as Madura responded to a lively demand from the Outer Provinces. Throughout Java, groups and communities benefited from the larger exports of luxury articles, such as cigarettes, sugar, tea, preserves.

To sum up, one may say that rubber restriction has brought great advantages, in the first place, to the rubber estates and the rubber-producing population; but these advantages have also played no unimportant part in bringing greater prosperity to other large parts of the archipelago.

Finally, a few words on the more recent extension of the rubber restriction scheme. For years to come, rubber cultivation in the Indies will remain in a state of overcapacity. In 1937, the productive capacity of the world, at a low estimate, was from 1.6 to 1.7 million tons as against a consumption that had reached 1.1 million tons. An abandonment of the restriction scheme, therefore, is out of the question. Indeed, renewal of the international agreement was unanimously demanded in 1939 and brought about in that year, though in a somewhat modified form.

The basic quotas were revised. As far as the Netherlands Indies are concerned, the quota of 540,000 tons at the end of the first restriction period was raised to 631,500 tons for 1939, to 651,000 tons for 1943, averaging 41.5 per cent of the joint basic quota. The maxima of permitted home stocks also were increased, so that any unexpected increase in demand could more easily be met. Some important changes were introduced also in the plantation provisions: unrestricted replanting was allowed for the years 1939 and 1940, and extension of cultivation by 5 per cent of the area under rubber. In addition, the international committee stipulated that an area corresponding to one per cent of the total area under rubber should be held in reserve for possible further expansion when and where this might be deemed necessary.

At the end of 1940, the situation was again reviewed. It was now made permissible to export rubber planting material between countries taking part in the restriction scheme. The position of the Netherlands Indies on the international committee was strengthened by raising the number of its members from three to four. The levy for research and promotion was made obligatory for all the participating countries. And a new article was inserted in the international agreement providing that the agreement might be suspended for one or more countries when this was considered necessary by the international committee for its or their national safety. However, the provisions concerning planting and prohibition of the export of planting material are excluded from this permissive article.

The Netherlands Indies' own provision for the execution of its part in the international agreement was formerly spread over five ordinances. It is now contained in a single rubber restriction ordinance, adopted in 1939. This is divided into four chapters: general restriction provisions, special regulations for estate rubber, those for native rubber, and general prohibitions and stipulation of penalties. The wording of the clauses was as far as possible brought into harmony with that of the cinchona restriction ordinance of 1937 and the tea restriction ordinance of 1938.

Everything pertaining to the enforcement of the restrictions on native-grown rubber is put in the hands of the Department of Civil Service. This means that administration of the restriction regulation for native rubber in Java has been merged in the general provision for the restriction of native rubber growing. The three categories of growers described above thereby have been reduced to two. Of course, this transfer involves a change in the basic quota allotted to estate rubber and to native rubber. Table XVI shows the somewhat greater increase of the estimated productive capacity of estate rubber compared with that of native rubber. Both together more and more surpass the internationally set basic quota for the Indies, so that the restriction is correspondingly felt more severely.

TABLE XVI:  ESTIMATED PRODUCTIVE CAPACITY FOR ESTATE AND NATIVE RUBBER
PLANTATION AND INTERNATIONAL BASIC QUOTA, 1939-1943

*In long tons*

| Year | Estate Rubber | Native Rubber | Total | International basic quota |
|---|---|---|---|---|
| 1939 | 330,193 | 325,600 | 655,793 | 641,634 |
| 1940 | 348,377 | 330,950 | 679,327 | 650,271 |
| 1941 | 364,474 | 336,300 | 700,774 | 655,859 |
| 1942 | 379,470 | 341,650 | 721,120 | 660,431 |
| 1943 | 391,825 | 347,000 | 738,825 | 661,447 |

Grant of a 5 per cent extension of the plantation area opened up the possibility of an added cultivation of 65,000 hectares. Of this total, 1,300 is reserved for general welfare purposes, namely, 1,000 hectares to establish a rubber estate in New Guinea, on which a beginning has already been made, and 300 hectares to extend the native rubber area on the west coast of Atjeh in North Sumatra.

Because a report on replanted areas must be sent annually to the International Rubber Regulation Committee, the replanting of estate grounds requires a license now; in 1939 and 1940, however, it could take place without limits. As far as extension is concerned, after a modest reserve of extension areas has been made for experimental purposes and to meet disasters and other special circumstances, the remaining area available for estate extension is allotted in accordance with the extent of area under cultivation, with permission to transfer from one unit to another.

To estimate the productivity of native gardens involves a more complicated process. There is a distinction not only between tapped and tappable but untapped gardens: those tappable but not yet tapped are estimated to be from one-tenth to one-fourth as extensive as the tapped gardens. But further corrections have to be made to allow for planting distances and the condition of the gardens. Eight hundred tap tests taken for periods of two months formed the basis for the estimate. On the score of these tests, the investigators finally arrived at basic figures for the production per tree in different rubber districts, varying from 0.52 to 1.91 kg., with an average of 0.85 kg., per year. At the end of 1939, the Government decided to organize a more accurate survey of the extent and productive capacity of native rubber areas, and this for two purposes: to implement international negotiations over the fixing of the Netherlands Indian quota, and also to guide the division of the basic quota allowed to the Indies as between estate and native production. The study was also intended to serve the further division of the native quota into district and individual quota allocations. In 1935-36, lack of time permitted no more than a tree count, but now measurements were taken by the topographic service, and the individual gardens were classified according to age, bark reserve, planting distances, etc.; and further tapping tests were made in the various classes of which four were distinguished. Although this involved a much dispersed area of at least 700,000 hectares, spread over a large region, the Government hoped to finish the classification in two and a half years.

As has already been mentioned, restriction on the native rubber plantations is in practice effected by the issue of three-monthly harvest licenses, transferable without limit but only in the particular restriction district. These harvest licenses, of which about a million are issued each time, can be changed for export certificates. These certificates, again, can be split into export tickets where this is necessary to equalize the quantities to be exported and their coverage. Limitation of transferability to the restriction district concerned serves to prevent a group of rubber garden owners in any one district from selling their harvest licenses through one large, joint transaction. For, if that happened, many of the native garden owners would become accustomed to receiving a regular income without doing anything for it; the tapping would be neglected or stopped altogether; and the existing apparatus for milling and sale would be lost. In short, it would be risky, considering the possibility that the restriction agreement may be brought to an end and many who now draw an essential part of their income from milling, processing, transport and intermediate trade in native rubber might lose these means of livelihood. The archipelago as a whole has been divided into thirteen registration districts for native rubber cultivation. Transportation of rubber from one to another of these districts is not forbidden but it could be checked if serious results of this freedom should appear.

As for the division of areas available for the extension of native rubber cultivation, two steps are necessary. First, a general division of the district is made in proportion to the areas planted with rubber. After that, further division among the individual planters is left to the local authorities of the native communities, acting under the directions given by the Residents concerned. Where such a native authority, or one with sufficient competence, cannot be found, the local government gives out transferable plantation coupons in proportion to the rubber area cultivated by each grower without the aid of a native intermediary.

Native no less than estate rubber contributes to the costs incurred in the maintenance of the restriction scheme, in international sales promotion, and in research. The dues raised for these purposes on exported native rubber are slightly augmented to pay for special information and advisory services and any special measures taken to strengthen the native sector of the rubber industry. By this means, the native growers are provided with valuable planting material; seed from good nurseries is made available in sufficient quantities at the price of one cent per seed; and through the services of the Agricultural Department 200 hectares of seed gardens are spread out over the various rubber districts and kept in reserve.

TEA

Signs that the tea market of the world was oversupplied were noticed as early as 1927. And it was feared that, with the large extension of plantations in the various tea-producing countries, overproduction would become still greater in the future. Prices which had averaged about 90 cents per kilogram in Amsterdam until the middle of 1926 had by the end of 1932 dropped to about 22 cents. In Batavia, the average price paid at the end of 1932 was only 13 cents per half kilogram; the position of tea cultivation in the Netherlands Indies had become so precarious that, in spite of a cut in expenses which had lowered the cost price to one-half of what it was in 1930, nine out of every ten tea estates worked at a loss. Some of the factories were closed down. Native growers, who had received up to ten cents per half kilogram of wet leaf in 1926, had in 1932 to be satisfied with 1.5 cents—a price which even for them no longer made picking worth while.

This crisis in the tea trade was serious because in the Netherlands Indies big as well as small interests are concerned with the cultivation. At the end of 1932, the total planted area of tea estates amounted to 135,704 hectares, and these estates provided work for about 270,000 laborers, including women and children. The plantations of native and small Eurasian farmers at that time were estimated to cover 39,375 hectares. (Later experience showed this to have been a serious underestimate.) In the same year, 69,500 tons of dry tea were manufactured by the companies from their own plantations and from the produce of small Eurasian farmers, in addition to 12,424 tons from native leaf. The question was, could so important an apparatus of production be allowed to go out of action?

The tea producers in the three most important countries of production, British India, Ceylon, and the Netherlands Indies, got together and decided to restrict exports and thereby also production, at least production intended for export. The different governments were asked to help, an agreement was made for five years, and a plan for centralized promotion of tea consumption was drawn up. This agreement was concluded on February 9, 1933. In April of that year, the Government of the Indies introduced in the Volksraad three draft ordinances, a tea export ordinance, a tea planting ordinance, and an executive tea export regulation for 1933, which was adopted on May 9. Some time later an ordinance prohibited the export of tea seed, tea plants, and plant material. The first of the three regulations was made retroactive to April 1, 1932, the date on which the international agreement was considered to have come into effect. The basic quota for Netherlands Indian tea exports had been fixed at about 21.5 per cent of the total exports of the three contracting producing countries. The restriction was fixed at the rate of 15 per cent for the first year and 12.5 per cent for the second. Each country was left free to determine how to divide among its tea producers the total amount allotted for export. In the Indies the first necessary step was to decide on the proportion of exports to be allowed for "estate leaf" and for "purchased leaf." This was settled at nine for the former and two for the latter.

To determine the leaf quotas for individual estates, the standard annual production of 320 of them was separately calculated. To these standard production figures, revised where it seemed necessary, the annual restriction percentages were applied. Since the sum of the standard estate production figures was greater than the nine-eleventh part of the export quota based on production in the previous year, and since further increases of production were to be expected during the five-year restriction period, the percentages allotted were higher than compatible with the international quota. Thus, the standard production of tea from estate leaf in 1933-34 amounted to 80.4 million kg., as against a total of 64.4 million kg. which would have been the nine-elevenths of the total Netherlands Indian quota allotted to estate leaf. In this way, an international restriction percentage fixed at 15 per cent for the estates in the Indies increased to 32 per cent, in the second year, with the increasing standard production, to 35 per cent, and in the following restriction years to more than 40 per cent.

The restriction regulation left open to estate owners the possibility of transferring export licenses in whole or in part from one of their own estates to another or even to estates of another owner—in each case, however, subject to the approval of the authorities, since public interests in the respective districts might be affected by these transfers. Of late, the number of such formal transfers has greatly decreased with the introduction of a system of joint licenses by which owners receive a single license for all the estates belonging to them.

So much for estate leaf. How does the native grower fare under the tea restriction policy? The export quota for tea from "bought leaf" was based on purchases in 1931 by 158 factories. Decreased by the uniform application of the restriction percentage, this purchase basis produced a quantity amounting to less than the two-elevenths of total exports allowed to the Netherlands Indies. This means that, in comparison with the assignment for estate leaf, that for bought leaf had been made too liberal. The surplus, given the name of "purchase reserve," was set apart to be distributed in special cases and in a special way among the purchasing factories. The manufacturers of "bought" tea also receive annual export licenses from the Indies Government.

In order to protect the native interests, purchases by the factories, traditionally taking place twice a year according to the seasons, was at first divided into two half-yearly terms, in the proportion of 40 to 60 per cent. It soon became evident, however, that the interest of the people needed more far-reaching protection, that it was necessary to keep a strict watch over the regularity of purchases and to insure a fair ratio between the purchase prices paid for native leaf and the tea prices on the export market. In each of the eight regencies where native tea plantations or plantations belonging to small Eurasian farmers were to be found, a beginning was now made with the appointment of mediation boards, under the presidency of the respective Regents. These boards have the task of seeing to it that native leaf is bought at a reasonable price and of trying to solve any difficulties that might arise in connection with these purchases. Further, a purchases subcommittee was appointed, with the task of looking after the special concerns of tea cultivation by the native population and by small Eurasian farmers; two lower civil-service officers in each case were associated with the subcommittee to supervise the purchases of wet leaf.

The difficulties which arose from the purchase of wet tea leaf could, as has already been intimated, in the main be considered under two headings: those connected with the fair distribution of purchases over the year and those connected with the fixing of a reasonable purchase price. As for the first of these difficulties, division of the purchases into two half-yearly periods did not go far enough; therefore six periods of two months each were decided upon. By this means the purchasing factories were obliged to distribute their purchases with greater regularity over the year. A third difficulty arose from the rationing of the purchases among the native tea gardens dependent on the local factory. This was because too large a proportion of leaf was offered from gardens in the immediate surroundings of the factories, to the disadvantage of the gardens farther away, so that in some outlying districts of the Preanger the local people often had no chance at all of selling their leaf.

As a first attempt to meet this last problem, extra licenses from the buying reserve were granted to purchasing factories on condition that purchases were to be made in specifically named remote districts. This, however, did not help enough. The most thorough-going remedy here seemed to be individual licensing to all the native producers of tea leaf, permitting each to sell only that part of the standard production of his tea garden to which he had a right, and no more.

Something like this had been done for native rubber production in Java, a system of individual restriction that had proved effective. A thorough investigation was now made of the applicability of such a system to native tea production. All of the authorities concerned with tea restriction were asked for their opinion: on the whole, it was felt that the granting of individual licenses to the small leaf producers, of whom there were many thousands, distributed over a wide area, would in practice meet with almost insuperable difficulties. The analogy with the use of that system in native rubber planting was not exact: while trees could easily be counted, the much denser planting of tea made a count much more time-absorbing. And the differences in quality also were much greater in the case of tea bushes. Since 55,000 hectares of tea gardens were in the hands of more than 50,000 owners, the separate surveying and taxation of each garden was altogether too expensive. Moreover, so continuous a stream of harvest and export permits would result from individual licensing as to demand an extensive and costly administration for which the existing civil service was not equipped. It was questioned also whether the negotiability of licenses in such large numbers really could be controlled or effectively prohibited; more probably an extensive trade in licenses would arise, and many growers no longer would work on their land, so that their gardens would go to rack and ruin, with the further result that not only the owners but the districts where the gardens were situated would become impoverished. Finally, it was considered inadvisable and incorrect to grant export licenses for a final product to planters who only supplied the raw material and were divorced from the actual export operations by the independent and non-native finishing manufacture of that material. Taken together, these objections make it understandable that the advisers unanimously advised against this system. The Government therefore did not follow this course, the more so since another system of control, one of registered purchase and called the Kingma system after the manager who first thought of it and applied it on his estate, had proved its usefulness. More about this will be told later. But here the other difficulties mentioned still have to be explained.

The second difficulty was connected with the price which the native planter received for wet leaf. In this more than in anything else his absolute dependence on the purchasing factory could be seen in all its ugliness. For the manufacturers exploited that dependence by forcing down the price of wet leaf to a point at which there no longer was any reasonable relation to the export price of tea. There were firms which for tea fetching 80 cents per kilogram on the market paid only 2 or 2½ cents, barely enough to keep the natives at the job of picking. In November 1933, the Government, considering itself responsible for the working of the tea restriction scheme, came to the conclusion that intervention was necessary; the director of Economic Affairs fixed a minimum price of 5 cents per kilogram for wet leaf. This regulation, however, was not satisfactory: the minimum came in practice to be regarded as the maximum and for that was too low and too inflexible. A very few months later, in February 1934, a better regulation took its place: all purchasing factories were obliged to pay for wet leaf a minimum price that was one-tenth of the price paid on the export market for dry tea. The last-named price was considered to be the average price secured by the leaf-purchasing factories on the Batavia market during the previous month. As a measure of control, each factory had to supply the Purchases Subcommittee with a monthly statement of the leaf prices paid and the prices fetched by their tea in Batavia. Careful investigation showed that this simple ratio fully met any reasonable demand for fair prices below the export price of 40 cents per half kilogram *loco* Batavia. Only after depreciation of the guilder at the end of September 1936, when tea prices on the Batavia market rose on the average above 40 cents, was it found necessary to revise the regulation. The Government decided that from March 1, 1937, calculation of a fair price for leaf purchases by any factory should be on the basis of a proportion of 1:9.5, a proportion by which the dealer's share in the final price was somewhat raised. With these new price relations, the leaf producer and the factory each received about one-half of the yield of the final product, the dry tea. The native income from the sale of wet tea, which had shrunk to 1.4 million guilders in the year before restriction began, subsequently rose to nearly 3.5 million in 1936-37, almost 4.9 million in 1937-38, and not quite 4.5 million in 1938-39.

There still was the third difficulty which threatened to offset the gain which the native tea planters might be expected to make from the regulation of buying and of purchase price, namely the intermediate trade in wet leaf, the so-called *tangkulak* system.[1] The purchasing factories found it easier to deal with a few leaf dealers than with a large number of leaf producers; and the dealers spared the latter the trouble of transporting their small leaf crops to the factory or buying shed. But the intervention of these middlemen made the dependence of the small garden owners even greater. Especially with the restriction policy there was little assurance either that they would receive a fair price or that a reasonable amount of their product would find a buyer. The buying factories, on the other hand, were interfered with only to the extent that they had to regularize their purchases of wet leaf and had to pay a fair price for it; for them the business ended with the intermediary trader, what part of the sum paid for a given batch reached the hands

---

[1] The *tangkulaks* were as a rule small Eurasian farms. The wet leafs bought up by their owners from native planters and resold to Western factories amounted in 1932 to more than 600 tons. In 1935, the quantity was reduced to almost nothing.

of the numerous small planters was not their concern. It took some time before a satisfactory solution was found for this difficulty; eventually it was provided by the Kingma system.

This system works in the following manner. In the villages from which a factory is accustomed to get its leaf, the aid of the native authorities and village chiefs is obtained to register the leaf producers. The productive capacity of each garden is then estimated as closely as possible by the manager of this factory and checked at village meetings attended by all the native tea growers. In this way, the latter's intimate knowledge of the productive capacity of the gardens in their neighborhood is utilized; and a valuation arrived at by mutual consultation between the parties primarily concerned takes the place of a technical survey. The total quantity of wet leaf to be supplied each year is determined with reference to the extent of a factory's buying licenses. The annual share of each grower in the total then is simply derived from the proportion of his productive capacity, as previously ascertained in common council, to total productive capacity. After that the order in which the various gardens are to be picked is regulated, and the day of delivery of his leaf fixed for each producer, as also the quantity that he is expected to deliver every two months. The schedule thus arrived at is posted in the factory. In this way, the leaf dealers feel that they have had a share in the regulation of purchases and are prepared to accept the result of the arrangement. Everyone knows on what day he is expected to make a delivery and the amount he has to supply; at least, he can easily find out, and he is certain of regularly selling a reasonable part of his crop. The factory, on its part, is assured of a regular supply of leaf apart from that which it grows itself. The *tangkulak,* now formally registered, is pushed into the background: his function has become that of a middleman for the small garden proprietors who live scattered far from the factory and who need his help; but they likewise no longer require his services where the factory is willing to open more purchase centers in the area from which it draws its supplies.

To make possible a satisfactory working of this system, the factory supplies one or more purchase books to each registered garden owner in its district. These books contain the name of the factory, the name and address of the holder, the size of his tea garden, its number in the village register and the estimated normal annual output, the quantity of leaf which he is authorized to offer in each buying period, and spaces to keep account of the dates of actual deliveries and the quantity delivered on each occasion. These books may, therefore, be regarded as non-transferable individual delivery license certificates. On delivery, the gross and net weight of the leaf supplied are entered in these books, together with the amount of money paid. The daily price per kilogram for wet leaf is posted in the factory where the producer can see it, so that he may check the accuracy of the amount entered to his credit. Payment is made, as a rule, after the deduction of advances if such have been made. These advances, in the nature of buyer's credits, used to be customary to insure sufficient deliveries; but they have considerably decreased after introduction of the Kingma system because the estate no longer needs to rely on such indebtedness of the producer to make sure of a regular supply. Occasionally purchase books are sold; but nearly all the firms oppose that practice. Incidental difficulties and obstacles arise from time to time but remain exceptional and are easily removed by the purchase supervisors. The Kingma system accentuates the common interest of manufacturer and leaf dealer; to the producer it brings a right to some return on his labor, since the manufacturer is obliged to accept delivery of the quantity of leaf agreed upon.

In 1938, the system was further improved by a decision of the Government to proceed to more precise estimates and surveys of the native tea garden areas. To this end, data available in the Land Revenue Offices were drawn upon and special assistant surveyors were appointed to re-value the productive capacity of the gardens. As in the case of the rubber groves, the tea gardens were divided into two classes according to their production potential; the owners themselves were consulted in making this classification. It was the intention to maintain the production of the individual native tea gardens in accordance with norms set for these two categories as long as the tea restriction was in operation, even though the tea planters might have other plans for using their land. The owner should have the right to dig up part of the tea bushes and replace them with other crops, provided the productive capacity of the part remaining under tea was sufficient to meet his obligatory leaf deliveries.

The quality of purchase leaf is generally good. Usually the system of fine picking is employed which, in contrast with the frequent former practice of coarse picking, saves from 25 to 30 per cent of the area that must be planted to secure a given quantity of leaves. This intensification not only insures a return on all the leaf deliveries demanded under the restriction scheme from a lessened area but also helps to improve the quality of the tea and therewith its price.

Although in subsequent years the position of the world stock of tea improved considerably and the former price level was recovered, potential production, that is, productive capacity, still remained in an unfavorable proportion to total consumption, with a ratio of 1,225 million lbs. to 950 or 1,000 million lbs. respectively. For this reason, continuation of restriction was unanimously deemed necessary. To provide the machinery required to carry out the obligations entered into under the renewed international agreement, the tea restriction ordinance of 1938 was issued in the Netherlands Indies, now including all the necessary measures in a single regulation.

Only in exceptional instances were new licenses issued. The possibility that a grower might use his license as an object of barter and sell it instead of working his own garden was checked by the provision that for such a garden the standard production was to be reduced to 90 per cent for 1938-39, to 70 per cent for 1939-40, and to 50 per cent thereafter as long as restriction might be in force. This stipulation was not to apply, however, if at the time of the license transfer the grower himself were to undertake to supply an equivalent amount of tea leaf. Nor did it apply to a transfer between tea gardens belonging to the same owner. Circumstances therefore could arise in which an owner would retain his licence unimpaired although he permitted the productive capacity of part of his holding to deteriorate, either by digging it up or through neglect. The purchase areas of each purchase factory, under the new regulations, were to be determined by the Government, and the purchases committees were to distribute the native and small Eurasian plantations between those areas. The "fair prices" to be paid the leaf producers by the factories now were fixed by districts, by decision of the director of Economic Affairs. In short, the Government penetrated more deeply into the organization of the tea industry and assumed greater powers in relation to it.

Another object, as we have seen, was to be that of stimulating tea consumption throughout the world. In this there has been a good deal of international cooperation. A uniform levy per kilogram of exported tea provides the needed funds; promotion activity takes place in part under national direction and in part jointly under the central supervision of an International Tea Markets Expansion Board. The Netherlands Indies carries on a strong promotion program of its own through a Board for Tea Propaganda. Thanks to its untiring efforts, native tea consumption has steadily increased, especially since 1936. In Java alone, the number of special itinerant tea shops (tea *waroengs*) has increased steadily to 5,843 in 1939. In the Outer Provinces there were 3,500 of them that year. The promotion campaign was supported from many sides: the Royal Packet Mail Company allowed a freight reduction of 50 per cent on tea in its coastal trade, the State Railways 20 per cent. The Sugar Sales Organization contributed 1,165 bags of sugar free of charge to encourage the use of sugar with tea among the native population. Thus no stone was left unturned to make the native "tea-minded" and to arouse in him a new need. In the restriction year 1938-39, the estates sold a total of 6,343,000 kg. of black and 2,118,000 kg. of green tea for home consumption, to which must be added about 4.5 million kg. of hand-prepared tea brought directly on the market by native growers and dealers.

## CINCHONA

In 1933, cinchona growers, through their representatives, petitioned the Government to intervene, as overproduction threatened to unsettle the market. As a matter of fact, bark producers and quinine manufacturers already had twenty years earlier concluded an agreement for the protection of cinchona cultivation, its regulation, and the promotion of sales. Extension of plantations could not, however, be prevented by this agreement, and between 1913 and 1933 the area planted with cinchona increased by 50 per cent, while potential production of sulphuric quinine was actually doubled to 1.2 million kilograms.

The consumption of quinine remained far below the greatly increased capacity for its production. World demand for this commodity seems to be rather inelastic; during recent prewar decades it oscillated between 450,000 and 555,000 kilograms of sulphuric quinine per year. Neither sales promotion, nor the offer of about 500,000 kilograms per year at greatly reduced prices to the League of Nations for use in poor countries ravaged by malaria, nor a general price reduction of about 25 per cent had an appreciable effect on sales. The disproportion between potential production and consumption increased, and stocks steadily rose. In 1933, there was a stock of more than 17 million kilograms of bark on the estates and in the warehouses at Amsterdam and Bandoeng—an equivalent of two years' consumption. Moreover, with postponement of the harvest, an additional large reserve of bark was still on the trees.

That year, the big producers, associated under the cinchona agreement, requested the Netherlands Indian Government to set limits to the extension of cinchona cultivation and to subject the export of bark to restrictive regulation. The Government readily agreed and as early as December of the same year laid before the Volksraad a project for a set of regulations which was promulgated in February 1934.

From that time, the export of cinchona bark and its delivery for local consumption was prohibited except with permission of the authorities.

The maximum quantity of bark that may be exported is determined annually, in terms of sulphuric quinine, by the Governor General. If an unauthorized rise in the price of quinine salts and quinine preparations takes place in the Indies, the Governor General can suspend the restriction. An advisory board, consisting of representatives of the producers with two government delegates, one in Amsterdam and one in Batavia, was assigned the task of keeping the Government informed of developments. The export of cinchona seeds and plants was prohibited.

The producers, for purposes of regulation, were divided into three categories. The first group comprises the members of the Association of Cinchona Bark Producers and producers connected with this organization by separate agreement, altogether 126 units, contributing about 97 per cent of total production. The second consists of the native cinchona planters who, under the restriction regulations, are for administrative purposes treated as one estate in each residency and at the outset contributed no more than ¼ per cent of the total area under cinchona. Third came the independent small estates, accountable for about 2¾ per cent. An inclusive export quota is each year fixed for the first group, while individual quotas are set for each "estate" in the second and third group. However, no restrictions were from the beginning placed on native gardens with less than ten thousand trees. The allotted quotas are supplied in the form of license certificates. The Assistant Residents, that is, the highest European officers in the districts where the gardens of the native planters are to be found, act for them as license holders. About nine-tenths of the native plantations are concentrated in the Tjiandjur Regency, West Priangan. The licenses are nontransferable. Expansion of plantations is prohibited; only renewed planting of areas already under cinchona is allowed, and this only with permission of the authorities. At the very start, in 1934, the restriction percentage was fixed at about 55 per cent of previous production.

The cinchona agreement for 1929 to 1938 concluded between the Cinchona Bark Producers' Association and three Netherlands quinine factories retained its dominating influence on the quinine market. This is hardly surprising, considering that the restriction legislation left that agreement untouched and protected its operation against the slowly increasing importance of outside producers. The interests of this private organization are looked after by the Cinchona Bureau in Amsterdam. However, the Government occupies an important place in this organization, too, since the oldest, best, and most productive cinchona estate, Tjinjiruan, is a government enterprise. In this way, the Government is in a position to influence the sales and price policy of the Cinchona Bureau.

About four-fifths of the cinchona bark is exported to the Netherlands where part of it is made into the final product while the remainder is distributed among quinine factories in other countries. The Cinchona Bureau strives to sell as large as possible a quantity of quinine at such profitable prices that it can afford to sell quinine for social welfare purposes at a lower price. It also tries to stabilize these prices and leads in the campaign for larger sales.

In 1937 the cinchona agreement was renewed. The Volksraad, however, amended the statute to provide that all native cinchona gardens, and not only those with less than ten thousand trees, receive licenses permitting full normal production, that is, to exempt them from all restriction. By this means, the share of that group of producers was slightly increased. Even so it still came to only about 1.5 per cent of the total in 1938. The new restriction scheme was to be valid for ten years. A new clause in the regulation was that the standard output for all non-native estates was laid down for the whole ten-year period. By this means an end was made to the unnecessary and, from an economic standpoint, unsound increase of the production apparatus. However, a separate category was established for estates that were not yet fully productive; for these the standard production is determined each year until they have reached the stage of full production. Furthermore, if, in spite of rational exploitation, the annual yield of any estate falls to less than two-thirds of the standard production entered for it, a correction is made. A new third category was formed of estates for which a declaration is given that the cultivation of cinchona either has or will be stopped and that replanting will not take place. The fixed standard production of these estates is recognized up to the time when the entire export of cinchona bark from them has either been exported or been delivered to the quinine factories.

## COFFEE

Coffee cultivation had got into a critical condition through chronic overproduction. For this not the Netherlands Indian producer but a foreign country, Brazil, was to blame. But this did not alter the fact that in the Indies, too, a considerable part of the coffee plantations was threatened with ruin.

Table XVII shows that neither the estates nor the native gardens have to any extent increased their output, and that there has even been a small decline of exports in the ten-year period 1929-38. The end column pictures the alarming fall in price. The year 1929 was by no means an exceptionally favorable one in this respect: in the ten preceding years the average wholesale price paid on the export market of the Indies had been 83.28 guilders per quintal. The later drop is serious when it is considered that on the average 72 per cent of the coffee is exported.

TABLE XVII:   COFFEE PRODUCTION, EXPORT, AND PRICE, 1929-40

*In thousands of tons and guilders per quintal*

| Year | Estate production | Native production | Export | Batavia price |
|---|---|---|---|---|
| 1929 | 55 | 58 | 83 | 89.57 |
| 1930 | 40 | 54 | 63 | 52.90 |
| 1931 | 49 | 54 | 70 | 36.30 |
| 1932 | 63 | 70 | 116 | 39.03 |
| 1933 | 57 | 50 | 72 | 31.87 |
| 1934 | 64 | 49 | 82 | 25.97 |
| 1935 | 55 | 56 | 81 | 20.12 |
| 1936 | 50 | 75 | 95 | 19.84 |
| 1937 | 62 | 70 | 99 | 25.74 |
| 1938 | 46 | 62 | 69 | 19.35 |
| 1939 | 58 | 55 | 66 | 17.85 |
| 1940 | 39 | — | 40 | 16.87 |

Coffee cultivation is very irregularly spread over the archipelago, and it is an industry requiring a comparatively large amount of labor. On a typical Javanese coffee estate from one to three thousand pickers find work during the picking months of a normal year, and a large number of native workers are employed all the year around for the upkeep of the gardens and other jobs. A relatively large number of Europeans, too, find remunerative work in this form of enterprise. The speedy and, after 1929, almost unbroken fall in prices threatened the existence of the industry: with production costs roughly amounting to 23 guilders per quintal, a price below 20 guilders cannot be sustained in the long run. The price had not been as low since 1811.

In Brazil, the valorization system, which had resulted in the increase of foreign competition, was replaced by a policy of holding down prices. It could therefore be expected in the Indies that the unfavorable price level would continue for the time being. Moreover, new difficulties were increasingly placed in the path of exports from the Netherlands Indies by foreign countries. It is understandable, therefore, especially in view of the help received by other agricultural industries, that the coffee planters made a request for aid to the Government, so as to save from complete ruin a historic colonial enterprise in the Indies which still took seventh place, by value, among the export industries. However, the Government was obliged to point out that the case of coffee was not comparable with that of rubber, tea or sugar, or even that of cinchona;

that the proportion contributed by the Indies to total world exports, only 5 or 6 per cent, was too small to justify a national restriction scheme, and that the Indies was in no position to take the initiative in the organization of an international restriction scheme.

On the other hand, perhaps remembering the revenues that coffee cultivation in the Indies had at one time provided for the mother-land, the Netherlands Government declared itself ready—as part of the plan of economic cooperation between the different parts of the Empire —to introduce a levy on the import of coffee in the Netherlands the profits from which would for the most part go into a fund to be estab-lished for the benefit of coffee cultivation in the Indies. This was to become a considerable help. That fund was estimated in 1936 at 780,000 guilders and in 1937 between two and a half and three million guilders. Administration of the duty and of the fund in the Netherlands was simple, since the Netherlands Agricultural Crisis Board already had power to raise levies on imports in behalf of Empire agricultural pro-ducers outside of Europe. The coffee fund would be somewhat similar to the Kapok Board (described below) and would be used not only to provide financial relief to the distressed planters but also as far as possible to strengthen the position of the coffee growers in all kinds of ways, including both the improvement of sales and that of the product itself. The Netherlands Indian Government decided that the financial aid should be given in the form of export premiums. In that way, it was assured, it would reach the planters through the exporters, who were not in distress; and among these enough competition would prevail to raise the cost price of the coffee exported by them by the amount of the premium. So as to be able to force the exporters, if this should prove necessary, to raise the prices paid on their purchases, especially of native-grown coffee, the export of coffee was subjected to a system of licenses and compulsory registration of exporters. The amount of the differed premium for the principal kinds of coffee, *Robusta* and *Arabica,* as the cost price of the latter was much higher.

While research in behalf of the European producers had already been done by their private experimental stations, financed through the Coffee Crisis Board, now the improvement of native-grown coffee could also be taken in hand from the coffee fund. But in order to be quite fair, it was planned that the expenses of the estate experimental station should also be aided by that fund, and that a sum equal to that spent in behalf of native cultivation should be added to its research budget. The work program was to include promotion and market research, especially in Asiatic territories. In this way the Netherlands Indian ordinance concerning coffee was re-inforced with a supporting program financed by the mother country.

The Government had no illusions that even with such assistance coffee cultivation could soon again become a paying proposition. There was no need to fear that the export-premium system might turn out to be an incentive to expand cultivation. But on the other hand it was reasonable to expect that this system would benefit also from higher prices obtained for the product sold at home on which it was not obligatory for the Government to pay the 30 per cent premium; the effect of the export premium would be felt on the home market in the same way as every fluctuation of the foreign market was immediately felt at home. No exporter expected that he would be able to keep the premium for himself.

However, before the regulation was embodied in the Statute Book, the situation in the world market apparently underwent a complete change, and the grant of financial aid to the coffee growers in the Indies became superfluous. At the end of March 1937, the prices for native coffee were twice as high as in mid-September 1936; and estate coffee, too, reached prices that removed all necessity for relief. The Governor General therefore decided to keep the ordinance in abeyance. The improvement in prices was supposed to have resulted from consultations between the South American producer countries, and it was hoped that this improvement would continue.

Nevertheless, it was considered advisable to strengthen the position of the Netherlands Indian growers by improvement of quality and of the methods followed in disposing of the crops. For one of these purposes, the Netherlands Government repeated part of its former offer of assistance, namely to contribute within the framework of economic cooperation between the Netherlands and the Indies a lump sum of 780,000 guilders from the Home Treasury to improve the quality of Netherlands Indian coffee. A more simply planned Coffee Concerns Ordinance, of 1937, reestablished in the Netherlands Indies a Coffee Fund, the chairman and secretary of which were officials of the Economic Affairs Department. The fund was allocated fairly equally between the European and the native coffee gardens. Its administrators paid attention mainly to the coffee trade on the home market and to efforts designed to check deterioration in the quality of native-grown coffee. An annual report on the working of the fund was made to the Volksraad. It was thought that with a program of diverse measures it might be possible in a period of three or four years to bring coffee production in the Indies up to the desired standard. But when the price of coffee dropped to a still lower level and, in 1940, the war caused the elimination of the major markets, the Coffee Fund was reestablished in a stronger setting, all required authorizations being obtained in a few days. Purchase and sale of coffee were centralized under government control; in this way losses on export could be compensated for by profits in the home markets where 34 per cent of the product is sold. Moreover, the Government used its monopolistic position to regulate sale terms and to standardize and improve grades; it succeeded to a remarkable degree in raising the quality of native-grown coffee.

## OTHER AGRICULTURAL PRODUCTS

*Kapok.* Three unfortunate circumstances had contributed to a constant fall in the price of this commodity when, at the end of July 1934, that is, before the harvest of that year could further have depressed prices, the price index, with 1913-14 as the basis, stood at 38. These factors were (a) the existence of a large stock of kapok in Java, (b) an annual overproduction which resulted from a former expansion of the area under cultivation when prices had been rising, and threatened to become still more widespread, and (c) a systematic bear policy on the part of some of the exporters.[2] In 1934, the situation had become untenable: under the influence of low prices, the quality of the native product had deteriorated steadily, and cultivation was no longer remunerative. The Government decided to intervene. As steps toward improvement, it took the following measures: market research and promotion of sales; better organization of sale and purchase, which would tend to increase the prices earned by producers without raising the prices of the exported product; and improvement of quality.

Kapok is in a real sense a native product: on the average about 89 per cent of the total volume exported from 1935 to 1939 was supplied by non-European growers.[3] Single trees, lining the roads and the banks between fields and clustered in the native compounds, are more numerous than those in regular plantations. The number of growers, therefore, is very large, and intermediate trade between growers and exporters prevails. Important in this industry also are the manufacturers who cleanse, gin, and press kapok, and the exporters who deal in the final product.

---

[2] It may be profitable for the exporter to sell a large quantity at low prices, provided he is able to lower his purchasing price to at least an equal extent.

[3] The steep decline in 1940 to 75 per cent (see Table III) is a result of sales from the valorization funds.

It was not feasible for the Government to get in touch immediately with the large mass of small producers. It felt confident, however, that if it could bring about a reasonable price on the export market this would, because of competition between the intermediary groups, ooze through to the growers.

The kapok plan of 1935 included the following measures. Export was made dependent on possession of export licenses, and these were fairly divided among the exporters of kapok. To meet the costs of maintenance and improvement of quality, of market investigation and sales promotion, an export duty of 0.40 guilder (about 1 per cent) was put on the licenses. With the returns from this, a Kapok Board was financed to which was entrusted the task which the Government had assumed in regard to the industry. This board was constituted to consist of twelve members, three of them officials, four representatives of the native producers, one from the Western estates, two from the factory owners, and two from the exporters. It set to work at once with great vigor. The kapok was divided into three standard qualities; a brokerage regulation, valid for the whole of Java, was introduced; on the manufacturers, who also had to take out a license, the obligation was imposed to purchase the raw material only in the pod and at a "fair price" which was set as a standard price for each category; and a regular information service on prices was organized for the interior. Although the Government had to overcome strong opposition on the part of the exporters, the results of the new policy were at the outset not unfavorable, as will be seen from Table XVIII.

TABLE XVIII:  KAPOK EXPORTS AND PRICES, 1934-40

*In thousand tons and guilders per quintal*

| Year | Export | Price |
|---|---|---|
| 1934 | 21 | 30.59 |
| 1935 | 25.6 | 26.96 |
| 1936 | 28.4 | 32.05 |
| 1937 | 19 | 47.42 |
| 1938 | 16.3 | 44.53 |
| 1939 | 21.8 | 44.53 |
| 1940 | 16.7 | — |

It so happened that during that period a tendency toward larger purchases by the United States, the chief customer, caused a rise in prices. But in 1937 the tide turned: prices went down and exports flagged. Forced to choose between acceptance of the fall in prices, which would mean failure of its kapok policy, and still more far-reaching intervention in market and valorization, the Government adopted the latter course.

A kapok fund was established, financed with a Government guarantee by the large banks, and a price-raising policy was started with purchases designed to take large stocks off the market.

When this measure was taken, the original stock was estimated to amount to from fourteen to fifteen thousand tons, while exports during the harvest year 1938-39 were supposed to take off some 1,500 tons per month. In both respects, reality proved less favorable than the expectation. The stock was about twenty thousand tons, and the sale during the whole harvest year, *i.e.* from September 1, 1938, to August 31, 1939, did not even reach the fifteen-thousand ton level but was more than three thousand tons below the estimate. Therefore, continually increasing quantities had to be taken off the market. In order to enable the kapok manufacturers to purchase the 1938-39 crop from the native population at the standard prices, the fund was obliged to relieve them of the greater part of their old stock. It had to buy more than eight thousand tons of the 1937-38 crop at the cost of 3.1 million guilders, and 7,300 tons of the 1938-39 crop at the cost of 1.8 million guilders. And still the position of kapok was not saved by these measures. On September 1, 1939, the fund disposed over a stock of 15,700 tons, while the kapok factories held 7,600 tons and the exporters 2,600 tons. It is true, the normal annual production was reduced to nineteen thousand tons by "unfavorable" weather conditions; but the export still had not reached fifteen thousand tons. The market was refractory in the expectation of a drastic price reduction.

In these circumstances the Government decided to recommend to the Volksraad that the Kapok Fund should be permitted to try to dispose of its stock as far as possible outside the supply of the normal kapok market and to destroy what was left over; further, that the manufacturers and wholesalers should be obliged to destroy one-third of the kapok pods which they intended to buy; that the export price should be fixed at the exceedingly low rate of 25 guilders which, with addition of the 2.50 levy imposed in behalf of the Kapok Fund, would amount to 27.50 guilders per quintal; and finally that the standard price for purchase from the native producers which, at a price of 25 guilders per quintal would amount to about 6 cents per hundred pods, should be fixed at 4 cents per hundred pods, so as to force destruction of one-third of the pods.

At this critical stage the European War broke out and became a means of deliverance. Confident that the demand for kapok would sharply rise, the Volksraad on September 9, 1939, discarded all plans for the destruction of kapok or kapok pods; and this confidence was not misplaced. The fund soon was able to liquidate its stock, and prices recovered. Still, this course of events obviously did not cure the basic illness of the kapok market; it only temporarily pushed the problem into the background.

*The Principle of the Commodity Boards.* Experience teaches that improvement of the system of selling raw materials cannot be left to the exporters themselves. If one exporter is willing to give himself the trouble and expense of placing his product on a new market his competitors share the new opportunities which he creates. Indeed, seeing that they have gone to no expense, they often enjoy at the start a certain advantage over the pioneer. In this matter, there is a great difference between trade in raw materials and that in finished products which it is sometimes possible to give a monopolistic position by pushing a special trademark. Those exporters of raw materials, on the contrary, who put themselves to the most trouble to serve the interests of the particular trade and the producers, come under the least favorable conditions, inasmuch as their working expenses increase without improving their position in relation to their competitors. Even a minority of exporters can thus render the majority in a given trade powerless to attempt improvements.

Above all, there are certain native products that are exported as raw materials, the export of which is threatened by particular dangers and that are therefore in urgent need of an improvement in export conditions. For example, exports of resin and essential oils from the Indies are threatened by the competition of other tropical countries and that of synthetic products of Western industry; cassava products are exposed to the dangers of too narrow a marketing territory, limited to a few countries; tobacco suffers from a market that is differentiated too little. Moreover, some of these native export products suffer from deterioration in quality.

How can the necessary improvements best be brought about? The Netherlands Indian Government, reassured by the initial success of the Kapok Board, at the end of 1937 thought to find a way out of the difficulty, which, as we have seen, it encountered with its plan, by a further extension of this system. Everything seemed to be in its favor. Such boards can, to begin with, concentrate on the exporters: the product then is dealt with at a level where it is in few hands and, moreover, since according to existing customs legislation it must be declared, regulation can be managed with only a small increase of customary formalities. As a matter of fact, all the exporters concerned have to be registered to be permitted to export at all, although thus far without restrictions either on the amount of exports or on the number of exporters. Now, at the same time that registration takes place and export licenses are issued, it is possible to make certain stipulations as to quality, packing, and trade usages; and these would form the basis of larger demands to be made by the board at a later stage. Moreover, it is not difficult to collect fees on the grant of export licenses to finance the operations of the board. It is only reasonable that the costs of these boards are charged to the product. Indeed, from the activities of such a board, made responsible for improving the quality of the product, for organizing market research, sales promotion, furthering cooperation between exporters, combating the abuses connected with purchasing from, and granting credit to, native producers, giving producers and manufacturers direct information and advice—from these varied activities, all concerned in the trade may be expected eventually to reap benefits.

The work program of all boards is much the same. They aim to improve the processes of cultivation and processing. They look into and try to improve the conditions under which the raw material is purchased and credit is granted the producer. They investigate possibilities of meeting the quality requirements that come from foreign markets and the commercial usages by which compliance with them can be controlled. They analyze sales and investigate new sales possibilities at home and abroad. They inquire into complaints about quality and faulty delivery. They engage in general trade propaganda, such as taking part in exhibitions, issuing publications, and the like.

After two years of existence, the Kapok Board was engaged in all these activities as parts of a continuing program.

Financing of the boards takes place by means of a charge on exports, ranging from $\frac{1}{2}$ to 1 per cent and fixed for each calendar year by government decree. This fee brings in a total of about 125,000 guilders per year.

In setting up regulations for new boards, a further provision is included, to the effect that the Government has the right to determine what qualitative requirements the product concerned must satisfy to permit its export. There is no other limitation on these exports; on the contrary, they are encouraged provided the conditions set are observed. The boards cover native products that cannot, or need not, be placed under restriction. Any dealer who is sufficiently equipped for this function may be recognized as an exporter even if he has never before done business in the commodity concerned.

The secretariats of the various boards are concentrated in the Export

Division of the Central Trade Office. Price fixing is undertaken by the boards only in case of need. How the commodity board system works out in practice will be shown in the following sections, concerning essential oils, cassava, natural oils and resins, and native-grown tobacco.

*Essential Oils.* This trade is almost exclusively concerned with sereh grass, the raw material for citronella oil. Its cultivation has developed in a remarkable way and this, curiously enough, during the years of general economic depression. Before 1932, production to no small extent took place on relatively small estates. There were good reasons for this: as a result of a sharp drop in prices, the development of Western enterprise in this field had been checked, but cultivation of this grass still was sufficiently attractive to the native producer and small Eurasian farmer, who found its cultivation more advantageous than that of other dry crops which also had sharply fallen in price and some of which were altogether unsaleable. The native-owned area under this crop in Java therefore grew proportionately ever larger, as will be seen from Table XIX.

TABLE XIX:  ESTATE AND NATIVE SHARE IN EXPORTS OF CITRONELLA OIL, 1931-39

*In thousands of kilograms*

| Year | Total Export | Estate Product | | Native Product | |
|---|---|---|---|---|---|
| | | Quantity | Per cent | Quantity | Per cent |
| 1931 | 893 | 360 | 39 | 533 | 61 |
| 1932 | 996 | 336 | 34 | 660 | 66 |
| 1933 | 1,529 | 411 | 27 | 1,118 | 73 |
| 1934 | 1,790 | 358 | 20 | 1,432 | 80 |
| 1935 | 1,664 | 328 | 19.7 | 1,336 | 81.3 |
| 1936 | 1,603 | 280 | 18 | 1,323 | 82 |
| 1937 | 1,414 | 248 | 17 | 1,166 | 83 |
| 1938 | 1,894 | 322 | 17 | 1,572 | 83 |
| 1939 | 2,509 | 379 | 15 | 2,130 | 85 |

The native plantations covered an area of 24,000 hectares at the end of 1939, 95 per cent being in West Java. However, the quality of the native product went down as a result of the drop in prices: less manure and less care was given to the gardens. Complaints about the oil prepared from citronella grass grew in number and were of an increasingly serious nature. This was all the more alarming as foreign producers competing with those in Java began to supply a product that could compare with the best Javanese consignments. The exporters did not deny the charges made but had to admit that they were unable to correct the situation without the help and guidance of the authorities. It was on this ground that the Government established the export board for essential oils.

The number of Western factories that bought the native product was on the increase. In 1939, 351,000 kg. of sereh oil was manufactured from bought raw material in addition to 379,000 kg. made from estate supplies. In addition, there were 191 native sereh-oil factories, most of them technically primitive installations, with a total production of 448,000 kg. of oil. There was also some manufacture in homes and in manufacturing establishments too small to come under statistical observation; and these together produced at least another 762,000 kg. of sereh oil in 1938. The exports in 1939 were larger than in any of the preceding four years.

At that time, the board interested itself exclusively in matters concerned with sereh oil. However, its plans included extension of that interest to such other essential oils as cananga, patchouli, cloves, cajaput and vetiver if further investigation should prove activity in their behalf to be necessary.

*Cassava.* This foodstuff is exported in the form of crude manioc *(gaplek)* as flake and siftings, as pearl and seeds, as refuse *(ampas)*, but especially in the form of coarse or finely ground meal (manioc farina). There were in 1939 about 39 estates which themselves raised the crop and 130 that bought up the material; but by far the largest part of the total export of 275,000 tons of the various cassava products is of native-plantation and -manufacture origin. Exports have increased continually but irregularly, as the native product is in the first place intended for domestic use. For the year 1940, native production in Java and Madura was estimated as 84 million quintals of fresh tuber of which less than 8 million quintals were available for export.

The development of manufacturing technique has endangered the export of cassava products in that it brings other starch-containing agricultural products into competition with them. It is a help, on the other hand, in so far as it leads to improvement and standardization of the local products and points the way to new industrial uses. However, to be enlisted in aid of the native producers, technical innovation requires government initiative. Only the large concerns are able to take care of their own interests and have managed to achieve a special position for their products on the world market. For this reason, the Export Board for Cassava Products does not concern itself with the problems of the estates. At the head of its program is the enlargement of the outlet for the native products which are still far too dependent on a limited number of buyers.

*Natural Gums and Resins.* In this group of export commodities a disastrous fall of prices took place. Damar and copal exports, which had reached a value of nearly 10 million guilders in 1929, fell to the value of 1.6 million guilders in 1934. The chief cause of this fall was the crowding out of these commodities by synthetic products that are of a much more stable quality and sold by the producers along with valuable services. To meet this competition, the Netherlands Indian Association for Trade in Gums was founded in 1931, in cooperation between exporters and the authorities. An annual subsidy of 12,500 guilders was granted to this association by the Government to carry on an investigation of ways in which the position of natural resins and gums might be improved. The New York Gum Importers' Association also took part in this project. The market position of these products certainly could not be considered hopeless: when correctly prepared, the natural product presents superior qualities. However, the association in the Indies had one defect, that some of the exporters kept aloof from it. Attempts to establish better standard qualities, to bring more unity into the excessive number of different kinds and categories, to simplify sorting and packing, ran up against the unwillingness of these outsiders to modify their trade usages in any way. The association therefore welcomed the establishment of the board which, now with official participation, proposed to attain the same ends and moreover was also to concern itself with much needed improvements in the remuneration of the native collectors of these forest products and in labor conditions in the sorting establishments. For the time being, the board confined its attention to the export of damar and copal which together accounted for 77 per cent, by value, of the total export of resins and gums and amounted to 2.3 million guilders in 1938. Already in that year the Government was able to announce that experiments to prepare a standard product from the natural raw material which could stand up against the competition of artificial resins and was suitable for direct use in varnishes, had to a large extent succeeded.

*Native Tobacco.* A recent decline in the export of unshredded native tobacco, or *krosok,* was a result, partly, of a falling off in quality; but it also was caused by a change in taste: this dark tobacco is less suitable for cigarettes than is Virginia tobacco. Moreover, the decline in sales resulted partly also from too restricted an orientation of the industry to a few markets in Western Europe. Especially since 1932 do the export statistics show a serious drop in the export of native-grown *krosok.* Where this had reached an annual average of 43,000 tons, it now dropped to 9,200. The producers of the tobacco were not to be blamed for this. The total area planted with that crop by independent native farmers did not vary much and in the period 1930-40 ranged between 130,000 and 170,000 hectares, with an average of 150,000 hectares—a slight increase, by ten thousand hectares, over the average of the previous ten years. Big changes had taken place in the destination of native-grown tobacco. While before 1933 about 60 per cent of the total production was exported every year to foreign countries in the form of *krosok*, export has since dropped back to 30 per cent of total production. This fact points to a steep increase in home consumption through the manufacture in the Indies of cigars, cigarettes, native straw cigarettes, and cut tobacco. At the same time, a transition took place from the use of *krosok* to that of cut tobacco and a sharp drop in the importation of tobacco for the cigarette industry and of foreign-manufactured cigarettes.

The machine-made cigarette industry is responsible for the utilization of about two-thirds of the native-grown cigarette tobacco and, under the regulation of that industry about which more will be said in a later chapter, is obliged to use native-grown tobacco to the extent of 80 per cent of its total tobacco consumption. Because of this, the two largest cigarette manufacturers, the British-American Tobacco Company and Faroka, have promoted the cultivation of cigarette tobacco in Java. The main center of this cultivation of Virginia tobacco is Bodjonegoro in East Java. The Tobacco Export and Import Company acts on behalf of the two manufacturing concerns just named in directing this new agricultural industry, the importance of which is rapidly increasing. Although the crop was poor in 1938, the growers of Virginia tobacco in the Bodjonegoro area that year reaped an income of 267,000 guilders from plantations with a total extent of 5,600 hectares. In 1939, cultivation of this crop was again extended by a few thousand hectares, and some estates in Besoeki and Banjoemas, but above all in Klaten (the Principalities), began to apply themselves to this crop.

It is clear that the Government's organizing board, the Krosok Board, will have to concern itself not only with export but especially also with the home market. As far as export is concerned, the first necessity is to make an end of the sale abroad of tobacco of inferior quality. In addition, the possibility of finding new foreign markets for Indies-grown Virginia tobacco will have to be investigated. As far as the home market is concerned, the Krosok Board enjoyed from the start the cooperation of the General Experimental Station for Agriculture which helped it to set up at Taloen, in Bodjonegoro, an experimental and selective seed nursery for cigarette tobacco. The Virginia seed which until then had been imported from the United States degenerates rather rapidly in Java. Besides, that country had for some time past been considering an export ban on tobacco seed—all the more reason why efforts were deemed necessary to find a variety of seed that would run true in the tropics.

The exporters expect great things from this board. The export trade alone cannot solve difficulties concerning planting, plant material, methods of harvesting and of dressing, or relations between producers, wholesalers and exporters. All this has to be done by the Government through the Krosok Board.

*Copra.* Another native product on which government interference has wrought a miracle is copra. This is a commodity difficult to handle because it is produced in almost every part of the archipelago, including outlying districts and islands, and because it is bulky. (The output is over half a million tons a year.) Two tasks were assigned to the Copra Fund: to dispose of the largest possible quantities of copra or its derivatives at the best price that could be obtained, and to secure by all imaginable means storage facilities for large tonnages of surplus product. In this case again, the Fund acted as the only buyer and seller. But the most remarkable feature of the work entrusted to it by the Government was the speed with which the Fund succeeded in raising the quality of the product. It did this by standardizing the processes of sun-drying and artificial drying. To bring this about and at the same time to keep a constant check on the prices paid to the small producers, a large staff of field workers was employed by the Fund—most of them young men, generally sons of farmers, who had gone through a short, practical course of copra preparation.

By the end of 1941, the average quality of the deliveries in the major producing areas of the islands already showed a substantial improvement. As for purchasing prices, these were calculated to cover the more urgent money requirements of producers and were rather higher than at that time could have been obtained in the few foreign markets that still remained open.

TIN

As in the case of tea, so in that of tin also suggestions for restriction of output originated with the interested private parties. In this case, too, the private interests were unable to form an effective organization and had to call on the Government to help them.

The increase in production during and after the first world war had been prodigious. As compared with the output of 4,600 tons in 1913, it was 41,900 tons in 1930. Even so, other countries had surpassed the Indies in this advance. In 1930, increased output was attended by a conspicuous fall in prices. In the following year, the four most important producer countries, Malaya, Bolivia, Nigeria and the Netherlands Indies, made an agreement that has since been renewed several times, last in 1937, and at that time affected more than four-fifths of the world's tin production. It is a strong international agreement because it confers large powers on the central committee set up by the governments concerned. This centralization of power was considered necessary because the demand for tin fluctuates strongly and quickly with the trade cycle and with changes in the political constellation, as is evident from the quantity and price of tin exported by the Netherlands Indies since the restriction agreement came into force. This is shown in Table XX.

TABLE XX: TIN EXPORTS FROM THE NETHERLANDS INDIES, 1931-40
*In thousands of tons and guilders per 100 kg.*

|  | 1931 | 1932 | 1933 | 1934 | 1935 | 1936 | 1937 | 1938 | 1939 | 1940 |
|---|---|---|---|---|---|---|---|---|---|---|
| Quantity | 27.8 | 17.1 | 12.8 | 20.5 | 21.4 | 32.4 | 40.4 | 21.4 | 31.9 | 45.3 |
| Value | 133 | 116 | 158 | 165 | 155 | 151 | 207 | 162 | 195 | 208 |

The International Tin Regulation Committee has done everything possible to give greater stability to both production and prices. To accomplish this, it formed a tin pool and, in addition, a buffer pool to which each of the participating countries contributed 5 per cent of its standard production. The extent of the buffer pool was limited to 15,000 tons; its purpose was, by purchase and sale, to keep price fluctuations between £200 and £230. By thus introducing a greater elasticity in export and supply, this method has achieved a considerable stability of prices, relatively speaking, as will be seen by comparing the quantity and unit value figures in Table XX.

The most productive of the tin mines in the Netherlands Indies are those exploited by the Government. The other two have been brought into a semi-official relation with the Government through the formation of the Billiton Company in which the Government holds a majority (62½ per cent) of the shares. Thus, the profits from tin sales form a not unimportant item in the budget of the Indies—an item, unfortunately, that is variable and difficult to estimate.

FORESTRY

More than two-thirds of the Outer Provinces are covered with virgin forest, as is shown in Table XXI. The impressive figure of more than

120 million hectares under forest does not, however, convey a very definite picture of the possibilities of production. Large parts of the forest territory, indeed, are not yet opened up, and other parts—those in the higher mountain ranges—are difficult of access and therefore will remain unsuitable for full and regular exploitation.

TABLE XXI:   VIRGIN FOREST AREA IN THE OUTER PROVINCES, 1938

*In square kilometers*

| Government Division | Total Surface | Virgin Forest | Per cent |
|---|---|---|---|
| Sumatra | 473,606 | 289,000 | 61 |
| Borneo | 539,460 | 416,000 | 77 |
| Great East | 759,105 | 499,000 | 66 |
| Total | 1,772,171 | 1,204,000 | 68 |

Only since about 1934 has the Government seriously concerned itself with the forest reserves of the Outer Provinces. Since that year, the forestry service has surveyed the wooded growth of ten million hectares and classified five million hectares of potential-use forest, spread over the whole archipelago in great varieties of admixture. Working schemes and plans of exploitation were drawn up for the east coast of Sumatra, Tapanoeli, Palembang, west and east Borneo, the Moluccas and some of the Lesser Sunda Islands. The collection of different kinds of wood at the Forestry Experimental Station and Herbarium has reached twenty-five thousand specimens. Important technical research to determine possible uses for the different kinds of timber and resin were in full swing before the outbreak of the war.

According to a general classification, four million hectares are grouped together as mangrove forests, 37 million hectares as swamp and lowland forests (that is, up to one hundred meters above sea level), 30 million hectares as hill forests (from one to five hundred meters above sea level), and 50 million hectares as mountain forests (above five hundred meters). The two first-named groups form the most valuable part of the forest territory from an economic point of view, because they contain the principal marketable kinds of timber and also supply considerable quantities of forest by-products. The hill forests are more difficult to exploit. Here actual cutting, especially in the higher areas, is confined to some of the more expensive woods, such as ebony, and to the collection of various forest by-products.

In 1938, the forests of the Outer Provinces supplied the world with timber to the value of 4.4 million guilders, and forest by-products to the value of 6.5 million guilders. The export values alone, therefore, come to almost eleven million guilders.

As regards the methods of forest exploitation, three types of private organization, apart from direct exploitation by the Government, may be distinguished: first, industries that buy from members of the native population; second, medium-sized industries in certain forest sections which are allotted to estate owners, where work is carried on with only a small investment of capital; and third, large mechanized Western industries which exploit large forest concessions and make use of considerable capital.

The first-named system usually involves cash advances. These industries do not work satisfactorily: the quality of their products is poor and they cannot meet standard specifications; on their part, they lack the certainty of a regular means to dispose of their product. Yet, for those who can put up with difficulties of this sort, the small industries that rely on bought forest material are quite profitable. Their costs are very low, so that the large and medium-sized concerns can hardly compete with them or be developed with expectation of adequate returns. In all of the archipelago there are, according to a recent report, only nine large lumber-cutting concerns.

After the depression years, the Forestry Service in Java and Madura for the first time showed a modest credit balance in 1936. After six years of deficit, the balance that year amounted to 121,000 guilders. In 1938, the annual balance had risen to 2.5 million guilders, in 1940 to 3.5 million guilders.

In the Outer Provinces, on the other hand, forest exploitation by the Government has not yet produced any noticeable profits. An exception has to be recorded for the Government's extraction of resins and turpentine in the Gajo countries (Acheen and its dependencies), where altogether some 12,000 hectares are exploited and where, in 1939, 5,800 tons of resin and 1,300 tons of turpentine were extracted. This enterprise was started in 1930 with an area of 1,650 hectares of virgin forest which produced 500 tons of resin and 133 tons of turpentine.

## ADVANCEMENT OF STAPLE CROP CULTIVATION

In 1933, an advisory committee was appointed to draw up a program for the advancement of staple agricultural crop cultivation. Nearly all the heads of bureaus, services, and government industries under the Economic Affairs Department have a seat on this committee, also the chief officials of several other departments. The setting up of this committee was connected with the restrictions that had been introduced for the most important agricultural industries. These had the effect of clearing considerable stretches of land of the commercial crops previously cultivated on them, and the job was to discover new crops at home or abroad that might have possibilities of remunerative production in the Indies. Such an investigation could not, of course, be limited to purely agricultural questions but had to concern itself also with questions of manufacture and of sale. The committee has been made as many-sided as possible so that an object of investigation might at once be tackled from all sides. For the cultivation of some new staple crop could be encouraged only if no grave difficulties stood in the way of technical success, of the manufacture or preparation of the material to become a trade product, and of marketing it.

In 1937, the committee was given a firmer financial •footing with a contribution from the twenty-five million guilder development fund, to be further explained below. When necessary, the committee tries to co-operate with private experimental stations and with the agricultural and commercial organizations in the Indies.

CHAPTER V

# GOVERNMENT INTERVENTION IN IMPORTS

QUOTA AND LICENSING SYSTEMS IN GENERAL

The foundation of the new Indies import policy was the Crisis Import Ordinance of 1933 (Indian Statute Book 1933, No. 349). This general measure was preceded by two specific import regulations, the Crisis Cement Import Ordinance and the Rice Import Ordinance, both of the same year. They are not mentioned without a purpose: the general statute originally followed the design of these particular regulations in order to protect the industrial life of the Indies where it was threatened by foreign competition. By the Crisis Import Ordinance the Government was empowered to take such measures as might be necessary to limit and regulate imports, provided such measures were in force for periods not exceeding ten months; the Government could take these temporary measures without having in each case to ask for the consent of the Volksraad. Only if extension of such measures beyond that time limit appeared to be desirable, further provision had to be made with the consent of that legislative body. As the general aim of these measures the ordinance indicated "prevention of excessive imports."

While this ordinance was still in preparation, the Netherlands Indian Government discovered that this general permissive statute could be used to serve even larger purposes. This appears clearly from the memoranda which at different times were laid before the Volksraad in support of the draft ordinance. In an explanatory statement dated July 24, 1933, which accompanied the draft, it is stipulated:

> "To change the principles of trade policy under these circumstances is not advisable. This takes too long, and it might become evident after some time that such change had taken a wrong direction."

And further:

> "The ordinance does not aim at procuring advantages for, or inflicting disadvantages upon, any particular social or economic groups or countries as against those held out to, or imposed upon, other groups or countries. Protection of the economic life of the Netherlands Indies in its entirety, in so far as it in itself is adaptable, is the sole aim of the measure."

85

But in a memorandum with which the Government answered a sectional report of the Volksraad, a memorandum, dated August 21, 1933, that is, which appeared only a month after the one previously quoted, it is stated:

"Further, the proposed regulation provides the opportunity to apply a quota system in the pursuit of certain other, no less desirable aims of trade policy."

and again:

"A quota system by countries makes it possible to set a different quota for each country."

In short, once the crisis import ordinance had come into force, it was regarded as a splendid enabling act which permitted the taking of all kinds of measures. These one might arrange in the following major categories: (a) those serving the protection of home industry in the case of an excessive supply of foreign goods at such prices as to make normal competition very difficult (this was the original intention of the ordinance) ; (b) protection of the distribution apparatus established in the Netherlands Indies against unusual competition (this, too, may be regarded as part of the original intention) ; (c) advance of export interests by showing some accommodation to importers who also are purchasers of Netherlands Indian products; (d) aid to the Netherlands within the framework of economic cooperation with the mother country.

All import regulations made under the ordinance have in common the fact that the admissible import of the article concerned is laid down in well defined terms of quantity and of the period during which the regulation is in force. The fixed quantity is shared out among the importers according to their reasonable interest in the import of the commodity or commodities concerned—an interest which usually is measured by the respective ratio of their imports of these goods in the basic years from 1929 to the end of 1933.

With reference to the fourfold aim of the import ordinance, the import regulations that have come into force can be divided into three groups: free quotas (category a), licenses (category b), and definite quotas for separate countries (categories c and d). In practice, however, several types of import regulation are used for more than one of the aims here mentioned. Only the license regulations are exclusively directed at the aim mentioned under (b), with the only exception that a few license regulations are used also in support of quota regulations for other commodities, so as to limit the import of the licensed goods, i.e. to prevent an expansion of imports, not to contract them. In such cases, it is the intention to prevent the import goods subject to the license regulation from being brought in as substitutes for goods subject to quota regulations. To assure the proper working of this protection of the import trade, or, in the wording of the ordinance, "on behalf of the trade and to protect the consumer," the Government in 1935 proclaimed the packing ordinance. This empowers the Government to stipulate the manner in which the origin, nature, quality, and quantity of packed articles are to be indicated. Specific rules under this ordinance have been issued for vinegar, margarine, flour, butter, cheese, milk, coffee, and other articles.

*Free Quota System.* Under this, the origin of the imports is left out of consideration; only the volume or quantity of the permissible import is limited to an amount which, together with that of comparable products of home industry, is deemed sufficient to supply the domestic market. Apart from such quota regulation for cement and rice, which preceded the crisis import ordinance, examples are quota regulations for frying pans, automobile tires, ready-made clothes, and copperas. The regulation of the import of unbleached cottons, although made in the form of a free quota regulation, aimed, at least at the beginning, not at the protection of a home industry but at the limitation of the import of materials which could in part have superseded that of bleached cottons, the import of which was made subject to a quota in favor of the Netherlands.

*National Quotas.* Under this term come, in the first place, those quota regulations the exclusive purpose of which is the protection of imports from the Netherlands; in the second place those which, together with such protection also are intended to serve that of a domestic industry in the Indies; in the third place those which promote the export interests of the Indies by protecting imports from those countries which figure among the most important buyers of Netherlands Indian products.

This system of national quotas usually grants definite parts of the quota set to particular countries. Especially when the purpose is that named in the third place—that is, with regard to foreign countries but not the mother country—the size of the national quota corresponds to the volume of trade advantages which it is hoped to secure by application of this quota system. In other words, the principle of the "most favored nation" dominates these international trade relations. In a later chapter we shall review the importance of the Netherlands Indian quotas for the mother country. It has been calculated that the quotas are responsible for the employment of about seven thousand wage-earners in the Netherlands.

*License Regulations.* In appearance, the license regulations are in no way different from the free quota regulations. The essential difference lies in the respective purposes for which they are issued. The license regulations are merely in aid of the established distribution apparatus which connects the Netherlands Indian importers with the wholesale and retail traders. These regulations certainly do not have in view a limiting of the volume of imports or control as regards their origins. They are not directed toward the protection of any particular group of producers at home or abroad but rather of a group of merchants, who deal in the goods concerned. This protection of an already well established distribution apparatus was necessary to curb a competition by numerous new importers who, taking advantage of temporary circumstances, tried to guide import and distribution into new channels. It therefore concerns exclusively branches of trade where a desire to eliminate the established import and distribution apparatus was seen to be actuated by dubious motives. Since in these instances the quotas exclusively serve as a basis for distributing the import trade, freedom is not interfered with: there is ample room for *bona fide* importers newly appearing on the scene, and the trade is not allowed to get into a rut.

In practice, license regulations are applied only to the import of goods mainly used by the poorer consumer groups. Since the importer retains the freedom of choosing the cheapest producers, there is no compulsion to raise prices. If at any time it should appear that an attempt is made to raise the prices of licensed goods in a line parallel to that of price increases for goods subject to quota—application of the quota tends to increase the difference in price between goods subject to it and those subject only to license—then additional import licenses can be granted; moreover, maximum selling prices can be fixed for the holders of these additional licenses, and importers can be obliged to keep up buffer stocks with respect to which the price control authority has the sole right to decide whether any part of them may be sold and if so in what quantity and at what price. For example, six groups of drygoods which are especially important for the mass of consumers have been selected for an order to set aside such buffer stocks. Since there is keen competition between the intermediary dealers and since, as a result, the price level of the wholesale trade in these drygoods determines the prices of the retail trade, it may be said that the price level at which the consumers can satisfy their needs in these textile goods is not very different from what it was before the import regulation came into force.

*Results of Import Regulation.* Every import regulation has the tendency of putting out of action certain factors that have determined prices while free trade prevailed. This does not mean that import regulations are affected only when there has been a rise in prices. There are many examples to show that an import regulation may be accompanied by a drop in prices. The regulation of import, nevertheless, has a tendency to cause a rise in prices. The license regulations show least the consequence of a rise in prices; for, they involve no interference with the participation of various countries of origin in the import trade: the importers retain the freedom to obtain their merchandise from those countries which are able to supply them most cheaply. A rise of prices in this case can in the first place result from too low an estimate of the quantity required to meet the demand when the total volume of the goods is determined for which import licenses are to be issued. It can be avoided by a policy of assessing the actual requirements of the market somewhat liberally. Nevertheless, the principle should be followed that the prices must contain a reasonable margin to compensate the *bona fide* import trade for its services and efforts; any steps that might lead to an excessive competition, disruptive and destructive in its effect on that trade, should be avoided, if only because this may eventually result in a rise of prices.

A more fertile soil for rising prices is to be found in the quota regulation system. Here price control forms a necessary complement to import regulation if the consumer is to be protected.

*Effects of the Import Regulations.* Even before the crisis of 1929, the Central Bureau of Statistics at Batavia checked very exactly the expenses of six different types of families. This bureau also calculated what the effect of import and excise duties is on the prices of imported goods used by the families whose expenses were checked. In this way it found, as Table XXII shows, that import and excise duties made up roughly from two and a half to four per cent of the family expenditures.

TABLE XXII: MONTHLY EXPENDITURES OF SIX TYPES OF FAMILIES AND INCIDENCE OF IMPORT AND EXCISE DUTIES AS PERCENTAGES OF THESE EXPENDITURES, 1929

*Expenditures in guilders*

| Monthly expenditure | Per cent spent on duties |
|---|---|
| 18.23 | 2.62 |
| 32.29 | 3.61 |
| 100.82 | 2.36 |
| 225.12 | 3.24 |
| 512.69 | 3.61 |
| 687.31 | 4.02 |

90   THE EVOLUTION OF THE NETHERLANDS INDIES ECONOMY

Of the total imports of the Indies, 59.23 per cent comes in free, 9.29 per cent is licensed, 11.13 per cent is subject to free quota and 13.82 per cent to national origin quota, while 6.53 per cent is made up of rice and soya beans which are also subject to restricted import. Since in practice only the national quotas result in greater expense for the Netherlands Indian consumer, these figures show that only about 14 per cent of the imports are weighted by import regulations with an extra charge on the cost of living.

In order not to leave to rough approximation the measurement of the social effect of the quota system, an exact calculation was made to determine which items of household expenditure represent purchases of articles affected in price by the import licensing regulations or by the import quota system. The expenditures of two families living in Batavia, each consisting of husband, wife, and two children, with family incomes of 225 and 18 guilders per month, were examined at the end of 1935; and those of a common laborer in Batavia with an income of 5 guilders per month in addition to free board and lodging were examined about the middle of 1936. The influence of the quota and licensing regulations on these three budgets is shown in Table XXIII.

TABLE XXIII: EFFECT OF QUOTA AND LICENSING REGULATIONS ON THREE
FAMILY BUDGETS, 1935 AND 1936

*Amounts in guilders*

| Monthly Income Amount | Bought Articles affected by import regulations | | Purchases in which rise of prices is noted as result of import regulation | | Increase of price | |
|---|---|---|---|---|---|---|
| | Amount | Per cent | Amount | Per cent | Amount | Per cent |
| 225.00 | 9.27 | 4.12 | 4.52 | 2.01 | 0.26 | 0.11 |
| 18.00 | 0.82½ | 4.42 | 0.31 | 1.62 | 0.07½ | 0.40 |
| 5.00 | 0.46 | 9.20 | 0.31 | 6.20 | 0.04½ | 0.88 |

One might formulate the following conclusions from these calculations. The quota system has doubtless caused a rise in the prices of certain commodities, often to a considerable degree. In the case of the second family, for example, the price of one article costing 31 cents was raised by 7.5 cents, or 24 per cent. For the most part, however, such rise of prices for articles in daily use can be held in check by the way in which the authorities handle the quota instruments; it was limited also in part by a further drop of prices for many imported and domestic commodities. The quota system, therefore, did not lead to a rise in the cost of living but only slightly checked a rather steep decline. The combined index number of the retail prices of forty domestic and imported commodities in general use in Batavia, with 1913 as base, in the years 1930 to 1940, took the course: 149.5, 133.5, 112, 99, 90.5, 87, 84, 90, 92, 93.5, 100. The figure for 1934, 90.5, reflects the start of the quota policy in the previous year, the rise in 1937, from 84 to 90, the abandonment of the gold standard by the Indies which occurred in September 1936.

*Principles of Policy.* A committee appointed in 1938 to advise the Government on concrete steps by which economic cooperation between the Netherlands and the Netherlands Indies might be further extended, wound up its deliberations with the following conclusions.

First, the system of quotas and licensing regulations in force in the Netherlands Indies in 1939 was to be regarded as an essential means of carrying out the economic policy of the Indies—not only in respect to cooperation with the countries of origin but also for the defense of the Indies' export interests and for the protection of the Indies' growing industry. For this reason, it was not necessary to reconsider each quota every year to see whether it should be done away with as an undesirable instrument, but only to reconsider each quota with an eye to the interests it was intended to serve, judging it as to the degree to which its advantages outweighed such disadvantages as might eventually spring from it and as to the degree to which it was answering the original purpose.

Second, economic cooperation between the Indies and the countries of supply did not under present circumstances make it necessary to introduce new quota or licensing regulations, although such additions were not to be regarded as excluded on principle.

Third, the continuance of several of the quotas then in force might be reconsidered after a certain period of operation. The main consideration in such possible discontinuance would be that the importance to the Indies of as low as possible a price level outweighed the interest of the countries concerned in the protection of their sales in the Indies. Apart from this, quota and licensing regulations remaining in operation as important for economic cooperation should be regarded as appropriate so long as no radical change occurred in the situation.

The duration of the quota measures introduced exclusively for the benefit of Netherlands Indian industry must depend on the development of that industry and the degree to which it remained in need of this special protection.

*The Import Licensing Policy and Its Objects.* The point of departure of any system of regulation by license is the desire that imports of the respective commodities shall take place only with licenses issued by the authorities. By means of such a system it is possible to ascertain in good time whether there is a danger of excessive imports, harmful to the economic interests of the importing country and, if so, in which districts and with respect to what commodities. As far as the Netherlands Indies are concerned, it also offered the only possible way of obtaining insight enough into the structure and working of the import trade and distribution of imports to prepare measures for the regulation of import in the interests of the domestic industry and that of the Netherlands, or as a return for support granted abroad to the export trade of the Netherlands Indies; the only way also of adapting the regulative measures to the interests of the existing import and inland distribution trade.

At the same time, such a system permitted the organization of cooperative relations between the authorities and the organs of trade with regard to the import of the more important articles, and this cooperation formed the framework within which further measures for the regulation of import on behalf of these interests could be fitted into the general trade structure in the least burdensome and most elastic manner.

Finally, by this means the existing carriers of the import trade, institutions which up to that point had taken good care of the import and distribution of the imported commodities required in the Netherlands Indies, were granted the necessary protection against the dangers which threatened their very survival from the Japanese import organization which did not offer as sound a guarantee as did the existing apparatus for the satisfactory distribution of imports over the extensive territory of the Indies. How deeply the established apparatus was rooted in Netherlands Indian society appears from the following facts. An investigation has shown that in 1934 sixty-four European importers in the Indies together had outstanding credits to the amount of 43 million guilders; and that this amount could reasonably be estimated to have grown to 60 million guilders in 1937. The import regulation system created during that period made it possible for the authorities to allocate an equitable share in imports to each of the institutions that had shown a reasonable interest in the supply of the Indies with the goods concerned.

On January 22, 1935, the first import licensing ordinance came into effect. After six subsequent amplifications of this ordinance, the following categories of import commodities were licensed by the end of 1935: glassware, enameled goods, bicycles and bicycle parts, toothbrushes, knives and scissors, paraffin lamps, various kinds of piece goods, earthenware and china, various kinds of metal goods, and soap.

The license regulations can thus in due time be replaced by quotas; however, such a move would modify the foundation as well as the aim and influence of the regulation.

Since 1940, the import licensing policy has become almost superfluous, because the Government preferred to regulate imports through the control of foreign exchange.

*Frying Pans.* To protect the manufacture of frying pans in the Netherlands Indies, importation of this article was, on October 1, 1934, made subject to a free quota. The quantity allowed to be imported was more and more limited with each renewal of the regulation. At the same time, production in the Indies, which threatened to expand too rapidly, has been consolidated under the terms of an industrial regulation.

The quota system has not, in this case, led to a rise of prices. On the contrary, the sale price per kilogram which amounted to fl. 0.125 at the time the quota came into force was fl. 0.11 in July 1935. Before a beginning was made with the quota system, an arrangement had been concluded with the principal producers by which they undertook not to increase the wholesale price in Java and Madura by more than 2½ cents per kilogram above the existing price at the time the quota system came into force.

The average annual consumption can be estimated at 1,220,000 pieces, weighing 2,515 tons. Of this, 2,200 tons is produced at home. In the Outer Provinces, frying-pan factories are unimportant. If they were to be provided with frying pans exclusively from the production centers in Java, a rise in prices probably would result. That is why a small import is allowed; it is destined almost entirely for the Outer Provinces.

The latest quota regulation dates from August 1941.

*Rubber Tires.* The free quota was placed on rubber tires in 1936 in behalf of the Goodyear plant in Buitenzorg. That plant is capable of producing a quantity of tires sufficient not only fully to supply the Netherlands Indian market but also a surplus. However, this industry, although located in the Indies, was not able to capture the market of the Indies. This was not because of the conditions under which the plant carried on production. But the Netherlands Indian tire market had long been characterized by the competition of many manufacturers whose principal means of contest were evasion of voluntary agreements and imitation of trade marks. To create a healthier situation, the quota system was put into force, originally for a period of ten months. One condition of the protection given the legitimate producer was that he had to reduce the prices prevailing on August 1, 1935, by 15 per cent;

the benefit of this price reduction was to be reaped by the consumer. The protection given has answered expectations but apparently cannot be abandoned. The last renewal of the quota regulation took place in 1941.

## COMMODITIES SUBJECT TO NATIONAL QUOTAS

*Portland Cement.* The quota regulation for cement had a twofold purpose. In the first place, it helped to protect the Netherlands Indian cement industry at Padang against abnormal competition from foreign producers. Besides, it provided the opportunity to grant import concessions to some foreign countries in aid of Netherlands Indian exports to those countries. The first quota dated from June 28, 1933. It was preceded by the Cement Agreement of 1932 whereby the importers of that commodity pledged themselves to pay the Padang Cement Factory a certain amount for each barrel of imported cement. The latest regulation, of 1941, was intended to be in force until the end of September, 1942.

*Beer.* The quota on this import also had for its principal aim protection against foreign competition. In addition, it was the object of several trade agreements. The first quota for beer came into effect on December February 12, 1934 and was renewed for the last time in 1941.

*Woven Colored Piece Goods.* The purpose of this quota was primarily to protect the growing weaving industry of the Indies. Also, it allotted a specific share in the imports to the Netherlands. The quota began on February 12, 1934 and was for the last time renewed in 1941.

*Bleached and Unbleached Cottons.* Originally only unbleached cottons were subject to the quota, primarily as a protective measure on behalf of exports from the mother country, while some bilateral agreements allotted quotas also to foreign countries. However, during 1934, and especially after the quota for bleached cottons had come into effect, it was realized that the import of unbleached cotton was excessive. As a result of it, the batik industry was shifting over from the use of cambrics to that of greys; and this formed a direct threat to the success of this quota and to the normal price relations between the two cotton materials. In order to put a stop to this substitution, the import of unbleached cottons also was made subject to quota on January 1, 1935.

The bleached cottons, the cambrics, form the raw material for the batik industry. Here, then, the relief given to the cotton industry in the Twente district of the Netherlands became a burden for an important domestic industry in the Indies which could not stand such an increase of production costs. Because of this, the Netherlands granted a subsidy from the national treasury of 813,000 guilders for a year and a half in order to neutralize for the batik industry the effects of the quota for cambrics and, later on, the quota for greys. This compensation only applied, of course, to the export from the mother country; it took the form of a premium to importers on their sales of Netherlands cambrics which they were obliged to sell at fixed, reduced prices. Meanwhile, the fact that the premium was paid only on Netherlands cambrics, while all cambrics had to be sold at the reduced price, meant a considerable loss of importers' profits on Japanese cambrics. However, working together under a "cambrics covenant," the importers declared themselves ready to cooperate fully toward the attainment of the desired price reduction. To make sure that the batik establishments actually had to pay no more than the agreed reduced prices, these through mutual organization secured the opportunity of buying directly from the importers, with elimination of the intermediary trade.

The quotas were last renewed at the end of 1940.

*Earthenware.* This quota formed a special case. It must be regarded as a preventive measure to guard against Japanese efforts—of which various indications appeared during the year 1935—to intervene in a coercive way in the supply of the Netherlands Indies' import market to the exclusion of the existing import apparatus. These intentions were abandoned soon after the measure came into force; and so it was decided to do away with the quota. When the licensing of certain other imports came into effect, this system was used also to regulate the importation of earthenware.

*Artificial Fertilizer.* Within the framework of the economic cooperation between the Indies and the mother country, the import of double-super-phosphates was placed under a quota, so as to protect this branch of Netherlands industry. The industry in its turn took on the obligation of offering the product at no more than cost price. The quota came into force on March 31, 1935 and was renewed at the beginning of 1941.

*Electric Bulbs.* From 1929 on, the Netherlands' share in the Indies' import of electric bulbs steadily decreased, whereas Japan's share increased by leaps and bounds, both in proportion and in extent. It was only a question of time when the Netherlands would be altogether crowded out of this market. In this state of affairs, with the economic cooperation that had been entered into between the Netherlands and the Netherlands Indies, there was every reason for protecting the imports from the Netherlands by means of a quota; the more so, as numerous experiments had proved that the cheap Japanese bulbs needed 25 per cent more current to give the same amount of light—in many cases, 30 and up to 70 per cent more—and that they were more quickly used up, so that the interest of the consumer was just as seriously injured by the substitution of these inferior bulbs.

In order to prevent an undesirable shift of the trade from the old importers to new ones, bicycle and pocket lamps also were brought under regulation, but only by means of licensing; no specific share of this import was reserved for the Netherlands.

With application of the quota system to this trade, which dated from March 12, 1935, some important conditions were imposed on the Netherlands manufacturers. They had to undertake that sufficient quantities of the low-powered lamps—of 10, 15, and 25 watt—were supplied to satisfy all of the Netherlands Indian demand; further, that at least one-half of the supply should be cheap lamps offered at a price agreed upon in advance; that the Netherlands supplies would be adequately advertized; that prices would not be raised during the period for which the quota was set; that care would be taken to make the cheap lamps satisfactory in quality, use economy, and power; and that the price would not exceed that of comparable lamps from other countries where similar conditions prevailed. This quota regulation was renewed in 1936 and again at the end of 1940.

*Piece Goods.* The import from other countries of piece goods, more than any other article, was threatened by Japanese competition and was therefore made the object of bilateral agreements with several countries. Since the difference in price between Japanese and European piece goods was the principal threat, the recovery of the latters' share in total imports of piece goods could be accomplished only by means of quotas. Great Britain and Italy more especially were concerned in this trade; but the Netherlands, too, were hard hit by Japanese competition. (The Netherlands' export of textiles, which in 1929 amounted to 55.5 million guilders in value, had by 1934 dropped to 8.5 million guilders.) It was unavoidable, however, that when quotas for different kinds of dress goods were assigned to some country or other there would be a rise in prices. Such a rise could not be allowed to take place in the prices of the more common piece goods that were bought by the poorer classes. This concern accounted for the policy of differentiating between categories, of placing under the import quota regulations only those goods which the poorer classes of the native population were not in the habit of buying. At the same time, the quota system could not be kept in hand unless the other kinds of piece goods also were subjected to some import regulation. It was decided, therefore, to license only the cheaper goods and to leave imports of them free as far as country of origin was concerned.

But because the quota system in this case was bound to lead to a rise of prices—and, indeed, may even be said to have had such a rise for its purpose—there was a corresponding danger that substitutes, not falling under the quota, would be imported in large quantities and would tend to hold down the prices of the articles placed under the quota. If that were to happen prices might fall below the level at which the European industry was able to offer supplies, and the quota would fall short of its aim. This is why the licensing of possible substitutes could not be avoided.

When these and other quotas were imposed, manufacturers in the Netherlands were placed under the obligation to allocate their supplies to the Indies on an equitable basis to all the recognized importers of piece goods. With this end in view, a board was formed in the Netherlands, of which all manufacturers were members, to distribute among them orders for bleached cotton goods coming in from the importers in the Indies. The board is referred to as Manex (Manufacturers' Export Centrale). On the initiative and under the supervision of the Netherlands Government, a similar body was later formed to regulate export to the Indies of other kinds of piece goods.

In addition to the arrangements here described for some of the major categories of imports, the following articles have been placed under import quotas, principally for the benefit of industries in the Netherlands: sanitary earthenware, bath towels, cotton blankets, cotton sewing thread, packing paper, sulphuric ammonia, and formic acid.

### BARTER AGREEMENTS

So far, this mode of regulation has taken place only on a very modest scale—as, for example, in the commercial relations with Siam. For instance, when in 1934 the Netherlands Indian Government had occasion to buy rice abroad, the opportunity was used to advance the sale of sugar. The possibility of such agreements always depends on opposing-but organizationally-connected needs and on the supply capacity of the two countries concerned. The Government can only stimulate and assist such exchange; and therefore the system is usually bound to rather narrow natural limits. In the above-mentioned case, for example, the transactions took place through a firm established both in Bangkok and in Java, which sold rice and bought sugar at the same time and was able to clear both accounts in the Netherlands Indies.

COMMERCIAL CONTROL

When a considerable portion of certain commodities required in the Netherlands Indies comes from particular countries, the possibility always exists that these supplies, whether temporarily or permanently, intentionally or unintentionally, may be stopped or greatly curtailed. A temporary scarcity caused by such stoppage might be misused by importers who happen to hold stocks. The Government, therefore, ought to have the power effectively to prevent such traders from holding on to their stocks if in so doing they seriously threaten the satisfaction of essential consumer needs. This consideration led the Netherlands Indian Government to proclaim the commercial control ordinance which empowers the Governor General, first, to appoint a committee to watch over the trade in any commodity and, second, to grant such a committee authority to further the collection of buffer stocks and to compel the owners of stocks to bring them immediately, either in whole or in part, into the normal channels of trade; if necessary to seize such stocks and to compel their sale and delivery for the account of the rightful owners.

The Committee for Commercial Control, composed of not more than five persons, also is empowered to investigate the character, causes, and effects of any rise in the price of commodities that are of importance to the masses of the people.

In the first place, this provision for control concerns import goods. However, if at any time it should become necessary to counteract a socially undesirable manipulation of home products, the ordinance covers action to that effect, too. For the regulation of trade is intended to be applicable under changing circumstances. Intervention can take place, therefore, also in the movement of goods that are both imported and produced in the Netherlands Indies.

To combat the holding back of stocks is the primary intention of the statutory regulation; to counteract the rise of prices is secondary. Yet, a rise in prices often is the visible sign of distress and the only symptom that justifies intervention by the Government. The Government desires to make its actions strictly contingent upon such outward manifestations, so as to make clear that it has no desire to intervene in business except where facts, which everybody can see, prove the necessity for such action.

The regulation is meant to work especially as a preventive, in so far as traders might try to create scarcity for their own benefit. In this its drafters had in view not only foodstuffs but also other goods, such as bleached and unbleached piece goods used in the batik industry and for other purposes; painted, printed and colored dress materials, earthenware, porcelain, ironware, and so forth.

The possibility remains that, forced by circumstances, importers may have to suspend the importation of certain goods. This eventuality, too, has been foreseen. A government organization has been set up in co operation with the importers to anticipate such difficulties.

SHIPPING AND IMPORTS

In the various import regulations which have been discussed above, the following far-reaching stipulation is practically always inserted:

> "If, as a result of any action, especially against shipping under the flag of the Netherlands, matters of vital importance to shipping under this flag between the Netherlands Indies and any other country are threatened the head of the Economic Affairs Department, after obtaining authority from the Governor General, is empowered with regard to the above mentioned goods, originating in or exported from the country concerned, to determine the percentage that may be carried in ships under the flag of the Netherlands."

It did not become necessary before the second world war to make use of this provision. The importers of their own free will increased the share of Netherlands shipping (including the ships of the Netherlands Indies which also sail under the flag of the Netherlands) in the transportation of their imports to such an extent that it was made clear to all foreign countries that the Indies would be quite able to maintain its position. Because of this, the Indies arrived at a satisfactory regulation of shipping even with Japan.

Generally speaking, one may say that the Netherlands Indies Government is not keen on foreign shipping services in the Indian Archipelago. This is apparent also from recent regulations of harbors and shipping. The Indies' shipping law of 1936 extended these regulations over the self-governing territories so that now they are in force over the whole archipelago. Moreover, it added to the regulations that govern the admission of vessels under foreign flags to seaports specified for overseas trade by the Government, and in principle it retained coastal shipping for vessels under the flag of the Netherlands—the trade between seaports in the Indies that are open to foreign shipping being included also in this ruling concerning coastal trade.

The new law recognized only two kinds of ports, overseas ports and coastal harbors. The first are open—not only for foreign trade but also for other than trade purposes—to seagoing vessels under the Netherlands flag and those sailing under foreign flags. Ninety-four seaports in the Netherlands Indies were so designated, with the proviso that their number might be further limited. Coastal harbors are in principle closed to shipping under foreign flags; they are open only to vessels under the flag of the Netherlands engaged in coastal trade or sailing for other than commercial purposes. Direct import from abroad in these coastal harbors was forbidden to ships of the Netherlands, too.

The right to engage in coastal trade can, under the general authority given to the Governor-General, be limited to holders of licenses for that purpose. Wishing to reserve all the internal sea transport of the archipelago for national shipping, the Government stipulated that not only the ships registered for it must be under the national flag but that the charterer also must satisfy the demand of nationality; and that the ship's certificate of registry can be refused, or be declared invalid, if there is doubt of the truly national character of the enterprise in question.

CHAPTER VI

COOPERATION BETWEEN THE NETHERLANDS AND THE
NETHERLANDS INDIES

In order to neutralize to some extent the effect of the policy of self-sufficiency which prevailed throughout the world, or at least to mitigate it, the governments of the Netherlands and of the Netherlands Indies, in regular consultation with each other, paid serious attention during the last six prewar years to means of strengthening the economic co-operation between both parts of the Empire. Only one foundation was possible for such an undertaking: a genuine mutuality of interests, willingness to render mutual economic aid according to the ability of the two territories without weighing the material value of their respective services. A policy of *do ut des* was considered contrary to the essence of imperial unity, the unity of the Netherlands and the Overseas Territories as parts of the Empire.

*Fourteen Principles.* In 1936, the Central Government of the Netherlands gave tangible expression, in fourteen principles of action, to the conclusions to which the consultation with the Government of the Indies had led. These may be summarized as follows:

1. In the economic cooperation between the Netherlands and the Netherlands Indies both the interests of the Empire as a whole and those of the two separate territories must be considered. The structure of the economic relations between the Netherlands and the Netherlands Indies is such that the services which, in this framework of cooperation, are rendered by the Netherlands to the Netherlands Indies in most cases at the same time promote interests in the Netherlands—as, for example, those of capital invested by the mother country in the colony. On the other hand, the services rendered by the Netherlands Indies, although they are of some importance to the Empire as a whole, are for the most part of *direct* economic importance only to the Netherlands. Consequently, measures taken by the Netherlands give a certain compensation for the sacrifices which they involve, while such compensation is lacking as a rule in the measures taken by the Netherlands Indies.
2. Present world relations require an energetic pursuit of the economic cooperation of both territories within the Empire. After the first experimental stage, which may be considered as having been concluded, this cooperation must now take place no longer

101

incidentally but as systematically as possible, so that the specific achievements may be fitted into a general framework of mutuality.

3. The economic cooperation inevitably requires sacrifices; whether these can be accepted or not must be judged in relation to the staying power and the structure of the territories concerned and to the help which they have obtained. Such a decision should not, however, rest on a policy of *do ut des* between the two territories.

4. The economic support to be rendered to the Netherlands Indies by the Netherlands consists chiefly of such aid as can be given by trade and clearing policies and would be very difficult to estimate in terms of money. Direct support by the sale of Netherlands Indian products in the Netherlands is possibly only to a limited degree. Further possibilities in this respect will nevertheless have to be examined by both sides and, where found practicable, to be utilized.

5. The policy concerning trade relations with foreign countries, for both territories, has to be formulated on the basis of Empire unity and in close cooperation between the competent departments of government. In so far as the colony in many cases is not capable of protecting its own exports to foreign countries, the mother country should as far as possible take over this task.

6. The assistance to be rendered by the Indies to the Netherlands is bound to consist chiefly in the promotion of imports from the Netherlands, the most important means of which is the grant of quotas. These quotas usually cause a considerable rise in prices, which often weighs heavily on the poorer sections of Netherlands Indian society and disturbs the adjustment [between income and cost of living] that has been attained. Nevertheless, within certain limits this rise in prices has to be accepted in the interest of industry in the Netherlands and of the needs of the Empire mentioned under (1).

7. The difference between the price levels in the Netherlands and in the Netherlands Indies, even with energetic adjustments in the Netherlands, is so great that the prices of goods the import of which in the Indies has been restricted in favor of the Netherlands must necessarily be made as low as circumstances in the Netherlands allow them to be. The Netherlands have to take the measures necessary to achieve this purpose and to stimulate an active relation between Netherlands industries and the Netherlands Indian market.

8. It is necessary in the interest of industry in the Netherlands and for the success of the quota system that there should be as great as possible a certainty, over as long periods as possible, as to quotas allowed to the Netherlands.

9. In cases where import restrictions without Government support do not on the whole achieve the end in view, the realization of the Netherlands' quotas must in the future be promoted by the Government of the Indies.

10. The interests of industry in the Netherlands should not be

allowed to stand in the way of such industrialization as is necessary for the Indies under present circumstances. But as industry is developed in the Indies, attention should also be paid to industry in the mother country. This last-named concern is valid also when a general limitation of imports becomes necessary because of increased domestic production in the Indies.

11. Both sides must strive to avoid differences between Netherlands Indian and Netherlands branches of the same industry. Among other things, the industrial investments of the Netherlands in the colony can be used to correct such differences where they exist.

12. When in the case of existing import restrictions it appears that the import duties imposed in the Indies prevent the Netherlands from filling its quotas, the question should be considered to what extent this might be compensated for by a lowering of these duties. If it should be evident that such a lowering is not feasible, either because of financial considerations or because of the character of the Netherlands Indian tariff law, then the Netherlands should carry this burden in cases where no third countries are concerned.

13. The Indian import restrictions in favor of the Netherlands are not in need of any considerable extension for the present. The measure of primary importance is consolidation of the important results already attained and still to be aimed at.

14. Financial aid is to be granted by the Netherlands to the Netherlands Indies to assist in measures for the general good, on the general grounds related to the facts mentioned under (1), (4) and (6), that is, as a fitting complement to other forms of economic cooperation discussed above. By this means, a certain amount of relief, comparable to that enacted in the Netherlands, can be given to the Indies which is economically so much weaker.

*Mutual Assistance.* The last of the points enumerated mentions financial assistance to be lent by the mother country to the Indies. The Central Government, taking seriously the first point of the agreement and recognizing the inevitable difference in the relative position of the mother country and the colony with regard to economic cooperation, did not leave matters to a general statement of principles.

In the same communication by which the fourteen principles were sent to the Volksraad, the Central Government announced to this legislative body that "both with a view to the principle of Empire unity, which brings with it a reasonable mutual sharing of burdens to the best ability of both parties concerned, and also because the successful adjustment—which has been carried out so consistently with the help of all groups in the Netherlands Indies—is an Empire concern of the first order," the Central Government had suggested to the States General that the Netherlands place an amount of 25 million guilders at the disposal of the Indies, in three annual instalments, without obligation of repayment, "in order to mitigate the effects of the depression in cases deserving special consideration in this connection, and to stimulate the achievement of new possibilities of prosperity."

This important financial contribution was justified by the Central Government in the following way: the deflation policy—consistently referred to in the document as a "policy of adjustment"—had in more than one respect caused particular difficulties to the Indies, so much weaker than the mother country; and the colony had been far less able to protect itself against the consequences of deflation, so that this policy had "incontestably led to the weakening of society in some parts of the Archipelago."

More will be said below about the spending of the 25 million guilder fund. Here we are concerned only with it as a gesture by which the mother country admitted, though in guarded terms, that the deflation policy which it had followed in recent years had primarily been in aid of Netherlands interests and had not been conducted in favor of the Netherlands Indies.

What precisely is the assistance offered to the Indies by the Netherlands under the fourth clause of the statement of principles? To begin with, it grants a privileged place to Indian products on the market of the mother country. This has happened with regard to maize, rice, feed-cake, copra, palm-oil, timber, and bags. In the second place, Netherlands import surpluses, among other auxiliary means, can be used in commercial negotiations to increase or maintain Netherlands Indian exports. Frequent and profitable advantage has been taken of this possibility, as for instance in bilateral trade agreements with Germany, the United States, Poland, Hungary and France. Third, the export possibilities of the Netherlands Indies sometimes can be maintained or extended by a clearing of accounts through the Netherlands, that is, by accepting foreign claims on the Netherlands in payment for exports from the Indies. Thanks to these trade and clearing agreements, the volume of exports from the Indies during the depression shrank but little. A fourth type of assistance from the mother country is illustrated by the remittance, already mentioned, of 780,000 guilders to assist coffee cultivation in the Indies. Fifth, there was the similar financial aid, also previously referred to, to the Javanese batik industry and to the Netherlands textile industry which took the form of premium payments spread over a year and a half on the importation of cambrics into the Indies from the Netherlands to an amount of more than 800,000 guilders per annum. Last but not least, there is the 25 million guilder contribution mentioned on a previous page and further to be considered below.

*The Netherlands' Share in Netherlands Indian Foreign Trade.* Events have shown that, notwithstanding an active desire on both sides to further this policy of economic cooperation, the importance of the mother country as a purchaser of Netherlands Indian products could not but remain within narrow limits. In this connection, Table XXIV is instructive. It is drawn from the Report of the Committee of 1938, mentioned above, one of whose objects was to watch for opportunities of economic cooperation.

TABLE XXIV: TRADE BETWEEN THE NETHERLANDS AND THE
NETHERLANDS INDIES, 1928-1939
*In million guilders*

I. Netherlands Imports from the Netherlands Indies
II. Netherlands Indian Imports from the Netherlands
III. Ratio of I to II, Per Cent
IV. Ratio between Total Imports and Exports of Netherlands Indies, Per Cent
V. Total Exports of the Netherlands Indies
VI. Total Exports of the Netherlands
VII. Proportional Share of the Netherlands in Netherlands Indian Exports, Per Cent
VIII. Proportional Share of the Indies in Netherlands Exports, Per Cent

|      | I   | II  | III | IV  | V     | VI    | VII  | VIII |
|------|-----|-----|-----|-----|-------|-------|------|------|
| 1928 | 140 | 175 | 80  | 154 | 1,580 | 1,987 | 8.9  | 8.8  |
| 1929 | 140 | 172 | 80  | 128 | 1,446 | 1,964 | 9.5  | 8.8  |
| 1930 | 92  | 136 | 68  | 129 | 1,160 | 1,694 | 7.9  | 8.0  |
| 1931 | 72  | 89  | 81  | 134 | 749   | 1,291 | 9.6  | 6.9  |
| 1932 | 60  | 47  | 128 | 150 | 544   | 836   | 11.1 | 5.6  |
| 1933 | 51  | 31  | 165 | 160 | 470   | 723   | 10.8 | 4.2  |
| 1934 | 58  | 30  | 192 | 188 | 489   | 709   | 11.9 | 4.3  |
| 1935 | 57  | 32  | 180 | 171 | 447   | 673   | 12.8 | 4.7  |
| 1936 | 79  | 44  | 182 | 189 | 533   | 743   | 14.8 | 5.9  |
| 1937 | 126 | 94  | 135 | 190 | 945   | 1,148 | 13.4 | 8.2  |
| 1938 | 102 | 100 | 102 | 139 | 558   | 1,039 | 15.5 | 9.7  |
| 1939 | 91  | 101 | 91  | 157 | 740   | 966   | 12.3 | 10.5 |

The figures of this table are eloquent, but we shall here consider only those features which relate to the subject of this chapter.

First, it is obvious from a comparison of columns III and IV that under normal economic conditions the export relations of the Indies with the rest of the world are much closer than those with the mother country—in other words, that the Netherlands as purchaser lags behind the foreign countries.[1] Only during the years of depression, 1933-35, was this relation altered and did the percentage of export-surplus to the Netherlands (column III) surpass that of the total export-surplus (column IV). No sooner had the tide turned and had again become more favorable to Netherlands Indian exports, than the colony again found its principal markets elsewhere.

The question is, can the increase of the Netherlands' share in the

---

[1] It should be kept in mind that for the Indies, as a region for investment of foreign capital, export—as has been shown in Chapter II—is of primary importance.

Indies' export surplus during the depression years be explained simply by the greater loyalty of the mother country to the colony that supplies it with tropical products? Column VII throws some doubt on this explanation. The share of the Netherlands in the Indies' total export during the depression years increased but slowly and by a few per cent. There was, in fact, a steep decline in the value of exports to the mother country. Greater headway was made only from 1934 on, when the Netherlands Government seriously set to work on an active program of economic cooperation. And yet, as soon as its exports gained once more some freedom of movement, the colony turned again to other markets.

In contrast, the effect of the depression on Netherlands Indian imports from the Netherlands (columns II and VIII) is much more obvious and much stronger. The figures show that, as economic distress in the Indies grew worse, the colony no longer could afford to buy the better but more expensive goods of the metropolitan; they also reflect the fact that at this time colonial investments and imports of capital goods from the mother country failed to materialize. One might also explain the phenomenon in this way: in years of depression, the mother country means a little more to the Indies than under normal conditions; but in the same period the colony means a great deal less as a purchaser to the Netherlands. Poverty prevents the Indies from defending itself against the effect of the unfavorable market situation; its resistance is much weaker than that of the richer mother country, weaker, too, than that of the other countries which it is in the habit of supplying with its products. But as soon as it is again in a position to cooperate with the mother country, the colony gives proof of its readiness to buy metropolitan products.

*In a general way,* it is true that the Indies means more, economically speaking, to the Netherlands than the Netherlands means to the Indies; because, as shown on the first page of this chapter, an interest of the Indies usually is at the same time also an interest of Netherlands investors. But economic cooperation if interpreted to mean exchange of products never is likely to become of major importance; therefore the distance between the two countries is great in more than one respect. One could hardly expect that the principle of Empire unity, which is a constitutional and cultural notion, should also be realisable in these economic terms.

The percentages in columns VII and VIII remain modest, but those in column VII prevail: the Netherlands means more for Indian export than the other way around.

*New Machinery of Promotion.* Another point in the report of the 1938 Committee deserves attention. The committee was of the opinion that industry in the Netherlands was not yet sufficiently adjusted to take advantage of the attractive opportunities afforded by the import market of the Indies, and that the capital interests of the mother country had not yet shown sufficient interest and concern in new investment possibilities in the Indies, particularly in connection with the industrial development of the colony. To fill this void, the committee proposed that the Government of the Netherlands should call into existence a non-official organization under the auspices of the Netherlands Public Treasury, in the form of a foundation under the Government's control. This institution, in which it recommended that a generous place be given to private industry, should then send a delegate to the Indies to be its permanent representative there.

The Netherlands Government readily acted upon this suggestion. On March 20, 1940, the Institute for Netherlands Economic Interests in the Netherlands Indies was founded at the Hague for the purpose of promoting the sale of Netherlands products in the Indies, to collect information on the industrial development of the Indies, and, with the aid of the collected data, to promote the investment of Netherlands capital in this development. A large board and a still larger advisory council were recruited mainly from industry—especially those industries that had some connection with the Indies. The Netherlands Department of Economic Affairs and that of Overseas Territories also are represented on the committee. An initial grant of 75,000 guilders was assigned to the institution in the Netherlands Budget of 1940.

The supplementary proposal of the Committee for Economic Cooperation, the "1938 Committee," to create a permanent organization in the Netherlands for the systematic promotion of exports from the Indies, which was to have been a charge on the budget of the colony, had not yet been realized at the outbreak of the world war. It was looked upon as less urgent, since the Indian (formerly Colonial) Institute in Amsterdam stood ready to further these export interests in the Netherlands.

*The Twenty-five Million Guilder Fund.* Concerning the large development fund previously mentioned, the following still has to be said. Because this involved the expenditure of a lump sum over a period of three years, some conditions had to be imposed. The grant could not be allowed to take such a form as to invite recurring demands on the budget of the Indies after expiration of the three-year period. On the other hand, the money was intended to be expended during that time and not to accumulate to form a reserve. There was no intention, either, that it should be used to decrease existing liabilities. Expenditure on works requiring much labor was preferable to expenditure on works requiring a large amount of capital. Although measures leading to a permanent strengthening of the Indies' economic position were regarded as of foremost importance, yet a place had to be made in the program for projects the main object of which was to increase employment opportunities. It was important, moreover, that such assistance should be confined to Java, Celebes, and the Great East (the many small islands east of Borneo and Java), since the rubber districts (mainly in Sumatra and Borneo) already had been generously provided for from the rubber export revenues, amounting to 85 million guilders.

Guided by these principles, the committee set up for this purpose has made the following apportionment of the Netherlands' gift: about 6.5 million guilders for irrigation works, about 3.4 million to speed up land settlement, about 3.3 million for roads and bridges, almost 3 million for building purposes, almost 2 million for sanitation, 1.6 million for forestry services, 1 million for relief of the metallurgic industry, 1 million for the advancement of agriculture and cattle breeding, 1 million for native industry, 1 million for release from debt bondage, 0.8 million toward a Madura welfare fund, 0.3 million for fisheries, and 0.2 million for various objects in those districts of Sumatra and Borneo that lie outside the rubber-producing areas.

CHAPTER VII

# GOVERNMENT INTERVENTION IN THE HOME MARKET

## FOOD PRODUCTION

Table XXV, below, is very instructive. For each of the four most important groups of food crops—cereals (rice and husked maize), the root crops (cassava and sweet potato), peanut, and soya bean—it gives the total production and consumption per head of the native population in Java and the proportion of the production consumed by that population. Account has as far as possible been taken of the growth of population.

TABLE XXV: PRODUCTION AND CONSUMPTION OF THE PRINCIPAL FOOD CROPS
IN JAVA PER HEAD OF POPULATION, 1929-1940
In kilograms

| | Cereals | | | Root Crops | | | Peanut | | | Soya Bean | | |
|---|---|---|---|---|---|---|---|---|---|---|---|---|
| Year | Prod. | Cons. | %* | Prod. | Cons. | %* | Prod. | Cons. | %* | Prod. | Cons. | %* |
| 1929 | 123 | 121 | 98 | 150 | 129 | 86 | 3.9 | 2.7 | 69 | 2.6 | 4.7 | 181 |
| 1930 | 139 | 134 | 96 | 155 | 142 | 91.5 | 4 | 3 | 75 | 3.1 | 4.9 | 158 |
| 1934 | 123 | 115 | 93.5 | 160 | 148 | 92.5 | 3.5 | 2.4 | 69 | 4.1 | 4.1 | 100 |
| 1936 | 141 | 128 | 91 | 200 | 176 | 88 | 3.8 | 2.3 | 60 | 5.6 | 4.9 | 87 |
| 1938 | 135 | 124 | 92 | 208 | 185 | 89 | 4.5 | 2.6 | 58 | 6.4 | 5.5 | 86 |
| 1939 | 138 | 122 | 88 | 215 | 190 | 90 | 4 | 2 | 50 | 7.1 | 6 | 93 |
| 1940 | 140 | 124 | 88 | 218 | 191 | 88 | 4.3 | 2.7 | 63 | 6.5 | 5.6 | 86 |

* Percentage of year's production consumed by native population.

The first four years, seemingly taken at random, actually have been chosen for a definite purpose. The year 1929 was a bad harvest year before the economic crisis; 1930 was a good harvest year before the crisis reached its greatest intensity; 1934 was a bad harvest year at the deepest point of the depression when state intervention was increasing; 1936 was a record harvest year with brightening business conditions. Information is added for the three years 1938-1940, for which exhaustive statistical information was available. What do these figures show?

Government intervention in the cultivation and trade of native crops increased considerably during, and as a result of, the economic crisis. New irrigation works were constructed; extensive measures were taken to improve plant material; fifty-two seed farms were established in Java with money from the twenty-five million guilder fund described in the previous chapter and later were augmented by five more and by seventeen auxiliary farms; agricultural methods were improved; cultivation of a crop during the east monsoon was encouraged as much as possible; diseases and pests were systematically combated; the use of artificial fertilizer was popularized; agricultural instruction spread over ever larger circles.

As far as the two major cereal crops, rice and maize, are concerned, this government intervention only achieved a rise in production of a few per cent. The volume of production of these crops fluctuates with good and bad harvest years but quantities per head have remained much on the old level. Much of the sawah land, suitable for dry cultivation of cereals, that had been leased to estates for the cultivation of tobacco and sugar was, as a result of the restriction on these crops, given back to the owners to dispose over as they wished; but this has exerted almost no perceptible influence on the volume of cereals produced. The native holdings already are subjected to a cultivation of more than optimum intensity and are not, therefore, susceptible with advantage to any large increase of productivity. Complaints about unsatisfactory yields have in recent times become more and more frequent.

The figures concerning consumption are more important. They can be arranged in a regularly descending series by placing the poor harvest years before and during the depression at the end. The consumption per head then is 134, 128, 124, 122, 124, 121, and 115 kg. It may, indeed, be assumed that the consumption of home-produced cereals has decreased; the greater provision of the Outer Provinces with rice grown in Java and the stimulation of the export of maize (although this comes to a large extent indirectly from the Outer Provinces) have been possible only at the cost of local consumption by the producers of these crops. Need of money induces the farmer to augment his sales, and government policy makes this possible; but the farmer's heart is not in it, he would prefer to keep his entire grain harvest for his own use. That, however, becomes less and less possible. It has correctly been pointed out that the export of food from densely populated Java to the sparsely populated Outer Provinces is paradoxical and can be regarded only as a symptom of Java's need—a need which, as far as one is able to judge, will be a permanent one. Meanwhile, the menu of Javanese households is changing with the increasing production of root crops and pulses. The successful advance of these "second" crops—including also soya beans—that are cultivated on dry land and during the east monsoon—can be credited to the Government. Its advice to farmers, encouragement, provision of seeds, and other activities have shown palpable and quick results. The most remarkable of these is in the cultivation of *kedelee* (soya bean) which, largely due also the sugar and tobacco restrictions, has in a few years been converted from an import into an export crop.

It is therefore with regard to these so-called second crops that further mention must be made of government intervention. The improvement of plant material particularly was accelerated by the establishment of seed farms established with an appropriation from the twenty-five million guilder fund. Of these seed farms there are now fifty-seven in Java and six in the Outer Provinces. The results achieved by these seed farms have been extended by the use of intermediaries: selected farmers, under the supervision of the agricultural advisory body, use some of their own fields to raise additional seed from that given them and so greatly increase the supply. The cultivated area of most seed farms is no larger than about five hectares. But attached to these are permanent showrooms where the farmers can give their orders for plant material, artificial fertilizer, agricultural implements, insecticides and fungicides. In this way, the seed farms have become local advisory centers. Agricultural courses are given here to both young and older farmers. In West Java, an increasing number of women take part in these courses—a development of great value considering the important role played by women in native agriculture. The area over which new and better methods of cultivation are put into practice already has reached hundreds of thousands of hectares. The problem of effective fertilization still is partly at the stage of investigation, especially as far as the use of artificial fertilizers is concerned. This use is on the increase, but the total quantities remain small: the amount applied in native agriculture in Java rose from 7,200 tons of sulphurous acid of ammonia in 1936 to 11,800 tons in 1939, from 1,700 tons of double-superphosphate in 1936 to 2,200 tons in 1938. The Government is thoroughly aware of the fact that every increase in the need for capital in native agriculture is a double-edged sword: in this matter the development of Japanese agriculture provides a warning example.

*Food Production in the Outer Provinces.* In the Outer Provinces, the population shows an increasing interest in the cultivation of rice on irrigated fields, in the cultivation of second crops on these fields, and in food cultivation generally. This development goes together with the very precarious financial results experienced in recent times with the growing of such staple commercial crops as copra, coffee, and pepper, the prices of which have dropped to a level at which they almost cease to be remunerative. For the Government this is certainly not an unalloyed advantage since the population of the Outer Provinces must depend on these staple commercial crops for its money income. The problem thus created will be discussed in a later chapter.

The cultivation of fruit—also mainly a branch of food production for home consumption—has with government help steadily extended over the whole archipelago. In Java six new government nursery gardens have been opened in recent years, in the Outer Provinces twelve, while at the same time the existing nurseries have been considerably enlarged.

### RICE POLICY

About the middle of 1930, a fall in the price of rice set in. Record harvests in the main production areas of South Asia and expansion of the area under rice in Java brought about a glut that could not have been absorbed by the Netherlands Indian market which has no great purchasing power. Through its connection with the prices of the other food crops, the drop in the price of rice affected the total agricultural income. The prices on the home market of the native agricultural products which usually show a strong seasonal fluctuation, now dropped continuously— even during the period of scarcity, just before the harvest. The farmer found it increasingly difficult to meet his financial obligations; arrears in taxes became serious.

In March 1933, the Government decided to intervene. It put an end to the free import of rice and restricted it by a system of licenses. This meant more than merely a checking of free importation; it signified the intention to work toward a system of self-supply with regard to rice. Javanese rice which until then had been offered chiefly in local markets had to find its way to all the Outer Provinces. In the few rice-surplus areas of these provinces, such as Bali, Lombok and South Celebes, an inter-insular rice trade had to be started. It was necessary to promote the establishment of rice mills to provide a product suitable for the new markets. The rice trade had to learn not to rely on foreign markets to replenish its stocks and had to become familiar with the intricacies of a purchasing system covering all of the scattered home supplies. Care had to be taken to insure a stable price so as not to raise the cost of living in the rice-consuming districts. In short, no failure of crops and no record harvest in a single territory of the vast archipelago could ever be allowed to become the occasion of a just reproach that the Government had neglected the obligation which it had undertaken to be responsible for a steady and regular supply of rice. How it fulfilled this task may be judged from Table XXVI.

TABLE XXVI: IMPORT AND EXPORT SURPLUS OF RICE, 1934-39

| | In thousands of tons | | | | |
|---|---|---|---|---|---|
| | 1934 | 1935 | 1936 | 1937 | 1938 | 1939 |
| Java and Madura .... | — 22.5 | — 79.3 | + 96.2 | +197.6 | + 53.4 | +134.0 |
| Other Provinces ..... | —243.7 | —287.4 | —306.0 | —344.5 | —370.8 | —390.5 |
| Netherlands Indies ... | —266.2 | —366.7 | —209.8 | —146.9 | —317.4 | —256.5 |

The increase in the excess of imports in the Outer Provinces is explained with the better price obtained for almost all native export products after 1934, with the restriction on individual native rubber production after 1936, and with the increase in the estate-labor population brought about after 1935 by the revival of the Western enterprises. The new task of the Government, as regards rice, was the more difficult in that the very unelastic demand for that commodity is exceptionally sensitive to any change in its relation to supply: even a small surplus depresses the price to a considerable degree, while a small shortage— whether actual or only anticipated—sends it up. Real strategy was expected of the leaders. Here a district might be temporarily closed to outside supplies and designated to supply itself; there it might be desirable to shut out foreign supplies and at the same time to organize an inter-provincial supply; in yet another place a primitive traditional barter had, as with a conjurer's wand, to be transformed into a modern export trade. Measures had to be taken on quality, packing, freight rates, time of delivery, etc. Rice mills had to shoot up from the ground. A rice trade accustomed to wait for customers had to be urged to adopt, and to be educated in, ways of conducting its business more actively.

It became necessary to intensify the observation of prices, so that the Government would always possess information only a few days old and could follow the food-price situation from tract to tract and from day to day. The price of rice on the world market also had to be kept in view; for, although the new rice policy had made the price of rice in the Netherlands Indies independent of foreign fluctuations, the country nevertheless remained dependent on the world market for deficits and had to be awake to the right moment for buying foreign rice. Thus, it became necessary in Java to import 150,000 tons of rice between November 1934 and the end of March 1935. This rice was, through the intermediacy of the Department of Economic Affairs, purchased at Saigon, Bangkok and Rangoon and was sold to the established rice dealers at prices which had previously been fixed and were quoted on the basis of the market values of corresponding kinds grown in Java. The prices at which the imported rice was sold to the public were controlled; if they appeared to be much higher than the c.i.f. value, the price level was reduced to reasonable proportions by the expedient of sending further supplies to the district concerned. Provision had to be made, too, that stocks were not left over at the end of the period of scarcity, which might be used by speculators to repress the prices of the new harvest. Furthermore, it was a task of the central direction to solve the problem of transportation in a satisfactory way; this was done through continual consultation with the railways and with the coastal shipping trade officials —especially with a view to lowering freight rates and to the expansion and improvement of services.

*Problems of Extended Rice Cultivation.* So much for the difficulties for which satisfactory and final solutions had to be found. However, the new rice policy also created other problems which may appear to be insoluble. For example, the policy followed since 1933 is possible only as long as there is an import surplus; if there were a recurrent production surplus the Government would be practically powerless. In spite of this, the common economic interests of the producers and of the treasury, and the defense of the far-flung parts of the archipelago under the Netherlands flag, demand that rice production be encouraged wherever possible. The export of rice is of vital importance for Java, but for the Outer Provinces self-provisioning is just as important. A decreasing ability to take advantage of unused arable land in several of the Outer Provinces, especially in Sumatra, makes essential an extensive substitution for *ladang,* or dry, cultivation of rice of an intensive *sawah,* or wet, cultivation by means of irrigation; but the increased rice production resulting from this change makes such districts competitors of Java. The settlement of the Outer Provinces with Javanese colonists thus begets an offspring which eventually may devour its parent.[1]

Another insoluble difficulty is posed by the contrary interests of producer and consumer. The price of the intensively raised Java rice will usually be higher than of that raised on the South Asiatic mainland. Is it permissible to keep the price of rice high by artificial means in times when the prices of Netherlands Indian export products are decreasing? Already it has occurred that the Government has had to support Javanese rice exports to the Outer Provinces with export premiums in order to hold down the price of rice in these provinces, while at the same time it was compelled to raise the import duties on foreign rice.

The establishment of mills to hull rice creates a similar problem. The present rice policy cannot by itself make Java rice a staple crop. The farmer raises it for his own needs, sells as much of it as he must to get

---

[1] In 1937 the excess of Netherlands Indian rice import was about one and a half million quintals, equalling three million quintals of unhusked rice. If we put the production of the rice fields in the colonization areas at thirty quintals of paddy per hectare, and if we assume that one-half of this is sold, an area of 200,000 hectares will suffice to provide the whole quantity now secured by importation; and this extent of rice cultivation will be reached in a few years of intensive colonization.

the ready money he needs and, later in the year, if he has any money left, will buy part of the sold rice back for consumption in his own household. The peculiar character of both the raw material and the final product of the rice hulling mills made it inadmissible to allow a free growth of these plants. Danger was seen in the withdrawal of too much rice from the producer-consumers in some areas and the increase of the share of the Java mills in the paddy crops sold in five years from 12 to 21.5 per cent. Therefore, in 1940, the provisions of the regulations under the industrial ordinance were applied to rice hulling mills with a capacity of $2\frac{1}{2}$ H.P. or more. In addition, the mills were organized and their sales centralized, on condition that they keep to the paddy purchase and rice selling prices fixed by government directive. To compensate for this restriction of liberty, the Government declared its readiness to take over any unsaleable rice surplus at the official price.

Every year, the Department of Economic Affairs issues a directive as regards prices for paddy. These standard prices serve no other purpose than that of indicating the amount which, with existing relations and prospects, can and should be expected to be paid by the hullers when purchasing paddy. These directive prices for 1939 amounted to 3.25 guilders per 100 kg. of unhusked and 2.90 guilders per kg. of husked paddy, delivered dry for milling in the rice mills. For paddy of inferior quality, or for an insufficiently dry product, also for paddy not supplied at the mills but at the village market in the *desas*, or still in the field or along the road, this standard price cannot, of course, be stipulated. However, it has officially been reported that in 1939 the purchase of paddy in Java generally took place on the level of the standard prices, and that in large districts of west and central Java even higher prices were paid.

Yet, there is no reason for optimism. The immediate cost prices of paddy do not come within the Government's sphere of influence. As long ago as 1878, an expert on the interior of Java shrewdly observed that paddy is never dealt with on the open market: "It is a fixed rule that those who buy paddy come and fetch it." And in 1936 a committee appointed to combat usury said about the granting of money advances on the green rice crop: "This is the practice of the Chinese rice hulling mills which in this way assure themselves of large supplies of paddy at low prices." Therefore, controlling officers were appointed in 1940 to check the prices paid for paddy.

The standard prices of paddy naturally do not settle the standard prices of hulled rice. Here local conditions have to be taken into account; and differences in quality, kind, cost of transportation and of processing make their influence felt.

In the beginning of 1934 the quota system for rice was extended also to soya bean (*kedelee*) and its products, soya and *taotjo*.

### PROMOTION OF INDUSTRY

Until the period 1925-28, production for export, measured in quantity, grew considerably quicker than did the population, while production for home consumption probably just about kept up with the increase of population. It is true, since about 1912, trade conditions had developed more and more in a direction unfavorable to export prices; but the increase in the volume of exports tended in large part to compensate for this disadvantage. Since 1929, however, the importance of production for export to the income of the people has declined considerably. This change resulted from restriction of the most important branches of commercial agriculture and a shifting of exports to the mining industries, the labor requirements of which are comparatively small. A return to anything like the respective position which existed in the period from 1920 to 1925 cannot be expected. As the population steadily increased, attempts in all directions to raise the income of the people became imperative. In these efforts the promotion of industry was assigned an important place.

What exactly is meant by industry in this connection? In Chapter VIII of my earlier book, *The Structure of Netherlands Indian Economy*, the following phases have been distinguished as leading from what is usually called "native production" to "industrial production": first, household industry, which produces for household needs and at most incidentally for a market; second, handicraft, which produces in close contact with the consumer and forms no stocks; third, home industry which, dependent on the merchant who is at the same time wholesaler and moneylender, produces for an unknown market; and fourth, the workshop where an entrepreneur brings together craftsmen and has them work with a certain regularity to accumulate a stock to be sold on the market. All these forms lead up to the capitalistic forms of industry which put capital in the place of labor and thereby lose to a certain extent the elasticity characteristic of pre-industrial production. Attempts to make domestic or household industry the object of industrial advancement inevitably lead to disappointment. The Government can effectively intervene only when the occupation has become a craft or business, working for the market.

Considering the point of departure for the promotion of industry in the Indies, it is understandable that the crafts and small shop industries must of necessity have a large place in the program, not only because by this means the welfare of the people is most effectively furthered but also because these forms of enterprise are often helpless when exposed to the demands of an exchange and money economy.

The industrial branch of the Economic Affairs Department is more especially responsible for the introduction of relatively simple improvements in technique, for the better organization of procurement of raw materials, for arranging the connection of such enterprises with central establishments that are better equipped to handle the technically more difficult processes and are in a better position to standardize and finish off the product, and for the regulation of sale.

*Methods of Encouragement.* To provide needed credit not covered from private sources, a "Fund for Small Industry" has been set up which makes loans under government guarantee and in conjunction with the People's General Credit Bank. Sales credits are in greatest demand. For workshop enterprises, likewise, it appeared necessary to provide special industrial long-term credits, secured more or less on a personal basis and by regular control of the industries concerned. The Government has established an organization for this purpose, too, in 1939, the "Fund for the Financing of Medium-sized Industries."

Generally speaking, only those industries are given encouragement of which it is expected that they will be able, within a measurable space of time, to manufacture their products at prices adapted to the Netherlands Indian standard of living. The price level should at least approach the Asiatic level. Protection, therefore, may not go beyond a point where it is compatible with the maintenance of the lowest possible price level on commodities that fill essential needs of the masses. In this framework, there is no place for special protective import duties; but the protection afforded Netherlands Indian industry by the ruling fiscal and protective tariffs may in general be considered reasonably adequate. On the other hand, industry is benefited by a decrease in import duties, or exemption from them on certain capital goods, raw materials, and auxiliary materials.[2] Import quotas should in this connection be regarded as, in principle, a temporary protection against competition of

---

[2] In August 1934, an amendment of the Netherlands Indian tariff came into force which authorized the Governor General to exempt machinery, tools, and raw materials from payment of import duties and to give retroactive effect to this provision for a period not exceeding two years.

exceptionally cheap imports from Asiatic countries further advanced than the Indies in industrial development. In the case of government purchases, home industry enjoys a ten per cent preference.

"Small" industry, as has already been mentioned, is assisted also by the organization of central boards responsible for the finishing plants. The aim of these central organizations is to bring about regularity of production, a standard quality, the prevention of onerous credit relations, and stimulation of efficient sales organization. By this arrangement, the small industry manufactures only unfinished products, the technically more difficult finishing-off processes being centralized. Finishing plants of this kind exist, among others, in furniture making and the manufacture of cigarette lighters, knives, forks, spoons and other kitchen utensils, earthenware, and agricultural tools. The central boards also accumulate buffer stocks. They are financed by the Fund for Small Industry at an interest rate of six per cent per annum. To start with, a central board is given disposal over only two thousand guilders. Its own task, apart from that connected with the finishing factories, is to finance, to organize, to supervise and to control production, and to promote sales. Several branches of industry may be grouped under one central board. So, for example, the "Batavia" Industrial Central Board has in its charge cooperative societies of cabinet makers, potters, and metal workers. The central board usually serves also as a sales office and as a joint purchasing office for raw materials, tools and equipment.

*Central Organization.* The administration of this whole apparatus heads up in the Industrial Service, a division of the Department of Economic Affairs, through which the Government's concern in the development of industry in the Indies is coordinated with the concerns of the interested private parties. The service is organized in four sections. One on "Industrial Policy and Factory Industry" deals with general problems and especially those of industrial planning. A section with the name "Consultation Bureau and Small Industry" is responsible for field services. It maintains six consultation bureaus, five of them in Java. Each of these bureaus is headed by an industrial expert whose duty it is to carry on local research and to collect data, to furnish information to all interested parties, and to organize and supervise small industrial enterprises. For certain branches of industry, such as textiles, ceramics, tanneries and leather works, the activities of the consultation bureaus are supplemented by workshops and by the appointment of handicraft teachers for village industries. According to the most recent available report, there were three of the former and nineteen of the latter. This

Industrial Service section also administers the Fund for Small Industry, established at the end of 1936, which, as we have seen, is especially useful in stimulating or carrying on experiments and in giving or underwriting credits to small industries. In 1938, it supplied credits to the amount of 114,000 guilders. The third section of the service administers the central laboratories for chemical analysis and for the examination of materials. These laboratories make investigations for other services of the department, too. The fourth section is formed by the Netherlands Indian Central Procurement Office which is of growing importance also for the promotion of home industries.

As for the results of these various efforts to further native industry, it may be stated that, generally speaking, domestic industry, working for household consumption, remains stable and shows some expansion here and there; that the small handicrafts, working for a limited local market, are losing ground; that the volume of production of the small industries has increased since 1934 but has remained at a standstill since 1938 and can maintain itself only by lowering prices.

### THE INDUSTRIAL PROVISIONING OF THE NETHERLANDS INDIES AND THE FOREIGN SHARE IN IT

The self-supply of the Netherlands Indies with manufactures of Western type increases rapidly. The following industries, among others, are represented: hardware; canning and packing, breweries; methylated spirits and arrack; biscuits; cocoa, chocolate and confectionery; carbonic acid; farinaceous products; preserves; food oils and fats, including margarine; soap; paint; ink; lacquer; office paste; wound-dressing requisites; glycerine and perfumes; insecticides and fungicides; sulphurous acid and ferro-sulphate; phosphate; shoes and leather goods; rubber tires and rubber articles; glass, paper; triplex boxes; textiles; resin and turpentine. Some of these industries are able to cover the whole needs of the Indies. The European war, before it merged with the war in the Pacific, provided a stimulus for the Indies to become still more self-sufficient. The cotton spinning and weaving mill in Tegal, for instance, was enlarged by ten thousand additional spindles, so that it was able to furnish all the yarn needed for its own weaving of a million yards of greys per month. The fact that the native operatives are very good spinners has contributed to this rapid expansion. In an experiment with five thousand spindles, 68,000 kg. of yarn was spun in twenty-five days, while in typical European mills, during a similar period, only about 60,000 kg. of yarns of the kinds necessary for unbleached cottons are obtained.

More recently, plans have been announced to start the weaving of other cotton textiles than greys.

Another example is the manufacture of bags for the shipment of sugar and other export products. It is true, the manufacture of bags from roselle fiber after some years still has a production capacity of only three million bags a year while the export need amounts to thirty million bags. It was expected, however, that production by the industry in the Indies would be increased to eighteen million bags in 1941. Further advances would depend on the results of future experiments with roselle.

At the end of 1939, a second paper factory was set going in East Java, and there were plans for the establishment of more factories to supply both paper made from wood pulp and paper made without wood. The necessary raw materials are to be found in the Indies in unlimited quantities.

An aluminum plant has been established in Sumatra, a joint enterprise of the Government and of the Billiton Company. Here the bauxite which is won in Bintan (Riouw Archipelago) is worked up with hydraulic electric power. More far-reaching plans to work the material into electric cables, tin foil for packing, sheets and alloys, and into household articles, have not yet been carried out.

Besides these realized enterprises, plans for others nearing realization are numerous.

*An economic evolution* may be seen in this development of the colony's industrial life. Commercial exploitation of the overseas territory by Western industries abroad has been succeeded by the growth of daughter enterprises in the consumption area itself. Foreign countries have taken part in this development also. The process began with the erection in 1926 of an assembling plant at Tandjong Priok, the port of Batavia, by the General Motors Corporation. In 1928, the British American Tobacco Company followed suit, and in 1934 the Goodyear Tire and Rubber Company, the National Carbon Company with a plant for the manufacture of electric batteries and torches, and the Unilever Company with a plant for the manufacture of soap, glycerine, and margarine, all of them in Java. The Dutch enterprise, Java Textile Company, established in 1937 at Tegal, on the north coast of Central Java, differs in design from those previously mentioned, in that here not one parent industry is concerned but about fifty concerns: Dutch textile mills, banks, commercial and shipping companies subscribed the capital.

Clearly, it is an essential advantage for such strongly mechanized industries if they can depend on a large market and especially a home market—even if its purchasing power is small. A large and cheap supply of good labor is an advantage, too, but not of first importance. There is, however, a third advantage afforded by the Netherlands Indies as a location for industry, and this of no less importance, an advantage which explains why this colony has been preferred for industrial investments, namely its geographical position in relation to surrounding countries. Together with Malaya, Indo-China, Siam and the Philippines, the Indies form a market that embraces more than 110 million inhabitants, more than one-half of them in the Indies, a market that can be cheaply served from Java.

The experience of the oldest of the foreign industrial concerns in the Indies, the General Motors Corporation, with a Javanese working personnel is that, while these workers need more working hours for a given labor achievement than those of any other of their plants, the low level of wages still makes the labor costs lower than they are anywhere else, and the quality of the product is not in the least inferior. The Goodyear company has reported similar satisfactory results.

Yet, the wage level in such industrial plants as these is many tens of per cent above the wage level to be found in native and Western estate agriculture. Only the Asiatic workshops and industries, such as the batik shops, the native cigarette factories, and the like, have a wage level not much higher than that of the surrounding agricultural world. Of great importance to the entrepreneurs, too, is that the wage level in this tropical colony is more elastic—shows far less lag and resistance in adapting itself to the changing business cycle—than is true of the wage level in Western, European industry. Trade unions are practically of no consequence in the Indies.

*Conclusions*: The following facts may help to give a clearer picture of the growth which Western industry in the Indies has attained. The use of electric power for industrial purposes has risen by more than 120 per cent since 1935. The export to the Outer Provinces of 34 industrial products made in Java is shown in Table XXVII. The total value of industrial production in Java in 1938 is estimated at 260 million guilders, in which Western industries participated with 80 million, domestic industries with 100 million and Asiatic enterprises with 80 million. The share capital of limited-liability companies of a purely industrial nature, with an original capital of more than 10,000 guilders, amounted to an average of 41 million guilders for the last ten pre-war years.

TABLE XXVII: EXPORT OF 34 INDUSTRIAL PRODUCTS MADE IN JAVA
TO THE OUTER PROVINCES, 1934-1938

*In million guilders*

| Year | Value |
|------|-------|
| 1934 | 30.6 |
| 1935 | 30.5 |
| 1936 | 33.7 |
| 1937 | 53 |
| 1938 | 47.9 |

## THE TEXTILE INDUSTRY OF THE INDIES

In a preceding paragraph, the Java Textile Company's mills at Tegal have been mentioned. This concern represents only the most recent branch of the textile industry in the Indies. The production of bleached piece goods demands a process of precision and closely integrated sequence, and because of this relatively large capital investments. This concern expected to reach its optimum size in 1942; at that time it hoped to be able to work into cloth some fifteen million guilders' worth of raw cotton annually and to give employment to twelve thousand native operatives. Its imports of the raw material were expected to be of commercial and political significance and thus of advantage to the colony's export interests, even though the company itself hoped to find at home the outlet for its entire output. The unbleached textile fabric which it produces came formerly almost entirely from Japan.

The production of multi-colored woven materials shows quite a different picture. Government intervention in this branch of the textile industry dates back to 1919. In that year a government textile institute was founded at Bandoeng to assist the native textile industry. Soon it applied itself to the improvement of the native handloom; and after many experiments it launched in 1926 the modern T.I.B. loom which very soon gained a well-earned reputation. Table XXVIII indicates the remarkable success of this venture.

TABLE XXVIII: NUMBER OF IMPROVED LOOMS DISTRIBUTED TO NATIVE TEXTILE INDUSTRY
BY TEXTILE INSTITUTE AT BANDOENG

| Year | Handlooms | Mechanical Looms |
|------|-----------|------------------|
| 1930 | 257 | 44 |
| 1931 | 524 | 44 |
| 1932 | 777 | 44 |
| 1933 | 1,299 | 46 |
| 1934 | 1,622 | 258 |
| 1935 | 3,919 | 414 |
| 1936 | 4,376 | 668 |
| 1937 | 12,000 | 2,000 |
| 1938 | 30,028 | 4,400 |
| 1939 | 35,000 | 6,600 |
| 1940 | 44,000 | 8,000 |

The handlooms came for the most part from the institute in Bandoeng. Especially the production of simple sarongs, the winding cloth generally used as the principal garment, threatened with the revival and improvement of the native weaving industry to attain such proportions that heavy competition was feared; for this reason restrictive regulations had in 1935 to be put into force for the small factories concerned. These regulations appear at first to have been unsuccessful. The wide dispersion over about 1,800 small units made it impossible to keep production under control. It had been thought originally that only the units with fifteen looms or more needed to be subjected to regulation; but it soon appeared necessary to extend the rulings to units with five looms or more and even smaller ones which often engage in only some of the processes which the dyed yarn has to undergo. And still the clandestine making and supply of sarongs seemed to be ineradicable. Partly, perhaps, because there was nothing to prevent anyone from buying, importing, and bringing into use as many weaving looms as he desired. The matter was further complicated by the frequent change of ownership of these small workshops, most often from native to non-native hands. In 1937, no less than 336 applications for such transfers were under consideration, 170 of them to non-native hands. Labor conditions in these small shops left much to be desired, and looms bought at heavy pecuniary sacrifices remained idle. In November 1940, a new regulation was introduced for the whole textile industry to take the place of the original regulation for the sarong industry only. To stimulate efficient business organization, regulation of production was substituted for regulation of equipment. By this means most of the problems just mentioned have been solved.

*Difficulties of the Native Weaving Industry—a Case Story.* How complicated the problem of such a native industry has become, can best be shown by a brief description of what happened in a certain district. The experiences of the weaving industry in Pajakoemboeh on the west coast of Sumatra illustrate the special difficulties which arise from the simultaneous encouragement by the Government of different industrial forms which in a socially homogeneous society usually lie far apart in time but in a dualistic society like that of the Indies operate next to each other. They also throw light on the effect of the close contact which exists between the crowded population of Java and the sparse population of the Outer Provinces. These aspects give the following picture a more than local significance.

From times immemorial, the population of the plains of Pajakoemboeh has been noted for its weaving. The most important center of this craft was the village of Koebang. The weaving, which was done with the aid of simple handlooms, formed an important source of income for the people of the district. When the weaving industry flourished, the output was one of more than 250 pieces per week which were sold at prices sometimes as high as fifteen guilders. When Buginese seafaring traders introduced on the west coast of Sumatra sarongs made in their villages in the south of Celebes, the weaving industry in the plains of Pajakoemboeh began to flag. Gradually the demand shifted from the old, expensive silken weaves—some of them with gold or silver threads—to the cheaper and more modern Bugi weaves which often were made of cotton.

Toward the beginning of this century, when European- and Japanese-made sarongs, too, appeared in that district in large quantities, the decline of the Pajakoemboeh weaving industry was accelerated. The local weavers could not easily adapt their craft to the altered circumstances; tradition proved a stronger brake on native production than it was on native consumption. As a result, the output of the local weaving industry had by 1922 shrunk to a fraction of what it once had been. Only the *negarie* Koebang was able to maintain itself as a center of this industry, though now on a much lower level than formerly.

To prevent the complete disappearance of this industry, the authorities in 1922-23 made efforts to revive weaving in Koebang and the surrounding villages. These efforts were directed into technical and organizational channels. The technical effort consisted in the introduction of new handlooms, the older models of the T.I.B. loom; the organizational effort, in an attempt to form a cooperative society. The technical effort was frustrated by the fact that the purchase price of the new handloom—yet far from perfect—was too high; the organizational effort, by an excess of individualism: the local weavers lacked a sufficient sense of the need for common action.

In the same year, 1922, Western competition penetrated more effectually to the west coast of Sumatra with the establishment of a power-using weaving mill at Padang, the capital of the district. As a result, ten years later almost all the weaving looms in Koebang and its surroundings stood idle. Still, the Government was of the opinion that the game was not yet lost. In support of this view, it could point to a Western hand-loom weaving workshop that had been started in Padang in 1933. Taking courage from this, it set up a permanent local advisory body in the former weaving center and opened in 1935 a model workshop there which within a year was enlarged to operate forty-three modern hand-looms. In addition, yarns were made available at reasonable prices, and opportunity was provided to sell the finished sarongs to the local central organization. These measures were supplemented, further, by import restrictions on multi-colored woven sarongs, the abolition of import duties on weaving yarns, and restrictions placed on the larger weaving mills in West Java. As a result of all these steps, the weaving industry of Koebang regained its feet. The new T.I.B. loom, the use of which was five times more remunerative than that of the old *negarie* looms, soon became popular. In September 1936, 338 of them were in regular use; and 16 shearing mills were in operation. The T.I.B. loom was worked by both men and women, alone or in turns. Such a loom became a keenly desired possession; to obtain it, irrigated fields, gardens and coconut trees were mortgaged, cows and buffaloes were converted into money. The center of the handloom industry came to be transferred from the *negarie* Koebang to the *negarie* Kotabaroe, and the model workshop of the Government was closed; the village weavers preferred to work in small units and thought they could get along without help from the Government. Although closed down in 1937 through lack of participation, the workshop may be considered to have been the means by which a flourishing industry was promoted which provided ample employment for 425 weavers who owned 441 T.I.B. looms and 23 shearing mills, and whose product was sold as far away as North Sumatra.

But there came a speedy end to this revival, too. At the end of the same year, 1937, the native weaving industry of Pajakoemboeh began to feel to an increased degree the competition of sarong imports to the west coast of Sumatra and to other parts of the island from Java where, because of a lower standard of living, labor costs were lower. So, one outlet after another was lost. At the end of 1938, only 17 per cent of the 517 T.I.B. looms, bought with such heavy sacrifices, were still in operation.

It is by no means certain that this is the end of hand weaving with colored yarns as a native industry in the Indies; but the chapter about the branch of that industry in Pajakoemboeh must be regarded as closed. When people rejoice over the rapid development of Java as the industrial center for all of the Indies, they should not forget that it brings with it the ruin of many and diverse native industries in the Outer Provinces, and that with its uniform cheapness the new industrialization is an instrument of social impoverishment.

SOME OTHER INDUSTRIES IN THE INDIES

To give even a sketch of the more important industries in the Indies would fall outside of the scope of the present discussion. That is why, for example, we must pass by the genuine Javanese batik industry which, although old, still retains its vitality. A few words will be said about only two other industries, not because they are more important than batik but because they throw a clear light on some aspects of Java's remarkable and complicated industrial development: the cigarette and the umbrella industries.

*Native Cigarette Industry.* The so-called straw cigarettes are cigarettes manufactured from tobacco mixed with cloves or other aromatic spices and wrapped with the outer leaf of the maize cob. The organized production of these smokes dates from the first European war; it began in 1918-19 in north-central Java, with Koedoes as its center. It still is an unusually scattered industry, at most concentrated in handicraft workshops but usually carried on as a household industry, with an army of middlemen and under either Chinese or native direction. Between 1921 and 1938 it increased fourteenfold; in the last-named year the value of its output amounted to 17.7 million guilders, since then to 19.5 million guilders—an amount all the more striking when it is remembered that it represents the return from an extremely cheap cigarette, the retail price of which usually is one cent for ten.

This industry is entirely in Asiatic hands; apart from that invested in the raw materials, no capital is at stake. But paralleling this straw cigarette industry, a Western cigarette industry has more recently grown up. This also originally used hand labor but was under Western management; and so the machine and with it the methods of modern big business soon appeared on the scene. In 1925, the British American Tobacco Company opened the first large factory for the machine-production of cigarettes; after some years, several others followed. In 1938, the total output of this Javanese cigarette industry was estimated to be worth 38 million guilders. In 1940, in spite of a much higher excise duty, its value reached 49 million guilders. The process of production is not, however, entirely mechanical. The handicraft stage of production was not altogether eradicated. On the contrary, it pushed itself as a wedge between the straw cigarette industry, with its traditional hand labor, and the machine cigarette industry.

This development was furthered in September 1935, by applying to the wholly mechanical production of cigarettes an industrial regulation under which minimum retail prices were set. As a result, the hand-made cigarette still constituted one-fourth of the total cigarette output of Java in 1940.

Although this measure made an end to the deadly competition between the machine-made and the hand-made cigarette, a struggle just as fierce continued within the hand industry itself. Everybody, it seemed, wished to take advantage of the additional elbow room which the hand-made cigarette industry enjoyed after the Government's price fixing for the machine-made product. As a result, the Government was obliged to extend industrial regulation to the hand-made cigarette industry, too. Because of the wider dispersion of this branch of the industry, that was much more difficult. And then there is the question whether, having gone so far, the Government will not have to go even further. For, once price fixing has been realized for the entire cigarette industry, then the straw cigarette industry will be encouraged to expand until it, too, goes beyond the limits of such remunerativeness as its outlet makes possible and must call upon the Government to help it out of that predicament. And that will not be the only way in which the authorities may, as it were, be forced to intervene. As has already been intimated, the large cigarette factories cannot but meddle with the native production of their raw material, tobacco. Although this is a native branch of agriculture, the Western enterprises are obliged to take an active part in it. The laying out and the upkeep of the tobacco nursery beds involve laborious and costly procedures, beyond the reach of the native population. Furthermore, the grower cannot manage without advances, and these, too, are supplied, either directly or through security of his credit, by the purchaser of his product. In this way the grower loses his freedom to dispose over his product. But the smaller cigarette manufacturers, who have not been concerned with the production of the tobacco, want their share in the business, too; and so a class of wholesalers has grown up who try to get possession of the tobacco that has been grown for the account of the big manufacturers. This clandestine purchase causes a strong deterioration of the product's quality, leads to the harvesting of unripe crops and insufficient drying, and makes for bad blood between the grower and the manufacturer. Again the result is that the Government has to come to the rescue, has to build up a system of licensing, and has to extend its control over the growing of and dealing in the tobacco product.

*The Umbrella Industry.* While the cigarette and straw cigarette industry may serve to illustrate the complications that may ensue from the development of a branch of industry in a dualistic society, the making of sunshades and umbrellas, *pajongs,* in western Java illustrates the traditional skill of the native population in the crafts, and the incredible cheapness of its labor. It is a very recent industry. In its center, Tasikmalaya and the surrounding villages, from where four-fifths of the product comes, there were only 70 small businesses in 1935, 120 in 1936, 200 in 1937. Most of these are limited to individual households, but there are also several small workshops or factories with from fifteen to twenty workers. The total output of the industry in 1937 was two million pieces in various styles—some with paper, others with cotton coverings—with an estimated total trade value of about 225,000 guilders, or a little more than 11 cents a piece. Of the total return, 93,000 guilders paid for the imported raw materials (material for covering, thread, dyes, and varnishes); 70,000 guilders for local raw materials (wood, bamboo, and glue), and 40,500 guilders for wages—leaving 21,500 guilders, not quite 10 per cent, as commercial profit for the entrepreneurs. The average wage that could be earned thus amounted to a little more than two cents for each *pajong*, a little less than one cent 'gold dollar'.

### REGULATION OF INDUSTRY

The economic policy underlying the regulation of industry received its first legal embodiment in 1924. In the beginning, its purpose was defense against immediate dangers that were threatening enterprises established in the Indies and already seriously affected by the crisis. With this aim in view, industrial regulation was introduced, to start with, in relation to branches of industry in which an excess of productive capacity had developed—amounting in some instances to several times the shrunken volume of sales—and where, in consequence, complete dissipation of the invested capital was feared. This capital, with a returning tide of trade opportunity, might still, it was thought, be profitable and render useful services to the economic upbuilding of the colony. Regulation was introduced also in branches of industry where, as a result of unlimited competition, a price war had been ignited that endangered the whole of the production apparatus and, moreover, made it too easy for new competitors to usurp the place of those enfeebled by the crisis. Examples of these uses of industrial regulation are those applied to the dairies around the city of Bandoeng, the capital of Priangan, to the dock companies, the printing offices, the foundries of frying pans previously referred to, the weaving mills, the ice factories and the cigarette factories. All of these regulations date from 1935. In all of these cases, inquiries were first made as to whether there existed, or was feared to arise, a competition leading to serious capital losses. Many requests for similar action from interested entrepreneurs in other branches of industry were rejected on the ground that government intervention of this sort was permissible only in cases of extreme necessity or where serious abuses had occurred.

With this rationale for a limited use of industrial regulation as an instrument of policy, the Government also appeared to favor its use, where needed, to prevent the forming of monopolies. An example of this is its action in the cigarette industry. Here regulation was originally confined to the mechanized enterprises: four licenses were issued to large plants with 97 per cent of the total capacity for turning out factory-made cigarettes, and ten licenses to smaller factories with a capacity of 3 per cent of the total output. When the licenses were granted, a schedule was drawn up giving the minimum prices at which the manufactured brands could be placed on the market—this to prevent underbidding. With this regulation, therefore, indirect protection was at the same time given to the as yet unregulated production of hand-made cigarettes and straw cigarettes; while the obligation imposed upon the industry to use in cigarettes of all makes at least 60—later 80—per cent of native-grown tobacco helped to assist the agricultural industry which lately had undergone a sharp fall in prices. Finally, it was hoped that as a result of this regulation the employers would no longer seek to lower their production costs by further forcing down wages.

Gradually, however, the aims of industrial regulation have shifted and taken on a more positive, constructive, and directive character. There is a growing interest in the development of industry in the Netherlands Indies. Typical of this is the remarkable modification in the composition of Netherlands Indian imports. Whereas before the first world war one-half of the imports consisted of textiles and foodstuffs, before the second the share of these two categories had diminished to one-fourth. At the same time, as a result of the quota system and of other official measures, the home market enjoyed a certain protection which was bound to exert a peculiar attraction to entrepreneurs. This was the case, for example, with foundries for making frying pans and with weaving mills, two industries which, for this reason, were in 1935 added to those subject to industrial regulations; it was the case also with rice-hulling mills which were brought under the regulations in 1940. Throughout that period, the Government more and more recognized its responsibility for the development of industrial life in the Indies.

This development has had other far-reaching consequences for the commercial policy of the Indies. The colony can never permit itself to forget that its income from exports must furnish the motive power for the growth of its money economy or, to use another simile, that export is the central pillar of the whole colonial economic structure. The international source of the Indies' capital investments assigns a fixed task to the colony; the plans for production, and especially those for industrial expansion, cannot disregard that task. This consideration is of special importance when a quota system introduced for the benefit of foreign countries, the mother country included, that is, a system of national quotas, provides an incentive for home production of the article which is thus placed under import control. A policy of restraining such expansion is justified by the even greater importance of not impeding the foreign trade: the export position of the Netherlands Indies and its treaty obligations must be protected.[3] This motive is even more pertinent in the case of a home industry that has no natural vitality and is able to keep alive only by virtue of the protection which it enjoys; it is especially pertinent also when the home industry which is to be protected is of less importance to the national income than are the export industries which are endangered by the limitation of specific imports. For these reasons, the growth of the industries in question is considered as undesirable and is checked by the authorities.

The fact that the principle of cooperation between the mother country and the colony clashes with the urge for the colony's industrial development makes the handling of industrial regulation extremely difficult.

Another positive purpose which the authorities can at times pursue with the aid of industrial regulation is that socially useful forms of enterprise, adapted to the native level of development, will not be pushed aside too often by Western mechanized forms of industry. In other words, the authorities may not forget that the somewhat primitive small and medium forms of manufacture—the household industries and small shops—may mean more for the income and well-being of the Netherlands Indian population than the large enterprises that work with considerable amounts of foreign capital.

With these newer purposes in view, the second industrial regulation ordinance, of 1937, declared emphatically that one of its objects was to care for the harmonious integration of new branches of industry into the existing economic structure and to prevent the establishment of undesirable branches of industry. In short, the regulation of industry was purposefully to be manipulated as a means of industrial planning. To carry out these new aims, an Office for the Investigation of New Industrial Opportunities was established in 1940, and an administrative apparatus set up. Even before, since 1936, an annual inquiry was circulated among interested industries to ascertain their views on the working of the regulations. These may be of two kinds. The first is that which restricts only the number of enterprises but does not exact that these must seek permission in advance for their extension. The

---

[3] The system of national quotas thereby changes its character and becomes a system of "free" quotas. An example of this course of development is the quota regulation of the trade in sarongs made of cotton and artificial silk. The protected exporters in the Netherlands could realize their quota only with the aid of the Netherlands Government which returned to them one-half of the duty of 25 per cent which they had to pay under the Netherlands Indian tariff.

second imposes more far-reaching limitations: it fixes both the number and the extent of the enterprises permitted and so makes expansion also dependent on special concession. The difficulty in the enforcement of this regulation lies in finding the right balance between the prevention of a destructive competitive struggle and the maintenance of healthy competition; it must seek to avoid a deadening protection, a slackening of initiative and enterprise, a lessening sense of responsibility and of independence.

With the new aim of industrial regulation, the restriction of the duration of legal regulations was abandoned in 1937. At that time, a General Regulation Board was called into being, which not only functions as an advisory organ but is also authorized to conduct independent inquiries with a view to the formulation of new proposals for regulation. The Government hopes, moreover, that through the institution of this body knowledge will be more widely diffused concerning the importance and character of the planning and regulation of industrial development.

### GOVERNMENT INTERVENTION IN FISHERIES AND FISH BREEDING

The interests of the sea fisheries are looked after in the Netherlands Indies by the Institute for Sea Fisheries in Batavia, a private institution subsidized by the Government and administered by a council composed of private persons and officials. This institute has fishery stations at Batavia, at Pekalongan, and at Soerabaya, and a temporary station in the eastern corner of Java, Banjoewangi. Its activities include, among others, the carrying on of industrial experiments, research in fishery techniques, biological research, economic research, supervision over fish auctions and over the granting of credits in connection with these auctions.

The part played by the Government in the development of mechanized fishing, that is, the use of motor vessels, is important. That branch of the fishing industry is, of course, much less a real people's business than is the extremely decentralized fishing from small boats. The use of motor trawlers in fishing has modified the character of the native fishing industry and is rapidly gaining ground because it is more profitable. First introduced in West Java, it has got a firm footing in the Straits of Madura (East Java), too. One phase of this development is the occasional combination of fishing from sailing boats with the conveyance of fish by motor boats and with salting a larger proportion of the catch.

A second form of government intervention relates to the development of the reef fisheries in the Thousand Isles, in the Bay of Batavia, in accordance with the Japanese method, the so-called muro-ami fishery.

In 1933 an experiment was made with this method: a Japanese muro-ami team was given a contract under which it carried on the industry for a period of two and a half months. Although this experiment was successful from a business point of view, it failed as a demonstration, since the fishermen of the Thousand Isles thought this system of fishing, which involved frequent and long dives, too laborious. When, however, in 1938 one of this island population's main sources of income threatened to dry up as a result of the very poor prices for copra, they made an attempt, on a small scale and of their own accord, to fish on their reefs with the muro-ami method. The test was successful; and, with the help of the authorities, the industry became more profitable.

A third initiative of the Government in the development of the fishery industry was the promotion of fish canning. This was advanced by setting up two experimental factories. One of these was soon given up; the other had not yet, when last reported upon, outgrown the early stage of a new industry with its accompanying diseases of infancy.

As regards fish breeding in salt water, Government intervention has been confined to technical advice and help given in the breeding of new species in fish ponds on the north coast of Java.

Throughout the 'thirties, the growing Japanese interest in the Java Sea as a source of fish gave the Government of the Indies a special motive to protect the national character of coastal fishing by means of stringent regulations. The local authorities were authorized to prohibit coastal fishing to a Netherlands subject when it appeared that this individual was merely a figure-head for a non-Netherlands subject, or where foreigners had a preponderating influence in a local fishing enterprise. Fishing enterprises organized as limited-liability companies were required, besides, to take out a license. For the rest, a Netherlands subject can fish along the coasts of the archipelago without a permit but may employ only Netherlands subjects in commercial fishing. These provisions are also valid for the mother ship of a fishing fleet and for the direction of the enterprise ashore.

Technical possibilities of a considerable expansion of the sea fishery seem to exist; the desirability of increasing the use of fish in the dietary of Java's millions is not open to question; but the realization of these technical possibilities and of the boon to the nutrition of the people is in danger of frustration from the lack of agrarian surpluses needed to pay for the sea products. The additional supplies will not fetch remunerative prices. However, the substitution of the home product for a fairly large import of canned fish—12 million guilders' worth, mainly from Siam— may reasonably be expected.

# Chapter VIII

# REGULATION OF THE PRICE LEVEL

## CONTROL OF COMMODITY PRICES

The control of pricing passed through three stages. Originally it was intended to prevent too big a drop in prices, a drop that would have meant that the importers had to face heavy losses. This control led to the licensing and restriction policy. After that, it became necessary to see to it that the imposition of national quotas on imports from Europe would not cause too sharp a rise in prices. To prevent this, it was assumed as a starting point when each quota was set that a rise of prices in the industries protected by them as long as they were in force would not be tolerated unless this were essential to maintain an otherwise efficient import enterprise. Where the quota system provided the opportunity for a business expansion causing a lowering of costs, producers might even be obliged to lower the prices on the respective commodity as long as the restriction of imports remained in force. This took place most often, of course, in connection with "free" quotas which aimed at the development of a home industry; but the same obligation also was laid upon importers of Netherlands products where the quota was imposed to advance imports from the mother land. Examples of the first type are the quotas for cement and automobile tires; an example of the second is the quota on electric bulbs. With regard to goods imported from the Netherlands and subject to import restrictions, the Netherlands Government has, as a rule, instituted a regular check-up by accountants of the cost-price calculations made by the protected firms. If this check shows a large enough fall in the cost price to make feasible a lowering of the price on exports to the Netherlands Indies, the factory owners are obliged to take this step, under penalty of the loss of their quota.

A similar method prevails in the control of the protected home industries in the Netherlands Indies. However, this check on prices at the fountain head is not enough; those who manage the distribution apparatus, the merchants, have an important say in pricing, too. First of all are the importers. A large part of the data necessary for price control is collected by the Central Bureau of Statistics which, under the authority granted it under the Statistics Ordinance, requires the importers concerned to report periodically the prices charged on sales in the preceding period. But the intermediary and retail trade have to be controlled, too. On many occasions it became evident that, when maximum prices had been fixed for the importers, the wholesale and retail traders were quite ready—either of their own free will or under compulsion—to pay more—"money under the counter," as the saying is.

The retail prices do not either automatically follow the maximum prices fixed for the wholesale trade. For this reason, the basic information collected from the importers is supplemented with data collected by market observers in various places and voluntarily by groups that are either directly concerned or only interested. If there appears to be a rise in wholesale prices, action can be taken, first, by giving out additional import permits and by imposing further conditions on the holders of import licenses. As another step, a stimulus may be given to the accumulation of buffer stocks to prevent a forcing up of prices. To make this possible, extra import licenses are issued to several importers on condition that the goods imported on the strength of these extra licenses be sold only at a time and place, and at a price, to be specified by the Department of Economic Affairs. In this way, the department may have at its disposal stocks of certain articles without having had to buy them.

The Government has no particular sanctions at its command, except those under the Usury Ordinance, to force the intermediary and retail trade to adopt a fair-price policy. Here a third form of price control must come into play. This was necessary in the first place after the devaluation of the guilder to see to it that the inevitable general advance in prices would take place as gradually as possible. In consequence of the prohibition to export gold from the Netherlands Indies, effected by the ordinance of September 28, 1936, and of the ensuing fluctuations of the rates of foreign exchange, some uncertainty had arisen in trade. In some instances, advantage was taken of this uncertainty to raise the prices of goods and services without reasonable grounds. Now, at the time of the devaluation, two legal regulations to combat such forcing up of prices already were at the command of the Government. First, there was the ordinance of November 22, 1918, under which the heads of the district civil service, after having been so authorized by the Governor General, were empowered to fix maximum prices. Second, the Expropriation Ordinance of 1920 contained certain articles allowing the taking over and selling of goods on behalf of the people where well-founded fears exist that the price of these goods is to be forced up to an unreasonable extent. In such event, the authorities could take possession under a set of rules laid down in the ordinance of 1918, just mentioned. Both measures, however, could be applied only with regard to victuals, raw materials for victuals, and household articles. In October 1936, both regulations were extended to cover all other kinds of goods and to services, under which rents were included, too. This extension was intended to remain in force only until March 1, 1937.

Another measure connected with leaving the gold standard was the lowering of a number of import duties, partly to absorb the unavoidable rise of prices on import goods if moderation of that increase were an urgent social need. Before the devaluation of the guilder, there had been a tendency to increase prices on many commodities, as a result of revived industrial activity in several countries, and this had raised the demand for raw materials. Not only Netherlands Indian export products, such as rubber, copra, kapok, and palm oil, but also imports, like textiles and metals, had experienced price increases because of this brisk demand which had been stimulated especially by the armament industry and the making of war supplies. Those officials in the Indies who were charged with the administration of the regulations designed to slow up a possible rise in prices saw clearly that to place price restrictions on export goods was not desirable but that, on the contrary, the native producers should be advised to take full advantage of the rise in prices; furthermore that, as far as import goods were concerned, a price increase by five per cent did not justify government intervention. This price policy with regard to export products was not, however, as self-evident as one might be inclined to suppose, mainly because there were among these products those intended both for the foreign and for the domestic market, as coconut oil, coffee, maize, and cassava. Which of the two conflicting interests should be regarded as of greater importance—the consumer's or the exporter's? For coconut and coffee, in which the quantity of exports far outweighs that which goes into home consumption, the interest of the producer was held to be decisive. But with regard to maize and cassava, mainly produced for the home market, the Government was of the opinion that it was not justified in limiting the advance of prices because, after a preceding drop in prices, it merely signified a recovery, to the advantage of the producer, which in the case of cassava (*gaplek*) was not even complete.

The prices of sugar and petroleum are controlled by monopolistic bodies which could be counted upon to pursue a reasonable price policy. For home industries, the devaluation of the guilder meant protection against competitive imports; their prices could follow those set for the imports.

As far as restricted and licensed imports were concerned, the Government could make use of the powers which it exercised through the regulations. For instance, it could require importers to import a considerable part of their quota within a given short period, thus insuring a larger supply of the market. With regard to the import of bleached piece goods from the Netherlands, an agreement was made that the prices should not rise more than was necessary to compensate for higher prices of raw materials and higher freight rates. All charges for services falling under the ruling of the Department of Transportation and the Department of Public Works remained unchanged. This affected, among others, the privately owned railways, gas and electricity companies, the coastal shipping trade, and motor truck transportation.

In the middle of October 1936, the margin allowed for price increases was raised to ten per cent, and luxury articles were committed to the free market. In November, the Government considered the time had come to abandon its more extensive intervention in price-fixing; the public control of prices thenceforth could be limited to commodities of vital necessity for the masses of consumers; the uneasiness about the stability of the guilder had disappeared.

By means of all these various manipulations of the powers vested in them, the authorities were able to keep in hand the movement of prices that had resulted from the devaluation of the guilder. Usually, an announcement of the Government sufficed to insure that certain steps were taken, since those concerned knew that the Government had the authority to take more decisive action if this should be necessary. The ordinance of October 1936 actually had to be enforced in only a few cases.

The period of six months, set for the validity of the legal regulations, seemed to be very ample. Nevertheless, the Government deemed it necessary, in March 1937, to prolong that period by another six months, since several new factors had in the meantime appeared which might cause a rise in prices—such as an increased demand for import products in the Outer Provinces causing stocks to disappear, and the increasing disparity between the rise of prosperity in Java and that in the Outer Provinces which necessitated a protection of Java against a rise in prices.

Further extension of the regulations did not appear to be necessary. Only when the international political situation in Europe became threatening, did the Netherlands Indian Government decide, in May 1939, to bring the regulations once more into force. At first this was for one year; and a new regulation was added by which the Government might prohibit or limit the movement of certain commodities or groups of commodities within the customs area. However, since it is not the purpose of this survey to deal with the special measures taken to safeguard and strengthen the economic position of the Netherlands Indies in an imminent state of war, we shall not discuss such matters as the establishment of a fund for the purchase of foodstuffs to insure the most adequate possible supply of the population in case of an unexpected breaking off of foreign or interinsular communications; or the ordinances adopted to permit if necessary the exercise of compulsion in the cultivation of foodstuffs and to increase temporarily food production in those districts which were especially dependent on the importation of food.

### THE CONTROL OF WAGES

*In Java.* As early as 1930, wages in Java were reduced considerably, almost all along the line; and this drop continued to such a degree that in 1936 the daily wages paid in most of the concerns amounted to only 25 to 45 per cent of those paid in 1929. Especially in many of the small workshops owned by Asiatics were daily wages reduced below the minimum necessary for the support of a workman's family. Thus, already in 1933, the daily wages paid in peanut-shelling factories, batik shops, copra drying establishments, nutcake (*tahoe*) bakeries, and similar native industries, were abnormally small. From some shops and factories, the wage-earners went home after an eight-hour work-day with only from one and a half to two and a half (guilder) cents. In the hat industry of West Java, few were able to earn more than two and a half or three cents a day, even in 1933.

The wage situation in the Western enterprises was, by comparison, considerably better. In this group, the lowest wages are those paid on the mountain estates, which are without exception devoted to the cultivation of perennial crops, especially those estates where the plantation manager is not dependent on the population of an estate settlement but has at his disposal an abundant labor supply from surrounding villages. On such estates, the wages in the years 1935 and 1936 amounted to between four and nine cents, as compared with wages between seven and fifteen cents paid on other Western estates.

At the beginning of 1936, the Government of the Netherlands Indies came to the conclusion that in a number of cases the adaptation of wage rates to decreased export prices, and thus to the paying capacity of the enterprises in questions, had surpassed reasonable limits. With a large and unorganized supply of labor, it was impracticable to set bounds to the cutting down of wage rates; but where the prices of the products raised showed a tendency to increase, the Government thought the time had come to intervene. It got into contact with the more important employers' associations to explain its views on the matter and to request their cooperation in an effort to obtain periodical information on wages. Thus, beginning with October 1936, a wage control was instituted for agricultural estates with an area of at least 200 *bouw,* or 142 hectares. Detailed information was collected concerning seven hundred estates, for the most part those engaged in the cultivation of mountain crops. The results of this investigation, which have been published, showed after some months that, except on some of the rubber estates, wages were showing only slight improvement in spite of a further continued improvement of industrial results and notwithstanding a rise in the prices of necessaries of life in the wake of the devaluation of the guilder.

In September 1937, the Government sent a circular on this question to the estate owners, stating the conclusions of the official inquiry and formulating some desiderata concerning the standard of wages. Many of the estate owners, who had not previously revised their wage schedules, gave ear to the expressed desires of the Government; but with about sixty of them a further step had to be taken. This took the form of a request for information as to why they had partly or entirely failed to comply with the wishes set forth in the government circular. Not all the answers received were satisfactory or convincing. Some said that, although individual wage rates had not been raised, the total wage roll had increased. Others pleaded that some of the wages paid should be regarded as supplementary to the income derived by the wage-earners from their own land. Still others argued that an increase in wage rates for piece work often led to decreased output.

Although such answers as these were not convincing as justifications for cutting down wages, they clearly showed the difficulty of finding a satisfactory solution for this problem. Where the economic law of demand and supply gives no assistance; where not the slightest help can be expected from the native population directly concerned; where, indeed, it is true that for a large part of the laborers the wages are merely supplementary to their agricultural income; where the employers can be induced to alter their conduct only by an appeal to their sense of decency; where the worst abuses occur in small enterprises which can practically not be controlled at all—in such a situation the Government is almost powerless. Still, it did not give up hope. As a next step, it decided to collect information in various estate districts on the minimum cost of living for the family of an estate laborer. With the aid of these basic household budgets, the Government hoped to arrive at a more exact judgment.[1] In the meantime it let it be known that it considered a system of legal minimum wages to be impracticable.

*Outer Provinces.* Outside of Java the problem is quite different. Here the planters' associations themselves fix the minimum wage rates; here the problem concerns laborers who find their only means of subsistence in wage labor; here the laborers have to be recruited at great expense since no inexhaustible labor reservoir is close at hand; here the fixing of wage rates is much more artificial and much more rigid.

It was not until January 1933 that the largest planters' organization, the General Association of Rubber Planters on the east coast of Sumatra, better known as the "Avros", decided to decrease the minimum wage from 37 to 32 cents a day for men and from 32 to 27 cents for women, with a withdrawable extra allowance of 2 or 3 cents for workers with a longer record of service. Two years of serious depression passed by before another wage decrease by 2 cents per day was announced—but not until an inquiry into the household budget of a typical laborer had shown such reduction to be reasonable. This precaution is in conformity with the legal regulation concerning "coolie labor" which stipulates that the income of the laborer must be adequate to supply his normal necessities, and which prescribes the drawing up of a complete household budget for a laborer as a basis for arriving at the cost of living with which wages are constantly compared.

The second largest central planters' organization, the Deli Planters' Association, was still more conservative in its wage policy and in August 1933 only started an indirect cutting down of wages by announcing that wages would no longer be paid for the fortnightly days of rest. In June 1935, there followed a decrease of the wage rate to 32 cents for men and 27 cents for women, augmented by a withdrawable extra allowance of 3 cents a day.

There is a striking difference in the wage level for similar work in Java and in the Outer Provinces; even for so-called half-day shifts the planters in the latter pay wages ranging from 20 to 25 cents for men and from 16 to 25 cents for women.

The wages paid to Chinese laborers are not much higher than those paid to Javanese. Tin mining in Banka, for example, which is heavy work, starts newcomers at a wage of 24 cents; this is increased by 12 cents at the end of 180 working days. All the workers also receive prepared meals free of charge. The *Singkehs* (Chinese newcomers) em-

---

[1] On one of the last days of December 1941, the Central Bureau of Statistics published the results of this extensive inquiry.

ployed in the workings of the Billiton Mining Company—in which the Government has an interest—receive a wage of 33 cents and, among the perquisites, a certain quantity of rice, salt and paraffine oil. This wage is augmented every two months by one cent until a maximum pay of 40 cents is reached. Laborers who enter a contract for a second time, called *Lohaks,* begin with a wage of 43 cents. In these mining concerns, of which the first is completely and the second for the greater part a government enterprise, the Government exercises control over the fixing of wage rates. But the Government, too, must take account of the fact that a raising of wages above the level that is considered adequate and decent by the laborers themselves is more likely to cause a decline rather than an increase in their output.

# CHAPTER IX

## THE POPULATION PROBLEM

### JAVA'S OVERPOPULATION[1]

What reserves of natural resources has Java in store for its growing population? An end will soon be reached to the possibility of extending the area of irrigated fields by the use of larger irrigation works. The technical possibilities of this method of enlarging the arable area are practically exhausted. Extension of that area by reclamation of waste land has little future, either. All land, including dry fields and village compounds,—7,646,000 hectares in 1920—showed by 1940 an increase of less than 282,000, an increase, that is, of less than 4 per cent and only about a third of that which would be necessary to keep up with the increase of population.

A government committee appointed to study this fundamental agrarian problem came to the conclusion, a short time ago, after having made careful estimates, that Java still can supply 300,000 hectares of new arable land—perhaps enough for five years, at the most. That food production nevertheless keeps up with the growth of population can be explained by the increasingly intensified use of the land. While in 1926, counting double crops, the arable land was used to the extent of 131 per cent of its surface capacity, the comparable percentage in 1940 was 145.4 per cent. It is not to be expected, however, that this intensification can go much further.

And what of the estate cultures? As far as tobacco and coffee are concerned, further extension will, within a measurable space of time, no longer be attractive. The three other agricultural industries of primary importance, sugar, tea, and rubber, are (or were before the war) restricted to respectively 45, 65, and 90 per cent of their potential capacity. It is very unlikely that the extension of these crops in the coming years will be by more than a few per cent at most.

There remains, then, the possibility of increasing the yield of land by the introduction of better agricultural techniques. Indeed, in this general

---

[1] The substance of this section is derived in part from a lecture given in 1937 by the then director of Economic Affairs in Batavia, amplified and corrected on the basis of later data.

field there are still some important opportunities, such as selection, use of better plant material, fertilization, combat of plant diseases and pests. However, improvements in these respects can only be slow. The problems that must be met are very old and have been studied for many years. The effect of such improvements on the larger problem here under consideration can hardly, therefore, be very great. In this, the small financial capacity of the population also has to be taken into account; it means that the limit to which it can take advantage of such opportunities is soon reached. The question may even be raised whether a forcing up of output by means of fertilization and the like, involving capital expenditure, really fits into the economic framework of an agriculture primarily concerned in food production rather than production for the market.

The chance of finding new sources of subsistence becomes constantly narrower. It is true, the population is no worse off today than it was some ten or fifteen years ago; but seeing that its means of subsistence have always been close to the border of insufficiency, this conclusion is not very re-assuring and does not mean much more than that the Government, all things considered, has taken advantage of every breeze in sailing its economic ship of state.

The reduction of the surface area used for the cultivation of sugar by 50 per cent compensates at most for a little over a year's increase of population by freeing for food production about 100,000 hectares of irrigated land. The loss of the money income from sugar, which exceeds in value a hundred million guilders per annum, probably is far more serious than the relief is helpful. There is reason to believe that the reduction of imports of rice and soya beans will be reversed in the near future. And where will the population be able to find the money to pay for these increasing imports? The self-sufficiency of the peasant, his slight dependence on the market, is not a result of prosperity but of small purchasing power: he has no reserves to fall back on. If another bad harvest, as disastrous as that in 1921, should occur, it would mean for the Government an additional expenditure of some forty million guilders —without a chance of restitution of any considerable part of it by the agricultural population.

Nor does the more and more intensive use of the land improve its quality. On the contrary, decrease in quality and a corresponding diminution of the yield lead to a further crowding of multiple harvests on the more and more exhausted soil, and a vicious circle is at work.

All in all, the future does not look too rose-colored for Java if the population continues to increase at the same rate; and one can understand why the authorities regard and treat the problem of the island's overpopulation as a very urgent one.

Where is a solution to be looked for? Some students of this subject expect much from the promotion of industry. Now, the annual increase of the population amounts to about half a million persons, and the population and vocational census taken in 1930 has shown that 35 per cent of the population are gainfully employed; so, every year 175,000 workers would have to find a new means of livelihood in industry to absorb this population surplus. Netherlands Indian industry is quite incapable of meeting such a demand. With a conservative estimate, it may be supposed that in the coming years industry can supply from fifteen to twenty thousand persons more with their main source of income, that is to say, absorb about one-tenth of the population increase. Besides, are we justified in looking upon such expansion of industry in the Indies as a long-term trend? The bounds which, as we have seen, already have had to be set to the advancement of industry, the relative slightness of the home market's purchasing power, and costs of transportation which too easily become prohibitive considering that purchasing power, all result in a scattered production distributed over numerous petty businesses. Our expectations, it appears, should not run too high.

Others have great hopes from an increased resettlement of workers. In this matter, too, the economic crisis has seriously disturbed illusions. The most important branches of commercial agriculture—which alone have a considerable need for labor since, in comparison, the mining industry can absorb only a small amount—are subject to restriction; no new estates have been opened for some years. Under these circumstances it can be hoped at most that the labor stream will remain constant. This implies that, whatever the number of Javanese laborers who are migrating to other parts of the archipelago, an approximately equal number return to Java. Moreover, the return stream largely consists of persons who will contribute little to production on this island but are merely consumers, have outgrown their village milieu and there form a disturbing element. Still another fact has to be considered: the importance of Java as a labor reservoir for the estates in the Outer Provinces is fast declining. In all the more important centers of Western agricultural enterprise a local labor market is developing. In this way, in 1940, 80 per cent of the newly employed estate laborers in Sumatra, 75 per cent in Borneo, were found within the district, all of them as free laborers. It is true that of the contract laborers 95 per cent still were recruited in Java; but as this category formed only 2 per cent of the newly engaged workers, this fact is negligible. While, therefore, the emigration of laborers must be rejected as a solution of the population problem, mainly because it is temporary in character, this does not hold good for laborers who are permanently settled on the estate that brings them to Sumatra or one of the other Outer Provinces. But estate settlement is not capable of considerable extension. Apart from the fact that most estates have no land available for such settlers, they can use settled labor only as a fixed nucleus of their labor force and must retain the freedom to adjust additional employment to their changing needs for labor.

Another form of permanent labor emigration is the so-called border colonization, an intermediary form between self-sufficient agricultural settlement and estate settlement. Its main feature is that the settler obtains part of his livelihood from a small piece of land on the borders of the estate, which he is helped to acquire, so that the wages earned on the estate need serve only as a supplement. However, this method of border colonization does not come into question, either, as a possible means of re-settlement on a larger scale. Not, at any rate, on the east coast of Sumatra where 65 per cent of Javanese migrant labor was, at the end of 1940, concentrated, since here the estates for the most part form united complexes. Nor elsewhere, because the demand for labor on the estates fluctuates and never really offers an opportunity for a large-scale experiment. In times of depression and restriction of output, the estate is not prepared to maintain or support unemployed laborers, even partially; in periods of boom and expansion it can only use labor which is at its disposal for the whole of its working time. Apart from this, the district authorities are not particularly keen on these half-farmers, half-laborers, who in the long run present the danger of creating a class of paupers when they fail to become either the one thing or the other.

Nowadays, the Government has great expectations from another form of permanent resettlement, that brought about by emigration from Java to the sparsely populated Outer Provinces for purposes of agricultural, i.e. self-sufficiency, colonization.

That kind of colonization has been an object of governmental interest since 1902 and was first put into practice in 1905. The Government has incurred large expenditures for experiments in this connection. Two colonies in South Sumatra, Gedong Tataan and Kota-Agoeng, are the only ones that can be considered entirely successful. They had more than 24,000 inhabitants in 1929; but they alone have in the course of years cost about five million guilders—three and a half million for actual settlement and one and a half million for irrigation—that is to say, more than two hundred guilders for every inhabitant, or eight hundred guilders on the average per family. "It is hardly surprising," says a report, "that in view of these enormous sums the Government came to regard this kind of colonization as one which in practice cannot be made to pay. When the crisis set in toward the end of 1929, things began to look practically hopeless for a continuation of the colonization project.

But "when bale is highest, boot is nighest." When the need was greatest, help came from an unexpected source nearby. It was found possible to connect the settlers themselves with the system of colonization and thus to insure its survival. Being rice growers, they found themselves short of hands at harvest time and declared themselves willing to take compatriots from Java into their service and shelter them for a season in exchange for their assistance with the harvesting. In 1932, this declaration was made the starting point for a new system of colonization, a system that proved entirely successful. In behalf of the seven thousand Javanese who were transferred to these colonies in 1932, the country needed to pay out only 48,000 guilders of which 26,000 guilders, representing the cost of travel, flowed back again into the treasury, so that actually the cost to the Government worked out at little more than three guilders a person.

The new system was gradually perfected in the following years. The "candidate colonists" are submitted to a medical examination and given treatment if necessary. Former contract laborers are excluded because they are deemed to be no longer easily adaptable to independent farming. Only families with not more than two children are sent out, so as not to make the struggle for existence too severe in the early stages. Where possible, an agreement is made with the colonist for a partial repayment of the cost of transfer and installation; this increases his self-respect and makes it possible to lend him additional aid.

The success of this type of colonization rests on the condition that settlements are formed only in suitable sections of the Outer Provinces, of an adequate area and easy to irrigate, where a beginning has already been made by a group of pioneers with the growing of rice. The costs attached to the forming of the pioneer nucleus are, of course, much higher per colonist, and the irrigation too costs money. But the larger is the territory open to settlement around the original nucleus, the smaller will eventually be the burden of the initial costs, for the filling up of the settlement with new colonists costs next to nothing. Yet, this condition brings with it a not unimportant limitation and perhaps also a danger for the new colonization scheme that is not altogether imaginary. In the choice of suitable settlement areas, the authorities are restricted to fields that can be irrigated, and the colonists have to be turned into rice growers—that is to say, they have to confine themselves to a form of agriculture which already is too intensive, which has made possible the unusual density of Java's population but which, because of this, practically excludes the possibility of changing over to some more extensively cultivated staple crop. In all the descriptive reports from successful colonization districts one finds a comparison with the settlers' place of origin. The Javanese village environment has been exactly reproduced, to be sure, but with the same limited chances of development which these village surroundings afford. Even at the time when the colonization grounds are for the first time extended, one meets with inhabitants of the nuclear colony who look on the extension as a means of securing arable land for their children, since no land is available in the original part of the colony. There are exceptions, but after a generation, at most after two generations, that lack must be felt in all these colonies.

The individual area of irrigated fields, which averages 0.072 hectares in Java and Madura, is only 0.09 hectares in a full-grown colony like Gedong Talaan which was established in 1905 and has a population of 42,000. The total amount of landed property per head of this population is not more than 0.234 hectares as against 0.168 hectares in overcrowded Java and Madura—that is, only a third more.

This does not imply that there is any other way out of the dilemma. This mass colonization is not one of enterprising pioneers with sufficient reserves to be able to hold out for a few years, nor of farmers with the technical knowledge and experience required to raise staple crops. They are all poor with nothing more at best than a knack and a traditional preference for the wet cultivation of rice. So, it is obvious that, accepting cold facts, the system of colonization cannot become the means of retraining the colonists as small planters; at any rate, this is impracticable for the time being.

This system of colonization thus remains a typical state project. The new settlements require the continuing vigilance of the authorities, as well as constant medical care. This is a reason for reclaiming for settlement only large tracts of land. The Government would be lacking in a sense of responsibility toward the settlers who by its propaganda have been induced to emigrate if they were simply left to their fate; on the other hand, the often intensive intervention which is required would be too expensive if these settlers were scattered in small groups. Besides, when recruiting new colonists, there is the attraction exerted by the large, well-known colonies where relations and friends from the village await the newcomer. For, the pace of colonization is not determined by the availability of land or of funds, but entirely by the supply of suitable candidate settlers. Propaganda is necessary and opposition has to be constantly cleared out of the way. The modest needs of the Javanese make him all too content with his circumstances at home, and obviously the poorest of the poor are not the most suitable material for making good colonists. Propaganda would not be necessary if it were the intention to use re-settlement as a sort of poor relief; but that would cause irreparable harm to the system. Little propaganda would be needed, either, if colonization could be confined to the most energetic persons for whom the Javanese environment offers too little elbow room and who feel the urge to rise above their surroundings; but their number is too small, and most of them can find an opportunity for success in Java. On the contrary, the success of mass colonization depends on the many who are barely able to keep their heads above water, who have to be aroused, encouraged, moved to make a new beginning in their struggle for existence, on another front. Long-term propaganda, carried out in the right way and begun at the right moment, is of decisive importance to appeal to this mass of the people. That is why the Government seeks the help of all who come in contact with the lower classes, the native authorities in the first place. That is the reason why it has *wajang*, shadow picture, performances; why it has had propaganda films made; why some of the older colonists are transformed into campaigners who travel through Java and Madura at government cost; why it organizes excursions to the colonization centers and issues literature about colonization for use in elementary schools; why it encourages correspondence between the colonists and their home folks, urging the latter to emigrate; in short, why the Government advertises migration as though it were a new article for mass consumption which it had just brought on the market. But every mass-consumption article is subject to standardization, and so is colonization: each colonist has to be treated in the same way, must be given the same amount of land, the same amount of credit. And so, since each colony must become a close replica of the original milieu, it is impossible to avoid the creation of little Javas wherever land is developed in the Outer Provinces. But in this way Java's problem also is transplanted, and not solved.

This transplantation of the Java problem may also be indicated in other terms. The Central Bureau for Statistics in 1938 made the following computations. If the growth of population continues at the rate of 1.5 per cent annually, and if no emigration takes place, Java which now has 46 million native inhabitants will have 116 million in the year 2000 —that is to say, 879 per square km. or 1,487 per square km. of cultivated land. With an annual emigration of 80,000 families, consisting of father, mother and one child, when the parents are between fifteen and twenty-four years of age and the child below five years, the population in 2000 would amount to 74 million. With an annual emigration of 120,000 families of the same composition, the population would have reached 57 million in the year 2000. If instead 120,000 childless married couples were to leave annually, then the natural increase of the population, with such annual emigration of 240,000 adults, could be absorbed. These figures assume, of course, net emigration, the number of those permanently staying out of Java after deducting those who have returned because of disappointment and homesickness, a number that may be high.[2]

These are hypothetical figures that need not be taken too literally. The actual number of Javanese who emigrated amounted to 33,000 in 1938, 45,000 in 1939, and 52,000 in 1940; the most optimistic of colonization propagandists does not dare to let his expectations soar higher than 100,000 per annum. On the other hand, it cannot be presumed that the rate of population increase in Java will continue unchanged.

The position with regard to the increase of population in the settlements, on the other hand, is quite different. The most productive age group is reduced in Java but now placed, to the extent of this migration, in an environment where, for the first time, conditions are completely advantageous for its reproduction. Because of the easier kind of life and the provision of good medical services, it must be expected that the natural increase of the settlement population will be high—if not immediately, then at any rate after some years when the situation has become more stable. But this means that the problems which it had been hoped would be solved by colonization re-appear in a new environment. With the land areas of the settlements cut into smaller sections and with the ampler local labor supplies, the colonies lose their value as population nuclei. Besides, the surplus from harvests available for marketing become smaller, although the colonists must sell the same quantities as formerly to maintain their standard of living; and with the increase of population the chance of earning money outside the colonies likewise diminishes. In many of the settlements, as a matter of fact, that chance will from the beginning be smaller than it is in Java. If a larger proportion of the harvest is sold then less will be available for home consumption; it means that the periodic scarcity of food, characteristic of life in Java, re-appears in the colonies; it means that good prices cannot be realized on supplies taken to market and that it will be difficult to

---

[2] In Soekadna, the biggest colonization center, the returning colonists in 1940 were 9 per cent of the population.

meet financial liabilities; in short it means that the present situation in Java will have been transplanted *in pessima forma,* and that Java itself will be worse off than before.

Even today, several estates in South Sumatra and the Lampong pepper plantations can satisfy their labor needs almost entirely by recruiting wage-earners in the local settlements—even though the colonists have a lower production ratio than the laborers formerly recruited in Java or the people from the Bantam district in West Java who have been in the habit to cross on their own initiative to the opposite shore to pick pepper. Even today, thanks to the settlements, the Lampongs are no longer dependent on rice imports from outside; for Java this means a double loss, of a rice market and of labor, perhaps even of a market for industrial products if the colonists should take up handicrafts as a supplementary means of livelihood and compete with the mother island in this domain, too.

All this is not put forward as a criticism of the system of colonization that has been followed in recent years. This system is excellent, no better can be found. But quite apart from the relatively small impact of such migration, thus far, on the population problem of Java, it should be made clear that colonization cannot provide the solution for that serious and urgent problem—a problem, moreover, with which not only Java but almost all the countries of East and South Asia have to wrestle and which has not yet found a satisfactory solution in any of them.

The Government of the Indies, too, has become more doubtful. In the summer of 1939 it declared before the Volksraad:

> "In spite of intensive propaganda, it has appeared in recent months that there is probably not enough keenness to emigrate to South Celebes to meet the requirements of the various places opened up to receive settlers. This experience shows that there is no reason as yet for optimism in this respect."

There seems, indeed, to have taken place a change of public opinion. The attempt to assist only the migration of selected families has had to be abandoned; to assist whole hamlets and villages to move now appears the best form of emigration and is encouraged as much as possible. There have been some surprising experiences. It has been found that in districts with a dense population and unfavorable economic conditions willingness to migrate is less pronounced than it is in more prosperous districts. The explanations given for this are that the attachment to the soil is strong in proportion to the demands it makes on the tiller; that the poor, illiterate crofter lacks energy and initiative; and that, in communities where there is only a slight differentiation in the levels of prosperity, consciousness of relative lack of it usually is absent or at least not very alive, while the community spirit is stronger. These are not very cheerful notes, but they harmonize with the analysis already given of the colonization problem and of the attempts made to solve it.

The direction of the Netherlands Indian Government's colonization policy, here sketched in outline, is in the hands of the Central Board for Native Emigration and Colonization, a committee of three presided over by a member of the Netherlands Indian Council and including the Directors of the Departments of Home Affairs and of Economic Affairs and the Adviser for Agricultural Affairs, the latter as secretary. This committee selects the areas suitable for the planting of settlements and also directs the propaganda and the recruiting of settlers. It had at its disposal a grant of 3.5 million guilders from the 25 million guilder development fund contributed by the Netherlands and described in an earlier chapter. This amount was spent chiefly on the clearing and preparation of new settlement territories. The general requirement laid down for the selection of these territories is that they must contain at least 5,000 hectares of land fit for irrigation and that it must be possible to lay out good roads for transportation of the products raised on them. The settlement area in South Celebes, mentioned in the above-quoted statement of the Government, was selected and made ready by the Central Board on that basis.

Mention should also be made of a special branch of native colonization, although perhaps it should be considered as belonging in the next section of this chapter, the colonization of young native intellectuals; this is placed by the Netherlands Indian Government in the same category as European colonization. Both come under the administration of the Council for Colonization which provides financial support, and also that of the Department of Justice. The plan differs from that which governs ordinary native colonization in that the initiative has come from a native association especially formed for that purpose. This organization prepares the future colonists for the tasks that await them by means of an educational work camp. The organization of this land settlement of native intellectuals is especially interesting because of the use it makes of feudal ideas that still prevail in native society. Each colonist is accompanied by five agricultural laborers, or *magersaries,* who have to assist him in his work. Each colonist is given five hectares to start with, an area that can be extended to ten hectares, while each *magersarie* has one hectare assigned to him. A preliminary impression gained from the first experiment with this type of colonization, which was set up in 1938, was favorable: it seemed to promise success.

## EUROPEAN AGRICULTURAL COLONIZATION

As has already been mentioned, government activity in behalf of European agricultural land settlement follows a different line from that adopted for native colonization. It was for this that the Colonization Council was set up to advise the Government. The Council gives help, direction and advice to associations and organizations concerned with colonization; it is charged with the allocation of funds made available for this purpose by the authorities—300,000 guilders appropriated from the twenty-five million guilder fund; when necessary, it makes suggestions to the Government for further action. The Government has attached to the Council an agricultural expert who is especially charged with the study of general problems connected with European agriculture on a small scale.

A sharp distinction should be made between such individual settlement for farming on a small scale which is practiced by Eurasians, chiefly in Java, and for which the Government provides small areas of waste land under long lease, and experiments in group colonization that originate with associations and take place exclusively in the Outer Provinces. However, both kinds have one thing in common, namely that they spring from the same urge of the Eurasian element in the colonial society which, remaining in the country, feels the need for a closer link with the soil of that country which it regards as its native land. Another thing which they have in common is that one cannot speak of either kind of land settlement as an outstanding success. To some extent this is because of a structural problem in Netherlands Indian society. The Eurasian group, especially the bottom layers of this element, have been crowded out of colonial society; and this has caused them to look out eagerly for new means of subsistence. Farming suggested itself. Between 1929 and 1938, the area of land given or assigned for small-scale farming in Java increased from 6,000 to more than 11,000 hectares, the number of holdings from 730 to 1,744, the number of tenants on long leases from 550 to more than 1,100. Yet, in 1938 these small farms occupied only 0.1 per cent of the cultivated area of Java and Madura, as against about 14 per cent occupied by Western estates and 86 per cent occupied by native agriculture. The Netherlands Indian Government asked a committee to advise it as to the extent to which the authorities should meet the wishes of the Eurasians to have land of their own; for, granting that wish would be contrary to the accepted principle that only the native population may have outright ownership of any agricultural land. This question remains unsolved. The small holdings mentioned above are on long lease and serve mostly for the raising of staple crops. The cultivators have a better claim on the Government when they ask for credit; but to grant this is not easy. These small farmers, as a matter of fact, do not often live entirely from the proceeds of their small holdings. Many of the small leaseholders are retired civil servants or former employees of the large estates.

The colonization of Europeans is even more completely a child of the structural changes that are taking place in Netherlands Indian society. It is obviously still in an experimental stage, both as regards the form of organization and as regards the choice of the most promising kinds of agricultural enterprise for the colonists. What is worse, it appears that a large part of these experiments must be regarded as failures. At the end of 1938, the Colonization Council decided to put a stop to the granting of subsidies to two of the three European settlements in New Guinea, since the closing of these settlements was under consideration. As causes of failure were mentioned: bad health conditions, insufficient knowledge of farming, lack of staying power, loss of soil fertility, and poor opportunities for the sale of the products. .

Such experiments require years of effort; and the resumption of assisted colonization on a fairly large scale will probably not be possible in the near future. This will not do any particular harm, as the number of Eurasians prepared to become colonists and possessing the necessary qualities and training is comparatively small and will not get any larger as long as all certainty of success is lacking. Moreover, the areas suitable for European colonization—which, in addition to the other requirements, must also satisfy exceptional climatic conditions—are so scarce that the Council intends to take an inventory of them and to apply for the reservation of the most suitable parts of such territories for this particular kind of project.

CHAPTER X

WELFARE AND SOCIAL CARE

THE COOPERATIVE MOVEMENT

It has taken the Netherlands Indian Government years to realize that cooperation might be a means of bringing about a further advance in the economic life of the people and that as such it deserves the support and aid of the authorities; to realize also that the cooperative principle and the cooperative mentality, as Western products unknown in Eastern society, must be taught from the beginning. The Government had been misled by considering the strong community sense in the native world as on a par with the cooperative mind and had not realized that cooperation, which moves entirely within the sphere of the money and exchange economy, lies quite outside that world and cannot be controlled by any of the forces working inside it.

So, the first cooperative ordinance, of 1915, an exact copy of the Netherlands law, was quite unsuitable for the native population of the Netherlands Indies. It was not until 1927 that the right legislative path was found. It supplemented the regulation of 1915, which had remained a dead letter, by giving the native section of the colonial society a legal regulation of its own, simple and positive in design and adapted to native concepts of law. With it, native cooperation was made an object of government care, to be advised, directed, and watched over by an official agency managed by experts.

Through this regulation, a private native corporate body was created for the first time, invested with all coded and customary rights of the native. In this way, the formation of economic organizations was made possible that would safeguard the rights due to the separate members of these organizations. Governmental intervention extended to instruction and help with the preparation of constitutions and rules of procedure, registration of the association's act of incorporation, supervision of its proceedings and of the conduct of its business.

The native nationalist movement, as appears from its earliest economic program, was well aware of the importance of Western-type cooperation; but it was not at the outset inclined to work with the Government. Numerous attempts were made by nationalist groups to form cooperative

153

associations of their own; but shortcomings in organization, unfamiliarity with cooperative working methods, lack of business knowledge on the part of the directors, insufficient administrative control, sometimes ignorance and lack of loyalty on the part of the members, led to the result that all these attempts soon failed. Only in 1929 did the interested native circles intimate their willingness to work together with the official staff set up to promote cooperation. From this step an organized cooperative movement soon developed which made it possible for the director of the cooperative service to transfer to native organizations part of his task of promotion, guidance, and supervision.

As far as these types of activities were concerned, the cooperative service had hoped at the outset to be able to make use of the existing technical social services, such as the various guidance services and the department of popular credit. But these agencies put the interests of cooperation in second place; and as a result the continuity and expertness of their intervention in this field left much to be desired, so that the hoped-for development and expansion of this form of organization failed to materialize. To build up its own regional services, although more expensive, appeared to the cooperative service the only satisfactory solution of the difficulty; and this was accomplished in 1935. The policy of delegating powers to the native nationalist organizations could be maintained, although in a somewhat modified form. In order to remove any appearance of being mixed up in politics, the official working relationship to the movement in the social and economic sphere had already in 1930 been moulded in the form of government-subsidized but independent cooperative central boards charged with organization, finance, and supervision. These central boards now supervise two-thirds of all registered cooperatives.

The application of social forms of organization to their own businesses, that is, the formation of joint-stock and other kinds of companies, also was taught the people; but although it was possible to provide the foundation of cooperative principles, ability and understanding were another matter. At the beginning, credit cooperation was the most general and the most successful form of cooperative organization, because it left the individual businesses of the members unchanged. However, it was realized that further to advance the native economy there was need for forms of cooperation that made more demands on the members and required of the participants a more developed understanding of the cooperative process. The pressure exerted to conquer the difficulties found to exist in these respects came from the side of the government committee which also accepted the task of educating the members in the cooperative conduct of business. It also undertook to investigate the possibilities of developing a native middle class. A home-trade advisory office, set up on a modest scale in 1934 on that committee's initiative, included native cooperation in its field of operations. The committee had the same experience which the cooperative service had had earlier, that the native tradesman at first lacked all ability for cooperative organization. The junction of both services now offered the opportunity for joint action directed toward the elimination of this cause of failure. This coordination was seen to be so fruitful that in 1939 it was decided to amalgamate the two offices into a single, independent office for cooperation and home trade. By this means there was achieved also a more intimate contact with the department of native industry.

That cooperation is a Western institution and that the need for its application in the Indies is most deeply felt by that part of native society which has the most Western orientation appears clearly from a grouping of the members of cooperative societies according to social background. Of the total membership at the end of 1940, 47 per cent were members of the civil service, 19 per cent were tradesmen, 9 per cent skilled workers, and only 20 per cent farmers—although the last-mentioned group makes up about 70 per cent of native society and although in other countries the rural classes have proved most susceptible to the advantages of cooperation. The promotion of cooperation has until now remained largely confined to Java, has indeed hardly as yet been taken in hand in the Outer Provinces. Table XXIX gives some indication of the growth of the cooperative movement.

TABLE XXIX: NUMBER OF COOPERATIVE SOCIETIES, 1930-1938

| Year | Consumers' Cooperatives | Credit Coop's | Coop's for freeing from debt | Central Credit Societies | Agric. Coop's | Indust. Coop's | Sale Coop's | Var. Coop's | Total |
|---|---|---|---|---|---|---|---|---|---|
| 1930 | 2 | 81 | — | — | 6 | — | — | — | 89 |
| 1934 | 25 | 215 | — | 8 | 5 | 2 | 2 | — | 257 |
| 1938 | 15 | 415 | 47 | 13 | 11 | 22 | 4 | 8 | 535 |
| 1940 | 23 | 478 | 53 | 14 | 43 | | 27 | | 638 |

## NATIVE LIMITED-LIABILITY COMPANIES

With the promotion of cooperative organizations it soon appeared on many occasions that the interested parties were more concerned with making profitable use of the capital raised than with cooperation in the usual sense of that term. What they really wanted was to be organized as a company. But since the native cooperative was the only form of association which was possible in the sphere of the native economy, the door had to be opened a little wider, and the leaders of the cooperative movement had to be prepared to a certain extent to modify cooperative principles. When this was done, the desirability of further extending the native forms of association was demonstrated. The Netherlands Indian Government also came to this conclusion and, in 1929, set up a committee to make recommendations as to this further extension.

Up to that time, experience had taught that the majority of official attempts to extend financial cooperation within the sphere of the native economy concerned over a longer period enterprises in the field of agriculture. It is understandable, therefore, that when charged with drafting regulations for other types of native corporate bodies, especially for native limited-liability companies, the drafters were mindful of the agrarian problem. They had to consider the effect of native law on the landed property of such companies; and they had to see to it that the chief principle of Netherlands Indian agrarian law, the inalienability to non-natives of indigenous rights to the soil, would not be undermined.

But the development of native society during the crisis and depression showed that, after all, it was not farming which promised to furnish the most important field for these new forms of association. Already in 1930 one could discern that it was the rising trading and industrial native middle class which in the first place felt the need for it. A striving for unity and organization showed itself more and more in the centers of small industry and trade. In the year 1937, for instance, not only owners of tea and rubber gardens, but also those of weaving and batik workshops, shipping enterprises and commercial firms, small credit banks, printing offices, and rice-hulling mills, were among those who requested the Government for advice and help in finding a suitable form of organization. In none of these cases was there any intention to obtain land; the petitioners only wanted to organize in one way or another so as to make a profitable use of the capital raised and to combine the preservation and applicability of their own customary rights with limited liability.

From this experience the Government learned to see the problem of the native company in truer proportions. It was still necessary to take care that these commercial associations would not become means by which the native peasantry might be dispossessed or become tools to serve the interests of the large agricultural industries, but although such dangers existed they no longer were a nightmare. The solution now accepted is this, that the native limited-liability company may not have at its disposal more than 75 hectares of the land belonging to the native population, and of this not more than 25 hectares of irrigated land.

Any leases above these maxima require advance permission by the head official of the district. Furthermore, as the company has to be re-registered every thirty years, any undesirable development can be stopped in good time. Abuse of this form of organization on the part of non-natives, whether by means of strawmen or by exerting pressure in any way, can be forestalled by dissolution of the respective companies. That the native limited-liability company will become an instrument to attract dormant native capital is unlikely. As the chairman of the committee which drafted the bill has correctly stated, economic cooperation undoubtedly is the foremost motive in the organization of these companies; the taking of shares purely as an investment without direct participation in the business is a notion for which native society is not yet ripe.

The legal regulation of native limited-liability companies first appeared in the Statute Book of 1939 and is as yet valid only for Java and Madura; its success cannot, therefore, yet be demonstrated from accounts of how it works. The authorities have great expectations as to its usefulness of which a few examples must here suffice: former pupils of agricultural courses form companies to rent land in common; concerns that work up agricultural products assure themselves by this means of collateral security on the land that supplies the raw material; companies that buy up produce similarly reduce their risks; small credit banks find security in lien and thus are able to provide themselves with real rights in cases of non-payment. In a variety of ways, the money economy, with the aid of such legal organization, can develop more safely in native society. All this is taking place under the watchful eye of the authorities.

### GOVERNMENT INTERVENTION IN THE PROVISION OF POPULAR CREDIT

One of the most characteristic peculiarities of Asiatic society is its constant need of money and credit. The closer contact of the village economy—precapitalistic, self-sufficient, and therefore managing without a regular exchange of money—with the Western capitalistic exchange economy has had as one of its chief effects this money famine and widespread need of credit. It is, therefore, understandable that the Government, when at the beginning of the twentieth century it began to interest itself more directly in the welfare of the native people, also paid attention to the organization of popular credit. It confronted the task of formulating a policy that really would meet the needs of the masses, a question of large-scale organization.

When taken in hand, popular credit was organized in four different forms. To begin with, the pawnshops were brought under public control and eventually organized as a government monopoly. Rice barns were set up as institutions of the native local authorities to grant credit in kind—also redeemable in rice. Small money banks, similarly under the local authorities, were established to furnish small loans, redeemable in weekly instalments. Finally, for larger areas, usually Regencies, semi-official popular credit banks were opened to lend out somewhat larger amounts to landowners, but as a rule not more than about fifty guilders and for periods no longer than twelve months.

Until 1930, these institutions, though not without ups and downs, on the whole took a favorable development. The 435 Government pawnshops that had been opened in Java and Madura lent in 1929 a total amount of 207 million guilders on almost 56 million pawns. Of these the small pawns, with an average value of 2.81 guilders, formed 99 per cent. At the end of the year, not quite 73 million guilders were outstanding. The 6,273 small village money banks lent nearly 55 million guilders to more than one million borrowers and at the end of 1929 had more than eight million guilders outstanding. The 71 popular credit banks had lent out more than 59 million guilders to 855,000 persons and at the end of 1929 had 48.5 million guilders outstanding. Finally, the village rice credit institutions—of which little more need here be said—were 5,900 in number and had lent a million quintals of paddy to more than a million borrowers.

Thus, at the end of 1929 the three types of money-credit institutions had between them almost 130 million guilders outstanding in Java and Madura, a not unimportant amount for a population of forty million requiring for the most part only small amounts of money. The interest received that year from these credits amounted to a little less than 34 million guilders, which means that the average interest rate was 26 per cent per annum. The credit, it will be seen, was not in the nature of a gift; but in popular opinion the need for cash had been met in a proper and not too expensive, although a rather stiff and awkward, way.

Yet, the official money credit presumably supplied only part of the need. Of the twenty-one thousand native municipalities less than a third had a small money bank of their own; and for the little man in need of money the two other kinds of money-lending institutions often were in more than one respect unattainable. More serious was the fact, brought to light by the crisis and the depression, that all these credit organizations really were fine-weather institutions which, instead of actively backing and promoting native financial exchange, on the contrary were themselves kept alive by it. In the years of depression, when all the financial resources of the population, the estates, the Government, and the markets for native products, quickly dried up, when the fixed charges weighed more heavily than ever and the need for money rose to precarious heights, the amount of money lent out by the pawnshops shrank to 38 per cent, that of the small village banks to 34 per cent, and that of the popular credit banks to 20 per cent of their former turnover. The need for credit was more urgent than ever, but the business principles to which the different institutions were bound paralyzed their activity. They stood helpless. As a matter of fact, the two last-named types of organization added to the general need for money by concerning themselves before anything else in the collection of outstanding debts.

Here, government intervention apparently had reached its limit, and organized credit had to yield the field to the private moneylender. The people always had shown a preference for this unorganized and therefore much more mobile, more informal, more widely scattered and therefore more accessible source of credit—in spite of the heavier interest charges; now they scarcely could get money anywhere else and were entirely in the hands of the moneylenders.

It speaks volumes that the committee set up by the Government in 1929 to combat usury, which used the years of the depression to prepare its proposals for the legal regulation of moneylending, was so impressed by the facts it found that it came to the conclusion that the business of moneylenders should on no account be impeded or hampered—and this at the same time that it had to report on a rapid spread of the evil of usury which threatened to become endemic, so that an intensive campaign to combat the disease should be considered a social task of the first magnitude.

There is an unpleasant knot in this chain of events. The Government itself increases the need for money by its system of taxation and Western administration; it then calls into being credit organizations to organize the credits needed to meet these requirements for money payments. These institutions, in turn, increase the shortage of money when it is most needed, during the years of depression, because the official credit policy has veered around to become an official policy to liquidate credits as much as possible. From this, again, a new stimulus emanates to inflate the private moneylender's trade to tropical luxuriance—and deterioration. As a final step, the Government at this point tries to devise new means to check the moneylending business—only to come to the conclusion that it cannot get at the root of that evil as far as the masses are concerned.

In the following paragraphs, we shall further discuss some particular aspects of this course of government intervention. All we have here tried to make clear is the general fact that *government intervention finds its inexorable limits in the economic ideas and in the peculiar structure of native society.*

### THE GENERAL POPULAR CREDIT BANK

In 1934, the semi-official A.V.B. (Algemeene Volkscrediet-Bank) was established by the amalgamation of the local institutions for popular credit, likewise semi-official, with the central financing and controlling office. This government child undoubtedly was an offspring of the crisis. The heavy demands which the continuing and rapidly increasing arrears had made on the resistance and vitality of the local popular banks made union necessary. Their semi-official character made it possible; all of them were able to sacrifice their individual existence without claiming exemption or special conditions. They were continued in ninety-four offices of the General Popular Credit Bank, the sphere of activity of which therefore embraces practically all of the archipelago.

The A.V.B. has no other business aim than to serve the welfare of the people. For this purpose above all it carries on its activities, by providing those needs for credit which are not met by other credit institutions —and this, of course, irrespective of nationality although chiefly on behalf of the native population. Another of its functions is the investing of the funds of public bodies (native municipalities, Regencies, self-governing districts, *etc.*) and of their institutions, also those of cooperative societies and of other private bodies. For all these it takes care of the keeping and administration of their bonds, shares, and other securities. Finally, it gives advice and assistance to other popular credit institutions, cooperative societies, and native municipal credit institutions, and exercises supervision and control over them.

From the main function of the A.V.B., as above described, it is clear that when any other institution can be considered capable of taking over the respective part of the A.V.B.'s task, this national institution withdraws from the domain of that organization. It cooperates regularly with the cooperative service, not only by granting working capital to cooperative societies but especially also by supporting the movement for freeing native landed property from debt—a type of action which wherever possible is performed by the cooperative societies. Further, it cooperates with the agencies set up to combat unemployment among Europeans, with anti-usury associations and other social institutions, with the British American Tobacco Company by granting loans to 8,157 native growers of Virginia tobacco; with the Government in many of its social activities—whenever these involve a grant of credit to the population, where necessary under guarantee of the Government. For example, the minute, difficult, and highly important economic investigations which served as a foundation for the Government's program of freeing the people from indebtedness could not have been carried out by any but the staff of the A.V.B.

### RELEASE FROM INDEBTEDNESS

Nearly all those actions that have brought native society in touch with the Western exchange economy have taken on a credit character. Whether the transaction concerns products, land, or labor, inevitably it develops into a credit relationship. The explanation for this may be found in the native's growing need for money, which does not go parallel with increasing production for the market. He is, moreover, keen on credit. The resulting "credit economy" is not dangerous as long as the terms of repayment are short. This was the rule before the crisis. The longest term of this normal credit is to be found in connection with the land leases of Western sugar estates, and there it was only one or two years. In other cases, it did not exceed one year, so that the effect of the amount of outstanding credit on the national income remained moderate and the indebtedness was nowhere general or precarious.

The depression in the 'thirties changed this. While the most important financial obligations (taxes, bank debts) remained the same or decreased very slowly, they became more urgent, as, with the restrictions on the estates, money incomes dropped rapidly. And this occurred because popular credit institutions suspended or limited their loans, through the retrenchments of the Government, because of the fall in prices and, in some instances, the total unsaleability of native products, and because of the enormous drop in wage earnings.

All this disturbed the labile balance of the native credit economy. But this disturbance led to a new and much more critical condition of indebtedness. A class of merchants in native products, sometimes even a single individual operating over a vast territory, took advantage of the disturbance to exploit the situation by granting new credits with the object of securing for themselves, under the most onerous conditions, the disposal over the still marketable native product (rice, coconuts, kapok, and other tree fruit) for a long time to come. The danger of this new kind of indebtedness did not lie in the extent of the amounts advanced but in the burdensome credit conditions and in the impossibility of debt redemption. In this way, debts became of long standing and increased in amount with an incredible rapidity so that, after a comparatively short period, the debtor was deprived of his power to dispose freely of his product and his capital goods, his land and his trees. Over vast regions, the farmer and the garden owner have in this manner become inextricably entangled in the net of credit which they formerly handled so smoothly and so lightheartedly.

When, after laborious, intense, and long investigations by the A.V.B. staff, the Government became aware of these new debt conditions, it proceeded energetically to free the people from the bondage of debt. In this it adapted its methods to local relations and circumstances in every part of the region. Where possible, it tried to obtain the active assistance of the interested persons by forming cooperative credit and sales societies. An amount of 750,000 guilders from the twenty-five million fund was set aside for this program of freeing the farmer from debt; 600,000 guilders of this amount were apportioned to serve as a guarantee fund for procuring credit from other sources. Since a guarantee of 20 per cent of the loans asked for was deemed sufficient, this 600,000 guilders made available an amount of three million guilders, lent out at an annual interest of 6 per cent.

Usually, the liquidation of debts was secured without the necessity to invoke any particular legal regulation. Where this was unavoidable, the ordinances adopted to combat usury sufficed, supplemented as they were with new provisions to be described in the following section of this chapter. Only one exception is worth mentioning: the legal regulation in 1938 of the copra contracts in the Manado district of North Celebes. This will now be described in more detail as an instructive illustration of the development and consequences of rural debt relations.

*Regulation of Copra Contracts in Manado.* The export of copra from Manado became important between 1890 and 1900, and the first world war greatly accelerated the extension of this crop. In the years 1914-16, exports averaged 40,000 tons; in 1923-25 they averaged 80,000 tons; in 1928-32, 170,000 tons; and in 1936 they amounted to 180,000 tons. The export from this district before the second world war was about one-third of that for the whole of the Indies. As a result, food production in that area no longer sufficed to meet the needs of the population. With a population of more than 1.1 million, the annual export of copra came to 160 kg. per head, the number of trees owned to an average of 85 per family of five, and the total garden area to between 150,000 and 200,000 hectares.

Neither the cultivation of coconuts nor the drying of copra demands

any considerable capital. The jute bags for the export of the copra
account for 3 or 4 per cent of the local copra price and are the most
important capital cost item. On the other hand, ship freights are very
burdensome. In the depression years, 1933 and 1934, they amounted to
65 per cent of the Manado copra price, and in 1940 they were estimated
at roughly 45 per cent of that price. Export duties, wages for loading
and weighing, and other costs make up 12 per cent of the local price.
The share received by the local growers from the copra yield is considerably less than one-half of the world market price, and that price
has shown itself very susceptible to the influence of the depression—
much more so than the prices that had to be paid for import goods,
especially rice and piece goods. This price relation is shown in Table
XXX, below.

TABLE XXX: PRICE INDEX OF COPRA, RICE, AND PIECE GOODS,
MANADO, NORTH CELEBES, 1931-1939

Base Year 1928

| Year | Copra | Rice | Piece Goods |
|---|---|---|---|
| 1931 | 37 | 54 | 68 |
| 1932 | 32 | 46 | 51 |
| 1933 | 19 | 35 | 45 |
| 1934 | 13.5 | 31 | 44 |
| 1935 | 25 | 42 | 43 |
| 1936 | 33 | 48 | 44 |
| 1937 | 40 | 62 | 56 |
| 1938 | 23 | 59 | 55 |
| 1939 | 22 | 58 | 54 |

The rice imports alone, in the crucial years, would require more than
one-half of the return on the copra exported.

How have credit relations developed in this situation? At the outset
it was only a question of small, harmless loans, such as those customarily
granted to producers by shopkeepers and by the middlemen who buy
up their produce: short credits for gradually increasing unpaid shop
bills and those advanced while the copra is in preparation. Then, in
the time of high copra prices, the debts were augmented by loans generously provided for the improvement of housing, the laying out of new
gardens, and all kinds of social obligations. The arrangements for the
repayment of loans, previously made by word of mouth, now were
replaced with written agreements; but the future still looked rose-
colored as incomes increased at about the same rate as did debts. The
producer held the upper hand.

The first reverse came in 1917-18, when the copra price suddenly fell
sharply as a result of the confiscation of shipping tonnage by foreign
countries at war. The copra merchants, however, continued to purchase; and as soon as opportunities for shipment returned, enormous

quantities were sold at extremely high prices. The dealers converted an important part of their gains into advances to producers, but the latter retained the high copra prices.

This went on until 1920. Then came a second sharp reverse with a convulsive but at the same time almost continuous decline of the copra price. This lasted until 1934. From then on, it was more and more the insolvency of the garden owners that produced a constant rise in debts. The loan contracts were not in themselves unreasonable: a moderate interest on the capital sum, delivery of the copra to the lender as long as the capital advanced had not been repaid in full—this at the price quoted for the day, and a fine if the supply of copra fell short of the quantity agreed upon. In practice, however, the price often was determined onesidedly by the copra merchant, and the garden owner bound himself to deliver a quantity of copra considerably larger than the proceeds of his garden. In this way, the producer was forced to pay the fine, and demand for its payment again could be held over him as a threat. The kind of contract under which the owner sells the yield of one or more gardens for a certain period and receives payment in advance, likewise, was customary. The merchant then arranged for the picking and drying of the nuts; and frequently the owner was denied even the right to set foot on his own property.

How high has the burden of debt mounted? In the years of depression, debts in Minahassa alone (the northeastern part of the northern peninsula of Celebes), amounting to more than one and a half million guilders, were converted into debentures attested by a notary or claimed in court. The yearly burden of interest on the considerably larger total of the debts at that time already was estimated as amounting to one and a half million guilders, while the value of the annual production was estimated as four million guilders. It is undoubtedly a fact that the copra production of the native population in Minahassa was tied up by advances from the copra trade, advances contracted for on terms by which, with the prevailing level of prices, many of the producers, even with the greatest precaution, could only run still deeper into debt.

And not only the coconut growers were harmed by the system under which the buyers of their product were at the same time also their creditors, the bona-fide copra merchants were harmed, too. The buyer-creditors had, because of the contracts, the chance of paying excessively low prices for the copra tied up by debt and in consequence could bid high prices for the relatively small lots of copra offered on the free market, in order to drive their competitors out.

So, everything pointed to the need for outside intervention. The A.V.B. was the first to take action. In 1937, it opened an office in Manado and straight away got busy on debt redemption with the aid of a government guarantee and in conjunction with a native cooperative society, the Minahassa Central Society for the Sale of Products. The latter took over the gardens on the security of the A.V.B., which acquired the debts on them, and made itself responsible for selling the copra. In this way, several hundred thousand guilders were lent out and a large number of private debts were extinguished, since most of the money-lending buyers were satisfied to receive repayment at a considerable discount when ready money was offered them. From a pedagogical and organizational point of view, this cooperative method, which compels the debtor to cooperate, offers only advantages; the only objections to it are its limited scope and its slowness. That is why it had to be supplemented later by legislative action.

The Manado Copra Contracts Ordinance of 1938 (Netherlands Indian Statute Book, 1939, No. 92) regulates the relations between the copra merchant and the native garden owner—that is to say, only those contracts by which a delivery of copra is stipulated for a date no less than three months after the day on which the agreement is signed, therefore practically all contracts that involve the usual credit element. Now such contracts may be concluded only by copra merchants in possession of a valid purchase license, and only such merchants may take over rights under contracts already concluded by others. Such a license is granted only to well-known merchants of good standing and repute—a somewhat elastic criterion which nevertheless allows the weeding out of those who primarily are moneylenders. Intensive government control remains necessary, however, to prevent the garden owners from again committing themselves to agreements which in the long run are fatal to their interests. The action of the A.V.B. will have to be continued in order to build up gradually a sounder credit relationship and a well organized sale of copra.

Copra was one of the "weak" products, the price of which, in consequence of the war, had fallen ruinously. Therefore already in 1940 the Copra Fund was established, and a valorization policy had to be applied. This institution monopolized the buying up from the import and production centers in the Outer Provinces. In Java, with its import surplus, the Fund controlled the inland prices by acting as the only seller. Its financial support has been valued at more than eleven million guilders, an amount raised by means of an extra export duty on the "strong" products: oil, tin, rubber, and cinchona.

## THE FIGHT AGAINST USURY

Until 1938 the direct attack on usury—as contrasted with the indirect attack on it by means of popular credit banks and other banks established purely for welfare purposes—was based on the usury ordinance of 1916. This legal regulation in turn is based on what used to be called the system of regulation by repression. It does no more than define what constitutes usury as a legal offense and leaves it to the judge to decide whether in a given case the elements mentioned are present. If so, the debt agreement can be cancelled or moderated by judicial procedure. The request for a judicial decision has to come from the injured party.

This last-named stipulation, more especially, in practice made appeal to the regulation a matter of only exceptional occurrence. The most frequent procedure was that the creditor caused his debtor to appear before the judge, and that the latter, after investigating the case, drew the debtor's attention to the legal remedy which the usury ordinance placed in his hands. Then it sometimes happened that the "injured" party, namely the creditor, did not dare to maintain his appeal to the court, or even denied the existence of a usurious agreement, so that the application of the ordinance to the case was frustrated.

In 1938, the single article of which the ordinance consisted was amended, so that in future the judge might be able if he deemed it necessary to apply the regulation by virtue of his office, and the duty of proving that the opposing party had taken advantage of the carelessness, inexperience, or need of the person on whom usury had been practised would no longer rest on the actually injured party. It is not to be expected that, as a result of this modification, the repressive regulation will suddenly become a frequently applied means of combating usury. In the way of such a likelihood stands the unavoidably vague description of what constitutes usury—which makes the task of the judge so difficult that he will not be inclined lightly to make use of this means. Besides, even with this new power, the judge must wait until a case of usury is brought before him by one of the parties to a debt agreement.

Of much greater significance is the legal regulation of the moneylenders' business which came into force at the same time as the amendment of the usury ordinance. It represents a preventive method of attacking usury and is sometimes called the American system, as opposed to the German repressive system. The field in which the moneylending ordinance operates is more limited than the other, in three respects.

In the first place, it is at present limited to Java and the east coast of Sumatra, whereas the usury ordinance is valid for the whole of the Indies. Further, the latter may be invoked in relation to all sorts of contracts with an excessive inequality of mutual obligations, whereas the moneylenders' ordinance applies only to contracts for money loans —although money loans disguised as transactions in goods also come under the regulation. For instance, it sometimes happens that a Mohammedan moneylender, in view of the Koran's prohibition of interest, disguises the granting of a loan as a simultaneous sale on credit and repurchase for cash of the same goods, in which case the cash purchase takes the place of the money loan, and the sale on credit that of its liquidation. Finally, under the usury ordinance each case is considered on its own merits; the moneylenders' ordinance, on the other hand, is applicable only where the lender is a person who makes moneylending his profession or business. (However, a person who practices moneylending as a regular side line still falls under the ordinance as a professional moneylender.) To be able to exercise this profession or business, he must have a permit from the head of the local civil service, and his license remains valid for three years unless for good reason it is withdrawn in the meantime. Provision is made that the lender cannot put pressure on the debtor by threat of imprisonment, that he cannot prevent the debtor from becoming informed of a judicial action brought against himself; and that a written receipt for each payment must be given the debtor in a language that is intelligible to him.

It is not to be expected of the moneylenders' ordinance, either, that it will have a profound effect on credit conditions in Netherlands Indian society. It will be of more importance for the Eurasian than for the native community, and this for two reasons. To begin with, it applies only to those moneylenders whose loans usually vary between ten and five hundred guilders, while private loans to natives, at least as far as the original sums borrowed are concerned, are nearly all below the minimum limit. Then, all those credit transactions in which the aim is not the lending of money but that of obtaining the right to dispose over produce or the means of production on native farms remain outside the scope of the regulation. The buyer who advances money on the crop or the nuts, the tenant who pays his rent in advance, these are not concerned. The ordinance does apply to the operations of the village moneylender, however, who lends out money with the obligation to be paid back in kind—provided the amount of the original loan does exceed ten guilders.

To carry on such transactions, too, the moneylender must bear a good repute. This is a powerful weapon in the hands of the civil service officers who have the right to refuse a license. Not the percentage of interest charged but the general conditions under which the loans are granted form the criterion as to whether the creditor is a *bona fide* moneylender or not. No maximum interest rate has been fixed, partly because it would be difficult to determine, partly because the legislators did not wish to make it impossible for people to borrow if they can give no security, or to prevent loans in cases where the risk for other reasons is exceptionally great. Partly also because, when the debt is discharged in kind, it is practically impossible to determine a legal rate of interest, and partly because an authorized maximum rate of interest would tend to be demanded by moneylenders in cases where it would not be justified.

The legislators were thoroughly aware of the fact that they were placing arbitrary powers into the hands of the license-granting local authorities. That is why not the native but the European civil service officer has been entrusted with this power, since only the latter can be supposed to occupy an independent position *vis-à-vis* the moneylenders. The victims of the moneylending business in the native civil service are so numerous that the Netherlands Indian Government has been obliged to draw up a special regulation for the redemption of their debts.

### PROTECTION OF LABOR ON WESTERN ESTATES

*Contract Labor.* The violent struggle that went on for many years over repeal of the penal sanction in labor contracts governing the employment of native and Chinese hands on the Western estates in the Outer Provinces ended in the decision that from 1931 on that repeal would take place gradually, in five-year periods, and that the first five-year period would have to result in the decrease of such contracts for up to 50 per cent of the total number of laborers employed on the older estates and a somewhat lower percentage for those on the newer estates. The organizations of estate owners at the time objected strongly to a proposed even more rapid elimination of the clause. Facts, however, proved stronger than theory. (See *The Structure of Netherlands Indian Economy*, Chapter XIII.)

Here it may suffice to mention the result, that between 1929 and 1938 the proportion of estate laborers under contracts with the penal clause shrank from 76.3 per cent to 5.6 per cent.

The restriction placed on the insertion of the penal sanction in labor contracts loosened the ties between employer and laborers. At the same time, it gave many employers who up to that time had from sheer necessity themselves looked after the recruitment and immigration of their laborers a reason for trying to take advantage of the labor supply available on the spot—men who had come there through the effort and at the expense of other employers. It was thought to be only fair that the employers who engaged in this "crimping" should be obliged to make a contribution to a general fund for labor recruitment in the normal way. With this aim, the Government established in 1931 a labor bureau at Medan, to register labor agreements and to collect the employers' contributions for this service. By fixing a maximum fee, the charge was kept low enough not to become an impediment to the transference of a laborer from one employer to another at the conclusion of his contract; for, the laborer's freedom of movement, one of the great advantages of a free-labor system, could not be allowed to become illusory.

In 1936, when the new plantation-labor law, the so-called "coolie ordinance," was for the first time amended, new regulations were adopted for the recruitment, in Java, of laborers to work on estates in the Outer Provinces. At the same time, the recruiting of "free" laborers also was placed under government supervision. The genuinely free migration—when a migrant intends to work on an estate—was not impeded by this. But henceforth it was no longer lawful to recruit native workers in Java other than through an officially recognized recruiting organization, in every case an agency operated by estate owners. The term "recruit" is understood in the broad sense of "taking action to induce a native to enter into a labor contract." Only those laborers are exempted who work on native-owned plantations or on small estates, those with an area of less than 100 *bouws* (709.6 sq. m.), even if they are recruited, according to this definition. Labor legislation and labor inspection do not extend to these small enterprises; it would therefore be useless to interfere with the recruitment of labor for them. All other recruited laborers are obliged to conclude, before leaving Java, a written labor contract in the presence of a labor inspector or employment officer. At that time they also must submit to a medical examination; and they must arrive at their destination free of debt.

*European Labor.* European labor employed on agricultural estates also enjoys legal protection since 1936. At the outset, this was limited to estate employees in the Outer Provinces; but after the Volksraad had expressed itself in favor of extending the regulation to managers and employees on estates in Java, and after a labor inspector's investigation had brought to light that only 73 per cent of 125 managers interrogated, and 43 per cent of 415 European employees similarly questioned, were in possession of an employment contract or a letter of appointment, and that there was some confusion as to the employees' right to days off, the so-called Supplementary Planters' Regulation came into being. It supplements the general provisions for the regulation of labor contracts in the civil code of the Netherlands Indies. The main reasons that supplied the authorities with the incentive for enacting this supplement on behalf of a special category of European labor were: that specialized training, of little value outside the estates, usually is required to obtain work in the large European enterprises; that employment on distant estates causes special difficulties and expenses in connection with the upbringing and education of children, medical care, freedom of movement, and in other respects; and that declining world prices are most severely felt in agricultural commercial enterprises, so that the position of their employees is less secure than that of those engaged in other forms of business. In this matter, too, small agricultural concerns, operating on areas of less than a hundred *bouws,* do not fall within the scope of the regulation. Apart from this, it applies to all persons who are subject to the civil law for Europeans, no matter what their nationality. In defining the group that falls under this regulation, two criteria have been applied: first, a labor criterion, namely that the person in question works under the manager of the estate and, as a rule, that he is charged with expert management or expert supervision of work carried on in field, factory, or workshop; second, a wage criterion, namely that he receives a compensation of at least one hundred guilders a month. Either of these criteria suffices.

The regulation requires a written contract, at least four free days in a month, of which two must be Sundays, and an annual vacation of at least two weeks. A right to leave abroad is confined to those plantation employees who have been hired or recruited outside the Netherlands Indies; this right can be exercised only after seven years of service. Only employees with such a record are entitled to a contract for a minimum of one year.

### STATE INTERVENTION IN UNEMPLOYMENT

The Government of the Indies has always been of the opinion that the care of the unemployed should not be considered a direct responsibility of the authorities but should be left as much and for as long as possible to private initiative—if necessary with financial support from the Government. This view is perfectly understandable if one keeps in mind that official intervention in this matter, to be consistent, would have to be extended to all groups of the population in the Indies and would entail a financial burden far beyond the Government's means.

Organized private provision is in the main limited to the European element. The relief committees set up in 1930 received in the first four years 3.8 million guilders for the grant of relief, 2.6 million of which came from private contributions. At the end of 1934, in the depth of the depression, 3,732 Europeans, 9,498 natives, and 864 Chinese received relief. Of these, 700 Europeans and 5,800 natives were out of work as a result of the sugar crisis and were given relief from a special sugar fund. In that same year the number of male European unemployed could be estimated as 10,000. Its age composition, as given in Table XXXI, deserves attention. It shows that the unemployment of youth, especially, was alarmingly high.

TABLE XXXI: AGE COMPOSITION OF EUROPEAN MALE POPULATION AND OF UNEMPLOYED MALE EUROPEANS IN 1934

| Age group | Census of 1930 | | Unemployed in 1934 * | |
|---|---|---|---|---|
| | Number | Per cent | Number | Per cent |
| 15-19 | 8,131 | 9 | 4,000 | 40 |
| 20-54 | 70,695 | 82 | 6,000 | 60 |
| 55 and over | 7,565 | 9 | — | — |
| Total | 86,391 | 100 | 10,000 | 100 |

* Estimated.

The Government of the Indies has tried to support the labor market by restricting the employment of foreign labor. To this end, a regulation was promulgated in 1935 and renewed in 1938. It requires employers of alien labor—which means other than Netherlands subjects—to secure permission in advance. It does not in any way interfere with foreigners who work independently in the Netherlands Indies. The many points of contact which, since the crisis, had been established between industry and various governmental agencies had made it possible for the authorities to exert some influence on the attitude taken toward labor recruiting in private enterprise. The existing predisposition to be helpful was made use of in relation to the labor market.

When, in 1939, it seemed to the Government that even the improvement in the economic situation after 1936 had brought little change in the employment of Europeans, and especially of young persons, and that the extent of unemployment was almost as great as it had been in the years of depression, it ordered an investigation, especially as regards the actual extent of juvenile unemployment. From this it appeared that, at least as far as unemployment among Europeans was concerned, the situation was not quite as dark as had been supposed. By enlarging the class of "juveniles" to include work-seekers between fifteen and twenty-four years of age, the total number of juvenile unemployed was found to be about 2,500. In addition there were some 4,000 older unemployed, 1,000 of them in receipt of a dole. This number, however, did not include 1,500 who had been withdrawn from the labor market under the unemployment relief program. Even if the last-named group is left out of account, and the number of male Europeans unemployed is put down as 6,500, it means that one-tenth of all employable male Europeans in the Netherlands were out of work, including not only employees but also those engaged in independent vocations, official as well as private, civil as well as military.

This leads one to ask: how many of the 65,000 positions and independent professional or business occupations that provide Europeans with a living will in the future be filled by natives in search of work? Indianization is in constant progress. Native youths graduating from the higher schools of the Indies number roughly ten thousand a year, and the total number of unemployed in this group of the population cannot amount to less than ten thousand. The Chinese element—those of Chinese stock, born and bred in the Indies—likewise, puts an ever increasing pressure on the labor market of the country. A solution for the unemployment problem of the Indies has yet to be found.

# INDEX

# INDEX

Africa—economic development of, 3-4; exports to, 27, 28; imports from, 28
Agave, 16, 23, 26
Agricultural—colonies, 144 *ff.*; education, 110, 111, 142; experiment and research, 1, 15, 16, 36, 52, 84, 110, 111; exports, 24 *ff.*, 84, *see also* Exports, various commodities; staple crops, 83-4, 109 *ff.*; techniques, 11, 18, 84-5, 110, 111, 141-42; tools, 111, 118
Algemeene Volkscrediet-Bank (A.V.B.), 160 *ff.*, 164-65
Aluminum industry, 120
Americas—exports to, 27; imports from, 28; *see also* Brazil, Cuba, United States
Amsterdam Trading Society (H.V.A.), 13
Animal husbandry, 52, 53; grant for, 108
Asia—exports to, 27; imports from, 28
Association of Cinchona Bark Producers, 66
Atjeh, rubber growing in, 54
Australia—exports to, 27, 28; imports from, 28
Autarchy, *see* Self-sufficiency
Automobile—assembling plant, 120, 121; tire manufacture, 93-4, 120, 121, 133

Bandoeng dairies, regulation of, 128
Bandoeng Textile Institute, 122-23
Bandoeroto Estate Company, 16
Banka tin mines, wages in, 139-40
Bantam, labor migration from, 149
Barnes, Leonard, 3-4, 7, 19, 20
Barter agreements, 97-99
Batavia Industrial Central Board, 118
Batik industry, 94-5, 99, 104, 121, 125, 126, 137, *see also* Textile industry
Beer—brewery industry, 119; import quota, 94
Bilateral trade, 27, 97-99, 104; with Netherlands, 101 *ff.*, *see* Netherlands
Billiton Mining Company, 81, 120; wages paid by, 140
Birnie, George, 4-5
Board for Tea Propaganda, 64
Borneo, 108, *see* Outer Provinces—estate labor, 143; forest resources, 82-3; public health work, 52
Brazil coffee—production, 67; valorization system, 68
British-American Tobacco Company, 79, 120, 126, 160-61
Buchanan, David H., 7, 18

Buffer stocks, 88, 98-9, 118, 134, 137
Burma, rice imports from, 113
Business—consolidation, 15 *ff.*, 19; cycle, 31, *see also* Depression, Foreign trade, Price fluctuation
Buying power, *see* Living standards

Cajaput oil, 77
Cambrics Covenant, 95, 104
Cananga oil, 77
Capital, Western, 3 *ff.*, 10-11, 12 *ff.*, 15 *ff.*, 24, 26, 27, 103, 129, *see also* Western estates, *etc.*
Capitalism and colonialism, 7 *ff.*
Cassava and c. products, 10, 12, 24, 77; prices, 135; production and consumption, 109
Celebes, *see* Outer Provinces; copra producers, 162 *ff.*; land settlement, 149, 150; rice production, 112
Cement—import, regulation of, 85, 94, 133; industry at Padang, 94; international agreement, 94
Central Board for Native Emigration and Colonization, 150
Central boards for small industries, 118
Central Bureau of Statistics, 89, 133, 139, 147
Central Trade Office, 76
Ceramics industry, 95, 99, 118, 119, *see also* Earthenware
Cereal consumption, 109, 110 *ff.*, *see also* Rice, Maize
Chadbourne sugar agreements, 1931 and 1933, 41, 46
Chemical industries, 119
Chinese—in cigarette industry, 126; labor, 139-40, 169, 171, 172; rice dealers, 10; tobacco growers, 12, 13; wholesalers, 29
Cigarette industry, 11, 17, 53, 78-80, 120, 121, 126-27, *see also* Tobacco—regulation of, 128-29
Cinchona and c. products, 23, 24, 25, 26 —exports of, 39, 40, 65-7; production and pr. capacity, 65; regulation, 65-7; sales promotion, 65; world consumption, 65
Cinchona Bureau, Amsterdam, 66-7
Cinnamon, 1
Citronella oil, 76-7
Clearing agreements with Netherlands, 104

174

Cloves, 1, 77, *see also* Spices
Coca, 16
Cocoa, 15, 16, 23, 26
Coconut and c. products, 7, 10, 25, 80, .104, 111, 135, 137—credit provision for, 161, 162 *ff.;* exports, 23, 24, 26; prices, 80, 163
Coffee, 7, 8, 10, 14, 15, 16, 24—estate labor, 68; experiment station, 69, 70; export premium, 69, 70; exports, 23, 26, 39, 67-71; import tax in Netherlands, 69; native-grown, 69; prices, 68, 70, 135; production, 67, 68, 111; regulation and restriction, 69-71; research and improvement, 69, 70, 71
Coffee Concerns Ordinance, 1937, 70
Coffee Crisis Board, 69
Coffee Fund, 69, 70, 71, 104
"Colonialism", 7 *ff.*, 27
Colonization, *see* Land settlement
Commercial Control Ordinance, 98-9
Committee for Commercial Control, 98
Committee for Economic Cooperation, 1938, 107
Commodity boards, *see* various commodities—principle of, 74-6
Commodity prices, control of, Chap. VIII: 133 *ff.*, *see also* Cost of living
Compulsory production, 1 *ff.*
Consumption, 25, 29, *see also* Living standards
Contract labor, 168-69, *see also* Estate labor
Coolie Ordinances—1931, 168; 1936, 169
Cooperatives, 9, 118, 124-25, 153-55—credit for, 155, 162
Copal, 78
Copra, *see* Coconut and products
Copra Fund, 80, 165
Cost of Living, 30, 89, 90-91, 102, 113, 117, 125, 133 *ff.*, 137, 139, *see also* Consumption
Cotton, 3, 16
Cotton textiles—control of stocks, 98-9; exports, 53; imports, 15, 88, 135, 136; industry, 17, 53—encouragement of, 118, 119-20, 122 *ff.;* premiums on Netherlands, 104; prices, 163; quotas, 94-5, 96-7; regulation, 129
Credit, 10, 15, 16 *ff.*, 29, 30, *see also* Debt, Usury—cooperative provision of, 155, 162; government provision of, 11, 157 ff.; provision for, agricultural colonists, 147; industrial development,

117 *ff.;* purchasers of native products, 10, 11, 13
Crisis Cement Import Ordinance, 85-6, 94
Crisis Rubber Centrale, 48
Crop—experiments, 1, 15-6; variety, 2, 15-6
Crops, *see* various—encouragement of second, 110, 111
Cuba sugar exports, 41, 44
Cubeb, 16
"Culture System", 3
Cultures, history of, 2 *ff.*

Dairies, regulation of, 128
Damar, 78
Debts of native cultivators, 29, 30, 52, 111, *see also* Credit, Usury—provisions to reduce, 108, 161-62
Deflation policy of '30's, 29, 30, 50, 91, 104, 134-35, 136
Deli, 12, 15, *see also* Sumatra, Tobacco
Deli Planters' Association, 139
Depression, economic, of '30's, 19, Chap. II: 22 *ff.*, 28, 29, 31, 41, 67-8, 85, 104, 106, 109, 135-36, 161, 171
Distribution of commodities, control of, 29, 86, 88, 92, 133 *ff.*
Dock companies, regulation of, 128
Drugs, exports of, 39, *see also* Cinchona
Dry land crops, encouragement of, 110
"Dumping" of sugar, 41

Earthenware, *see also* Ceramics—control of stocks, 99; industry, 118; quota, 95
East India Company (Netherlands), 3
Economic Affairs, Department of, 21, 34 *ff.*, 48 *ff.*, 60 *ff.*, 70, 83, 99, 113, 115, 117, 118, 134, 141, 150
Education, 33—agricultural, 110, 111, 142; industrial, 118
Electric batteries industry, 120
Electric bulbs—Japanese imports, 96; quota, 95-6, 133
Essential oils and products thereof, 10, 23, 24, 76-7
Estate—consolidation, 16 *ff.*; expansion of area, 32, 141 *ff.*; labor, 31, 32, 68, 113, 143-44, 168-69; management, 16
Estates, Western, 3 *ff.*, 10, 11, 13-4, 15 *ff.*, 32—share in exports, 22 *ff.*; wages paid by, 137-38
Eurasian—agricultural colonists, 151-52; employment, 33; growers of—sereh grass, 76; tea, 59, 61, 62
Europe—exports to, 27; imports from, 28

European, *see also* Western—agricultural colonists, 151-52; employment, 33, 169-70; unemployment, 33, 171-72

Export, 22 *ff.*—composition, 26; destination, 27; government intervention in, Chap. IV: 39 *ff.*; licensing and regulation principle, 74-6; Netherlands share in, 105; organization, 16 *ff.*, 64-5, 74-6; prices, 12, 136; promotion, 39, 64-5, 74-5, 87 *ff., see also varom.* commodities; restrictions, 26, 27, 41 *ff.*, 47 *ff.*; statistics, 22, 24, 26, 27, 39, 40; tariff, 48, 49, 52

Export Board for Cassava Products, 77

Export Division of Central Trade Office, 76

Expropriation Ordinance, 1920, 134

Faroka Cigarette Company, 79

Fertilizer, 11, 110—increased use of, 111, 142; industry, 119; quota, 95

Fiber and f. products, 13, 14, 17, 24, 104, 120—exports, 39

Financial aid from Netherlands, 103-04, *see also* Twenty-five Million Guilder Fund

Finishing industries, 11, 23, 71, 77, 118, *see also* Processing

Fish canneries, 132

Fisheries, 108, 131-32

Food—consumption, 109 *ff., see also* Living standards; crops, land for, 44; value of, 25; processing industries, 17, 119, 120, 132—wages in, 137; production, 109 *ff.*, 141 *ff.*

Foreign exchange control, 93, *see also* Deflation

Foreign trade, 22 *ff., see* Export, Import—organization, 29 *ff.*; regulation, Chap. III: 34 *ff.*; statistics, 22, 24, 26-8

Forest—area, 82; experiment station, 82; products, 22, 23, 81-3, 104; reserve, 82

Forestry services, 82-3—grant for, 108

"Fourteen Principles" of imperial economic cooperation, 101-03

France, bilateral trade agreement with, 104

"Free" native enterprise, 6

Fruit growing, 8, 10—encouragement of, 109

Frying pan industry, 93, *see also* Hardware—regulation of, 128-29

Fund for Financing of Medium-sized Industries, 117

Fund for Small Industry, 117, 119

Gambier exports, 23

*Gaplek, see* Cassava

Gedong Talaan agricultural colony, 144, 146

General Association of Rubber Planters (A.V.R.O.S.), 139

General Motors Corporation, 120, 121

General Popular Credit Bank, 11, 117, 160

General (Industrial) Regulation Board, 131

Germany, bilateral trade agreement with, 104

Gold exports, prohibition of, 134

Goodyear Tire and Rubber Company, 120, 121

Government—agencies, 38; budget, 36, 52; economic policy, Chap. III: 34 *ff.*, 91 *ff.*; extension of powers, Chap. III: 34 *ff.*; initiative, 37; intervention in—crop production, 110 *ff.*; exports, Chap. IV: 39 *ff.*; imports, Chap. V: 85 *ff.*; protection—of native enterprise, 14, 18, 19, 30-1, Chap. III: 34 *ff.*; of Western enterprise, 19-21, Chap. III: 34 *ff.*

Grants in aid, 52, 107-08

Groundnut, 23

Gums and resins, 77-8

Handicrafts—economic importance of, 25, 116 *ff.*, 149; education in, 118; losing ground, 119, 126; promotion of, 118-19, 122-24

Handloom improvement, 122-23

Hardware—control of stocks, 99; industries, 93, 118, 119, 120, 128, 129; market in Outer Provinces, 53

Harvest—effect on food consumption, 109, 110, 112, 142

Hat industry—wages in, 137

Holding companies, 17

Home consumption of—export products, 25, 109 *ff.*; food products, 143

Home industry, 116 *ff.*, 133—preference in government purchases, 118

Hospital construction, 52

Household industry, 116 *ff.*, 127 *ff.*

Housing improvement, 52

Hungary, bilateral trade agreement with, 104

Ice plants, regulation of, 128

Import, 22 *ff.*, 27, 28, 90—barter against exports, 97-9; change in character of, 129; government intervention, Chap. V: 85 *ff.*; Chap. VI: 101 *ff.*; 129-31—

through control of foreign exchange, 93, *also see* Deflation; of shipping, 99-100; through quota and licensing systems, 85 *ff.*, 91 *ff.*, 102-03, 117, 129-31, 133 *ff.*; through restrictions, 30, 85 *ff.*—effect on prices, 90-91, 102, 135; through tariff, 117, 135

Import Packing Ordinance, 1935, 87

Imports—mechanism, 29-30; Netherlands share in, 105-6; origins, 28; statistics, 25, 26, 28

India, British, 7, 18—sugar imports, 45; tea agreement with, 57

Indigo, 3

Indo-China—market for N.E.I. manufactures, 121; rice imports from, 113

Industrial—advice and education, 118; central boards, 118; equipment exempted from import duties, 117; labor, 121; market, 121; population, 143; production, 121-22; research, 52, 118; self-sufficiency, 19, 119; service bureaus, 118-19

"Industrialization", 19, 103, 116 *ff.*, 121 *ff.*, 126 *ff.*, 143

Industry—promotion of, 116 *ff.*, 128 *ff.*; regulation of, 128 *ff.*; share in exports, 23; "small", 118 *ff.*, 130; Western (European), 11, 14, 18-21, 119-21

Industry, native, 2 *ff.*, 9 *ff.*, 17, 18-21, 53, 116 *ff.*, 121 *ff.*, 127 *ff.*—cottage (household), 17, 116 *ff.*, 127, 130; small, 118 *ff.*, 130; workshop, 116 *ff.*, 123 *ff.*, 126, 127, 130—promotion, 108, 116 *ff.*, 128 *ff.*; protection, 85 *ff.*, 130-31; regulation, 128 *ff.*

Institute for Netherlands Economic Interests in the N.E.I., 107

Institute for Sea Fisheries, 131

Intermediate trade, *see* Middlemen, Wholesale

International Rubber Regulation Committee, 47, 50, 53-5

International Sugar Board, 46

International Tea Markets Expansion Board, 64

International Tin Regulation Committee, 81

Investment, 14, 26, 106, *see also* Capital, Credit—policy, 103; trusts, 17

Investors, European, 15 *ff.*

Irrigation, 5, 52, 109, 111, 114, 145, 146—grant for, 108, 150

Japan—aggressive trade policies, 29, 92, 95-6; exports to, 27, 28; imports from, 17, 28, 29, 30, 95, 96; method of sea fishing, 131-32; part in distribution trade, 29, 30

Java—"exports" to Outer Provinces—food, 110, 136; manufactures, 122, 136

Java Bank, 51

Java Textile Company, 120, 122

Juvenile unemployment, 171-72

Kapok and k. products, 7, 10, 12, 16, 71-74, 161—brokerage regulation, 72; crop destruction proposed, 73; exports, 23, 24, 26, 71 *ff.*; native production, 71-2; prices, 71, 72, 73, 135; production and pr. capacity, 71; regulation, 72; research and improvement, 71; sales promotion, 71

Kapok Board, 69, 72-4, 75

Kapok Fund, 73

*Kedelee, see* Soybean

Kingma system of tea purchase, 60, 62-3

Koebang weaving industry, 123-25

Koedoes native cigarette industry, 126-27

Kota-Agoeng agricultural colony, 144

Krosok Board, 79-80

Labor—Chinese, 168; conditions in native shops, 123; contract, 168-69; cost, 121, 125, 127, 137 *ff.*; division of, 5-6, 19, 32-3; efficiency, 121; European, 33, 169-70, 171-72; industrial, 121; migration, 31—*see also* land settlement—encouragement of, 147, 150; recruitment, 143, 168-69; supply and wage rates, 137-38; surplus, 116, 143—*see* Unemployment

*Ladang, see* Rice, dry cultivation of

Lampong pepper plantations, 149

Land—clearance, 8, 31, 141, 144 *ff.*, 150; holdings, size of, 9, 110; leases, 3, 5, 110, 156-57, *see also* Estates; rents, 44; settlement, 108, 114, 141, 143 *ff.*—and labor supply, 149; utilization, 44, 83, 110, 111, 114, 141 *ff.*

Leather industry, 17, 119—encouragement of, 118

Lemon grass, 7

Living—cost of, 30, 89, 90-91, 102, 113, 117, 125, 133 *ff.*, 137, 139, *see also* Consumption; standard of, 52, 53, 109, 110, 146, *see also* Consumption

London Sugar Convention, 1937, 45, 46

Madura welfare fund, 108

Maize, 23, 24, 104, 110—prices, 135
Malaria, 65, 108
Malaya, market for N.E.I. manufactures, 121
Manado copra contracts, 162-65
Manioc, see Cassava
Manufactured consumer goods, import of, 119-20
Manufacturers' Export Centrale, 97
Market—local, 10; native farmers', 6, 10 ff., 18 ff., 24 ff., 27, 28; sugar, 41 ff.
Metal industry, 17, 93—encouragement of, 108, 118; regulation of, 128
Metals, imports of, 135
Middle class, native—colonization scheme for, 150; growth of, 33
Middleman, see Wholesale trade—as creditor, 161; between native grower and European purchaser, 11, 62, 127; between small industry and native market, 126
Minerals, see Tin—exports of, 39, 40
Mining, 17, 22, 23, 116—labor, 143; wages, 139-40
Moneylenders, 166 ff., see also Debt, Usury
Monopolies—as price regulators, 135; prevention of, 128-29
Muro-ami method of sea fishing, 131-32

National Carbon Company, 120
Nationalist movement and cooperation, 153-54
Native—agriculture, 9, 31, 32; industry, 9, 11, 12, 116 ff., 121 ff., 127 ff.; intellectuals as colonizers, 150; lim. liability companies, 155-57; middle class, 33, 172; producers, 2 ff., 23—attitudes, 2, 6; characteristics, 2 ff., 23; dependence, 9, 10-13, 18-21, 28; prospects, 19-21; share in exports, 22 ff., see also Rubber, Sugar, Tea; share in sugar production, 44, 45
Native products—home consumption of, 25; value of, 25
Natural resources and population growth, 141
Netherlands—benefit from exports to N.E.I., 69, 87-88; economic cooperation with N.E.I., 91 ff., Chap. VI; 101 ff., 130; exports to N.E.I., 27, 66-67, 101 ff. —of cambrics, 94; electric bulbs, 95-6; fertilizer, 95; piece goods, 96-7; financial aid to N.E.I., 103-04; import tax on coffee, 69; imports from N.E.I., 28,

87-8, 101 ff., 129, 136; investments in N.E.I. 106, 107, 129; sales promotion in N.E.I., 107; share in N.E.I. trade, 105-06, 129-30; shipping, 100
Netherlands Agricultural Crisis Board, 69
Netherlands Indian Association for the Sale of Sugar (N.I.V.A.S.), 20, 41
Netherlands Indian Association for Trade in Gums, 78
Netherlands Indian Central Procurement Office, 119
New Guinea—European colonization in, 154; rubber growing in, 54
New York Gum Importers' Association, 78
Nienhuys, Jacob, 12, 15
Nutmeg, 1, 15, 16, 23, see also Spices

Office for Investigation of Industrial Opportunities, 130
Oil, see Essential oils, Palm-oil, Petroleum, Vegetable oils
Operations, size of, 8, 9, 16 ff., 110
Opium growing, 15
Outer Provinces, 4, 8, 48, 50—employment, 31, 168; European settlement, 151; food imports, 110; food production, 111; forestry, 81-2; "imports" of Java manufactures, 122, 136; labor opportunities, 143-44; land settlement, 144 ff.; market for Java products, 53; population, 25; rice "imports", 112-13, 136; rice production, 112, 114; share in grants, 108; surveyed for rubber production, 56; wages, 139-40
Over-production, 28-9

Padang weaving industry, 124
Pajakoemboeh weaving industry, 124
Pajong (umbrella) industry, 127-28
Palm-oil and p. products, 14, 23, 24, 26, 104, 135
Paper industry, 119, 120
Paraffin, 25
Patchouli, 77
Peanut, consumption and production, 23, 109
Peasant producers, see Native
People's General Credit Bank, 11, 117
Pepper, 1, 7, 15, 16, 23, 24, 26, 52, 111, 149—disease, 52
Petroleum, 25—export, 39; price control, 135
Philippines, as market for N.E.I. manufactures, 121
Plant diseases and pests, 14, 52, 110, 142

Poland, bilateral trade agreement with, 104

Population—density, 147-48; problem, 25, 31-2, Chap. IX: 141 *ff.*

Ports, categories of, 100

Price—control, Chap. VIII: 133 *ff.;* fluctuations, 24, 29, 30, 41, 47, 111, 112, 114; level, 30; regulation, *see* Government intervention

Printing industry, regulation of, 128

Processing industries, 11, 14, 17, 23, 118, *see also* Industry, var. industries, Western industry

Production—costs, 30, 40, 43, 44, 121, 125, 127, 137 *ff.;* regulation of, 42 *ff.,* 47 *ff.*

Productivity, rise of, 28

Public health, 52—grants for, 108

Public utility companies, 136

Public works, 52, *see also* Irrigation—grants for, 108; service charges, 136

Pulses, increased production of, 110

Quinine, *see* Cinchona

Railway freight rates, 114, 136

Raw materials, *see* Export, var. commodities—purchase by Western factors, 10 *ff.,* 14, 44; sales promotion, 74-6

Reclamation of waste land, 141 *ff., see also* Land clearance, settlement

Relief measures, 52, 108, 109, 169-72, *see also* Depression

Resins and gums, 77-78, 83—industry, 119

Restriction—of exports, 26, 27, Chap. IV: 39 *ff.;* of imports, 30, 85 *ff.*

Rice and r. products, 1, 10, 12, 15, 110—barter agreements, 97-8; consumption, 109, 110; dry cultivation, 114; export, 23, 24, 104; import, 90, 114—licensing, 112, 113; inter-island trade, 112; marketing, 115; mills, 10, 113, 115—regulation of, 129; policy, 112 *ff.,* 142; prices, 113 *ff.,* 163; premium on shipment to Outer Provinces, 114; production—encouragement of, 114; in Outer Provinces, 111

Rice Import Ordinance, 85

Rice-growers—colonies for, 144 *ff.;* indebtedness, 161

Road improvement, 52—grant for, 108

Roselle and other fiber bags, 104, 120

Root crops, *see also* Cassava, Sweet potato—production and consumption of, 109, 110

Royal Mail Packet S.S. Co., 64

Rubber, 7, 8, 12, 14, 16—area under, 141; export tariff, 49; exports, 23, 24, 26, 39, 40, 47 *ff.,* 51, 52, 55; improved production, 52, 56; industries, 119, 120; licenses, 50 *ff.;* native-grown, 40, 48, 50, 51, 52, 54, 55-6; prices, 51, 135; production and pr. capacity, 49 *ff.,* 51, 53, 54-5; regulation, 47 *ff.,* 113; research, 53-4, 55, 56; reserves, 52; restriction, effects of, 51-2; survey, 50, 55; tires, 93-4, 120, 121, 133; wages, 138, 139; "wet", proportion in exports, 52

Rubber Fund, 52, 108

Rubber Institute, 48

Salt imports, 15

Sarong weaving industry, 123

*Sawah, see* Rice

Schumpeter, Joseph A., 16

Science and technique, 4, 8, 11, 18, 84-5, 110-11, 118, 141-42

Second crops, 110, 111

Seed selection and distribution, 11, 79, 80, 109, 110, 111, 142

Self-sufficiency, economic, 19, 24, 25-6, 31, 142—in industry, 19, 119

Sereh grass, 76-7

Shipping—coastal and inter-island, 64, 99-100, 112, 114; control of, 99-100, 113; freight rates, 136; organization, 17, 29

Siam—barter arrangement with, 97-8; market for N.E.I. manufactures, 121; rice imports from, 113

Silk weaving industry, 124

Soap and cosmetics industries, 119, 120

Soil investigations, 52

Southeast Asia, N.E.I.'s natural market, 41-2, 121

Soybean and s. products—export 23, 111; import, 90, 111; production and consumption, 109, 110; quota regulation, 116, 142

Speculation, 51, *see also* Price—fluctuation

Spices—early trade in, 1; exports, 39; production, 15, *see also* Pepper

Staple crops, advancement of, 83-4, 109 *ff.*

Stock raising, *see* Animal husbandry

Sugar, 3, 7, 8, 11, 12, 13, 20, 25, 31, 141—barter arrangement, 97-8; convention, 45, 46-7; crisis, 171; exports, 23, 24, 26, 28, 39, 40, 41 *ff.;* gift for tea sales promotion, 65; market in Outer Provinces, 53; mills, 12, 13, 41 *ff.;* policy, 40 *ff.;*

# 180 THE EVOLUTION OF THE NETHERLANDS INDIES ECONOMY

price regulation, 135; production, 44—
cost of, 44, 45; restriction, effects of, 45;
sales promotion, 45
Sugar Fund, 171
Sugar Sales Organization, 65
Sumatra, 14, 15, 50, 54, 108, *see also* Outer
Provinces—estate labor, 143, 149—
wages, 139; forest resources, 82-3; handloom weaving, 123-25; industrial development, 120; land settlement, 114,
143 *ff.*; land utilization, 114; rice cultivation, 114; rubber surveys, 50, 55
Sweet potato, consumption and production, 109, 110
Syndicates, 17

Tapioca and t. products, 13—exports, 39
Taxation, 25
Tea, 3, 7, 8, 10, 12, 14, 24, 56-65—area
under, 141; exports, 23, 25, 39, 40, 57 *ff.*;
international regulation, 38, 57 *ff.*; native production, 57, 58; purchasing factories, 59 *ff.*; prices, 56-7, 60-1; production and pr. capacity, 56-7, 62, 63; production and export licenses, 58 *ff.*; sales
promotion, 64-5; survey, 63
Tegal cotton textile mills, 119-20, 122
Textiles, *see* Cotton, Fiber, Silk
Thousand Isles fisheries, 131-32
Timber, 82, 104, *see also* Forest products
Tin—exports, 40, 80-81; international
regulation, 81; mining, 81—wages in,
139-40; prices, 81
Tobacco, 3, 4, 6, 8, 10, 11, 12-13, 15-16,
25, 78-80—area under, 110; exports, 23,
24, 39, 79; growers—credit provision
for, 127, 161; native, 78-80; research, 79
Tobacco Export and Import Company, 79
Trade, *see also* Export, Import, Foreign
trade, Wholesale—balance, 26-7;
evolution of, 1 *ff.*; restrictions, 26-7
Trade Unions, 121
Transportation, *see also* Railways, Shipping—costs, 14, 45, 64, 136; improvement, 52; organization, 17, 113-14

Turpentine, 83
Twenty-five Million Guilder Fund, 84,
104, 107-08, 150, 151

Umbrella industry, 127-28
Unemployment, 31, 32-33, 170-72—
Eurasian, 33; European, 33, 171-72;
juvenile, 171-72; relief grants, 108
Unilever Company, 120
United Java Sugar Producers
(V.I.S.P.), 20
United States—bilateral trade agree-
ment with, 104; exports to, 27, 128;
imports from, 28, 72
Usury, combat of, 134, 166-68, *see also*
Credit, Debt

Van Gelderen, J., 47
Vegetable growing, 10
Vegetable oils and fats, *see* individual
products—exports, 39
Visman, Frans H., v-vi
Volksraad, 36, 57, 65, 67, 70, 73, 85, 103,
149, 169

Wage labor, 11, 25, 31, *see also* Labor
Wages, 30, 137-40—control of, 137-40;
relation to other production costs, 44,
45, 121 *ff.*, 126 *ff.*
War, economic effects of, 18, 28, 73, 119,
135, 137, 163
Weaving industry—a case history,
123-25; regulation of, 128, 129
Welfare policies, Chap. X: 153 *ff.*
Western—capital, 3 *ff.*, 10 *ff.*; commerce,
1 *ff.*, 10, 12, *ff.*; estates, 3 *ff.*, 10, 11, 13-4,
15 *ff.*, 32—area under, 32, 141; share
in exports, 22 *ff.*; wages, 137-38
Western-type—commercial agriculture, 8
*ff.*, 12 *ff.*; consumer goods, 119 *ff.*, 126;
industry, 119 *ff.*, 126-27—wages in, 137
Wholesale trade, 8, 29-30, 86, 88, *see also*
Distribution, Middleman
World market, dependence on, 24, *see also*
various commodities, Export